ADAMS

The Small Business Legal Kit

Business titles from Adams Media Corporation

ADAMS

The Small Business Legal Kit

J. W. Dicks, Esq.

ADAMS MEDIA CORPORATION
Holbrook, Massachusetts

Dedication

To the legal professionals who truly try and serve their clients.
To Larry Pino, John Dicks, Jim Redman, Don Rhett, David Ferguson,
Phillip Snyderburn, Steve Berry, Anthony Palma, Perry Mason, Marvin Rooks,
Chip Brosokas, and Cathy Brown, all lawyers I respect and have learned from.
To my Mom and Dad, who encouraged me to become an attorney.

Published by Adams Media Corporation
260 Center Street, Holbrook, MA 02343

ISBN: 1-55850-699-3

Printed in the United States of America.

J I H G F E D C

Library of Congress Cataloging-in-Publication Data
Dicks, J. W. (Jack William)
    The small business legal kit : ready-to-use forms, agreements, and contracts for small
businesses / J. W. Dicks.
        p.   cm.
    ISBN 1-55850-699-3 (pbk.)
    1. Small business—Law and legislation—United States—Forms. I. Title.
    KF1659.A65D53   1995
    346.73'0652'0269—dc20   94-19160
    [347.3066520269]   CIP

This publication is designed to provide accurate and authoritative information with regard to the subject matter covered. It is sold with the understanding that the publisher is not engaged in rendering legal, accounting, or other professional advice. If legal advice or other expert assistance is required, the services of a competent professional person should be sought.
— From a *Declaration of Principles* jointly adopted by a Committee of the American Bar Association and a Committee of Publishers and Associations

This book is available at quantity discounts for bulk purchases.
For information, call 1-800-872-5627 (in Massachusetts, 781-767-8100).

Visit our home page at http://www.adamsmedia.com

Table of Contents

Chapter 4

Chapter 5

Chapter 9

Chapter 10

Note to the Reader

How to Get the Most Out of This Book

The book is divided into nine stand-alone chapters. Chapter 10 includes an array of special forms. I have carefully selected the chapters as those areas of the law a majority of entrepreneurs deal with.

Before you use any of these forms, you should read the chapter introduction, where I have tried to give a brief overview of the subject. You may find that the introduction gives you a hint as to which form will be best for you in your particular circumstances.

Once you find the form you are looking for, you will see that there are two copies of it. The first copy is filled out as an example of what you might want to do. You will quickly see not only where everything goes, but generally how the form should look and read when completed. I am convinced that concern over where to write in words has kept most people from using forms in the past.

Above each sample form is a special section labeled "Commentary." This is a brief discussion of the form, how it should be used, and anything I think is unusual or critical in the form's use. Please read the commentary before using any form.

My closing thought on using this book is a warning. You have bought this book because you want to be your own attorney and save legal fees. That's great; this book will do it for you. However, please understand that filling out the form is not what you pay an attorney for in the first place. An attorney should be paid because of his or her ability to look at your situation objectively and give advice based on his or her experience that will help you. You will miss this if you do it all yourself.

Although the forms are useful starting points for any small businessperson, each of the fifty states has its own body of law, and federal law is also applicable to some matters. What's more, the law sometimes changes. These are additional reasons why it is often useful to consult a lawyer.

Introduction

I grew up in a small-town community where your word was your bond. People made business and personal commitments on a handshake, with seldom anything put down on paper between them. They lived by an unwritten code of honor and arguably died by it.

Life has become more complicated today. While there are still times when a written contract isn't necessary, in most cases you will get burned if you don't have one. There is no doubt in my min that today every agreement should be put in writing. Nostalgia would say that this is bad, but it is really just a change in times. It isn't good or bad, it is just the way it is. Once you accept this fact, you will learn to put everything in writing. Even your correspondence will become written confirmation of understandings. If communication is confused at a later date, you will only have to review your written file, and your paper trail will prove your case.

If the only lesson you glean from this book is the importance of a legal paper trail, I will have accomplished a great service, and you will have saved much more than you paid for this information. I hope I can do more; I intend to teach you about contracts and even pass along to you those that I have found successful in a variety of circumstances.

Will this book eliminate your need for a lawyer? Not a good lawyer. Ultimately, your goal is to find an experienced lawyer who is also an experienced adviser and confidant. Such a person is hard to find, but if you do, he or she will save you much more than you will pay. On the other hand, many of you will have the confidence born of your own experience to use some or all of these forms on your own. At a minimum, all of the forms will give you a starting point so that your lawyer need only complete or review them, thereby dramatically reducing your fee. Under most hourly billing schedules, the cost of this entire book is less than ten minutes of an attorney's legal time. You'll save that if you use one form and let your attorney review it.

Chapter 1

Contracts

For me, the contracts class in law school was what law school was all about. I'm sure it's because I watched the movie *The Paper Chase* many times and my contracts professor was seemingly cut from the same cloth as Professor Kingsfield in the movie.

Whatever the reason, contracts became "the law" to me and was a major impetus for this book. If you are going to be dealing with legal forms, and especially if you are going to be filling out your own forms, you need to have a basic understanding of contracts. What a contract is and what makes it legal are two questions that you are sure to ask yourself.

First and foremost, a contract is an agreement. You can have an oral contract or a written one. Some types of contracts (real estate, for example) must be in writing. Since you will be dealing with written forms, the law in this area won't be a concern.

The second question, regarding legality, is a bit more cumbersome to answer, but we will. Many people believe that a contract must be written in legalese. Not true. Perish the thought. Legalese may have been the accepted form at one time, but simplicity and clarity are the important characteristics today. Although some lawyers would argue that contracts have always been simple and clear, I would argue that for the most part they have been shrouded with far too many wherefore's and whereas's. Although some of the forms you find in this book still contain the older language, you will see a vast improvement.

Why write a contract? If some contracts don't have to be in writing, why are we writing them?

Good question and an important point. We are putting them in writing because we want a record of the true agreement. If you think that means that I'm concerned about people changing their mind or having a different recollection of events, you're right. *People hear what they want to hear and believe what they want to believe.* If you do nothing more than memorize that phrase and act accordingly, the cost of this book will be repaid a thousandfold. Amazingly, what you will really find is that even the written points are debated as to their "true meaning." A contract is a written example of Murphy's law—what can go wrong will.

What do you have to have in a contract?

Historically, there are certain legal elements that every contract must have to make it enforceable in court. Note that I didn't say that they were required to make the contract valid, because you can have a valid contract that a court won't enforce. Consequently, we will deal with the elements that you want to have to get the court to at least recognize that you have a contract. Heaven help you if you actually have to go to court to try to enforce one, but if you do, at least make sure your contract will stand.

There are five essential elements of a contract:

1. Identify the parties
2. Consideration for the contract
3. Terms
4. Execution
5. Delivery

■ *Identify the parties.* In the old days of legalese, most contracts used phrases like "party of the first part" and "party of the second part." These were so confusing to me that by the end of the document, I wasn't sure who the party of the second part was.

In most of these forms, you will simply use the formal names of the people making up the contract and a short abbreviation after that in parentheses. For example, United World Bank Incorporated might be followed by (United), letting you know that the contract will be using the single word *United* rather than the full corporate name.

Individuals' names are also commonly shortened. Frank A. Johnson (Johnson) would tell you that the last name would be used throughout the agreement, but that it stood for Frank A. Johnson as opposed to anyone else in the Johnson family.

To help in identification, it is also customary to give the parties' street address, but this is for clarification.

■ *Consideration.* With great apology to my law professor for the weeks he spent on consideration, let me simply say that it is something you give or give up for the agreement. Generally speaking, it will be your promise to do or not to do something. Sometimes the consideration will be money, but that does not have to be the case. What is important is that there is something mutual between the parties and that it is acknowledged in the agreement. The acknowledgment does not have to recite the specific consideration, such as $20,000, because the parties may not want others to know. Instead, you can say, "For and in consideration of the mutual promises and benefits to be derived by the parties." That language alone is sufficient to have consideration. You do not need to put a token dollar amount like "For one dollar..." unless that is the *only* consideration paid.

■ *Terms of the agreement.* This is the main part of your agreement. You will state in as clear a fashion as possible what the parties are agreeing to. The language you use should be adequate to allow a stranger reading the contract to understand what everyone wishes. This is important because if the contract ever goes to court, the stranger will be a judge, and you want to make sure he or she is reading the phrase the way you intended it to be read.

■ *Execution.* It would seem clear that the contract should be signed, but things get confusing when you have corporations and partnerships. A good rule of thumb is to get everyone on the other side to sign. The important thing is to make sure you get the authorized party to sign. If you are dealing with a corporation, make sure the person signing is an officer or director of the corporation. Such as person still may not have the authority to sign, but accept that as a minimum. If someone is signing on behalf of another individual, make sure he or she is authorized in some legal fashion to do so. A power of attorney would be evidence of such authority.

If you are dealing with a corporation, it is also a good idea to get the document "sealed" with the corporation's seal. This is an old custom, but some states still give credence to the seal, so be safe and get it.

The need for witnesses on a contract can create confusion. This doesn't usually affect the validity of the contract (except in the case of wills), but the number required if a contract is to be recorded differs among jurisdictions. If you want to be ultra safe, get two witnesses and a notary. Alternatively, call your local courthouse and ask the clerk how many witnesses are required for recording in your jurisdiction.

■ *Delivery.* The delivery of the contract is an old formality, but it is still a necessity. Even though the contract is signed, unless you deliver it before the opposing party cancels, you don't have a valid contract.

Commentary

The first contract we will review is the basic vanilla contract. This contract does not even contain a lot of the "boilerplate" language typical of many contracts. Nevertheless, I think it is very important because it can be used for many purposes to get your agreement down on paper.

There are definitely two sides to business contracts: the legal and the practical. A good business lawyer will argue into the wee hours of the night about various nuances to clauses that can be developed in your favor. These may very well be helpful to your case. Unfortunately, however, sometimes these arguments of law between the attorneys can result in a deal's never getting done. I don't think this helps anyone.

An alternative method of developing a contract is to use a vanilla form like this one to get your basic agreement down on paper. Once you do that, you at least have some sort of an agreement. If both parties like, they are now free to turn the lawyers loose to hammer out details that can be added to the contract later.

I would be remiss if I didn't tell you that the last paragraph was me talking to you as a fellow entrepreneur and not as a lawyer. In fairness, the lawyer would probably argue that you are better off without the deal if you can't agree on every point. As an entrepreneur, I believe this is unduly restrictive and doesn't help pay the overhead.

Contract

THIS CONTRACT, entered into this the _8th_ day of _June_ , 199 _5_ , by and between _Charlie Jones_ (_Jones_), whose address is _147 W. Bay Street_ , city of _St. Petersburg Beach_ , state of _Florida_ , and _Brown Printing_ (_Brown_), whose address is _421 E. 2nd Avenue_ , city of _St. Petersburg_ , state of _Florida_ .

FOR AND IN CONSIDERATION of the mutual promises and benefits to be derived by the parties, they do hereby agree to the following:

1. _Jones will deliver to Brown a six-page newsletter on the second Tuesday of each month, camera ready for printing._
2. _Brown agrees to print and deliver the newsletters to Jones within three days of receipt for a price of $0.20 each._
3. _This agreement shall extend for twelve months._

This contract is the entire agreement between the parties and can only be modified in writing with both parties' signatures. The contract binds and benefits both parties, their successors, and assigns. Time is of the essence of this contract. The contract shall be governed by the laws of _Florida_ . Venue shall be _Pinellas County, Florida_ .

The parties have signed this contract on the date specified above.

Frank Adams
Witness

Kathleen Shuman
Witness

Sue Smith
Witness

Chris Johnson
Witness

Charles Jones
Signature

Brown Printing, Sean Brown
Signature

Contract

THIS CONTRACT, entered into this the _____ day of
_____ , 199 ___ , by and between _____ (_____),
whose address is _____ , city of _____ , state of
_____ and _____ (_____), whose address is
_____ , city of _____ , state of _____ .
　　FOR AND IN CONSIDERATION of the mutual promises and benefits
to be derived by the parties, they do hereby agree to the
following:

_____
_____
_____
_____
_____
_____

　　This contract is the entire agreement between the parties and
can only be modified in writing with both parties' signatures.
The contract binds and benefits both parties, their successors,
and assigns. Time is of the essence of this contract. The
contract shall be governed by the laws of _____ . Venue
shall be _____ .
　　The parties have signed this contract on the date specified
above.

_____　　_____
Witness　　　　　　　　　　　　　Signature

_____
Witness

_____　　_____
Witness　　　　　　　　　　　　　Signature

_____
Witness

Modification of Contract

THIS MODIFICATION OF CONTRACT, entered into this the _10th_ day of _December_ , 199 _5_ , by and between _Charles Jones_ (_Jones_), whose address is _147 W. Bay Street_ , city of _St. Petersburg Beach_ , state of _Florida_ , and _Brown Printing_ (_Brown_), whose address is _421 E. 2nd Avenue_ , city of _St. Petersburg Beach_ , state of _Florida_ .

FOR AND IN CONSIDERATION OF the mutual promises and benefits to be derived by the parties, they do hereby agree to the following:

1. The parties entered into a contract dated _June 8, 1995_ , a copy of which is attached to this modification and incorporated.

2. The parties agree to modify the contract as follows: _The newsletter shall be expanded to six pages and the price increased to $0.25 each._

3. All other terms and conditions of the original contract remain in full force and effect. This modification binds all parties and successors.

The parties have signed this agreement on the date first above written.

Frank Adams
Witness

Charles Jones
Signature

Sarah Barnett
Witness

Sue Smith
Witness

Brown Printing, Sean Brown
Signature

Greg Taylor
Witness

Modification of Contract

THIS MODIFICATION OF CONTRACT, entered into this the
_____ day of _____ , 199 ___ , by and between
_____ (_____) , whose address is _____ , city of
_____ , state of _____ , and _____ (_____) ,
whose address is _____ , city of _____ , state of
_____ .

    FOR AND IN CONSIDERATION OF the mutual promises and benefits
to be derived by the parties, they do hereby agree to the
following:

  1. The parties entered into a contract dated _____ , a
      copy of which is attached to this modification and
      incorporated.

  2. The parties agree to modify the contract as follows:

_____

_____

_____

_____

_____

_____

  3. All other terms and conditions of the original contract
      remain in full force and effect. This modification binds
      all parties and successors.

    The parties have signed this agreement on the date first above
written.

_____   _____

Witness   Signature

_____

Witness

_____   _____

Witness   Signature

_____

Witness

Extension of Contract

THIS EXTENSION OF CONTRACT, entered into this the _8th_ day of _June_ , 199 _6_ , by and between _Charles Jones_ (_Jones_), whose address is _147 W. Bay Street_ , city of _St. Petersburg Beach_ , state of _Florida_ , and _Brown Printing_ (_Brown_), whose address is _421 E. 2nd Avenue_ , city of _St. Petersburg Beach_ , state of _Florida_ .

FOR AND IN CONSIDERATION OF the mutual promises and benefits to be derived by the parties, they do hereby agree to the following:

1. The parties entered into a contract dated _June 8, 1995_ , a copy of which is attached to this extension and incorporated.

2. The parties wish to extend the time period called for in the contract as follows:
   From June 8, 1996 to June 8, 1997

3. There are no other changes in the contract, which shall continue to bind and benefit both parties and any successors or assigns.

The parties have signed this extension on the date first above written.

Mary Smith   _Charles Jones_
Witness   Signature

Sarah Barnett
Witness

John Simmons   _Brown Printing, Sean Brown_
Witness   Signature

Greg Taylor
Witness

Extension of Contract

THIS EXTENSION OF CONTRACT, entered into this the _____ day of _____ , 199 ___ , by and between _____ (_____), whose address is _____ , city of _____ , state of _____ , and _____ (_____), whose address is _____ , city of _____ , state of _____ .

FOR AND IN CONSIDERATION OF the mutual promises and benefits to be derived by the parties, they do hereby agree to the following:

1. The parties entered into a contract dated _____ , a copy of which is attached to this extension and incorporated.

2. The parties wish to extend the time period called for in the contract as follows:

    _____
    _____
    _____
    _____
    _____
    _____

3. There are no other changes in the contract, which shall continue to bind and benefit both parties and any successors or assigns.

The parties have signed this extension on the date first above written.

_____   _____
Witness   Signature

_____
Witness

_____   _____
Witness   Signature

_____
Witness

Assignment of Contract

THIS ASSIGNMENT OF CONTRACT, entered into this the _4th_ day of _April_ , 199 _6_ , by and between _Brown Printing_ , Assignor, whose address is _421 E. 2nd Avenue_ , city of _St. Petersburg Beach_ , state of _Florida_ , and _New Press_ , Assignee, whose address is _832 Century Blvd._ , city of _St. Petersburg Beach_ , state of _Florida_ .

FOR AND IN CONSIDERATION OF the mutual promises and benefits to be derived by the parties, they do hereby agree to the following:

1. Assignor entered into a contract dated _June 8, 1995_ with _Charles Jones_ , a copy of which is attached to this and incorporated.

2. Assignor hereby assigns all rights, interests, burdens, and benefits described in the contract to Assignee.

3. Assignor warrants that the contract is still in full effect and has not been modified except as indicated in writing. Assignor agrees to indemnify and hold harmless the Assignee from all claims resulting from Assignor's failure to perform under the contract prior to the date of assignment.

4. Assignee agrees to perform all the duties and obligations called for under the contract. Assignee agrees to indemnify and hold the Assignor harmless from all claims which may result from Assignee's failure to perform under this contract.

5. This contract binds the parties and all successors.

The parties have signed this agreement on the date first above written.

Kathleen Shuman
Witness

Sarah Barnett
Witness

Greg Taylor
Witness

Chris Johnson
Witness

Sean Brown, Brown Printing
Signature

Mark Barts, New Press
Signature

Assignment of Contract

THIS ASSIGNMENT OF CONTRACT, entered into this the _____ day of _____ , 199 ___ , by and between _____ , Assignor, whose address is _____ , city of _____ , state of _____ , and _____ , Assignee, whose address is _____ , city of _____ , state of _____ .

FOR AND IN CONSIDERATION OF the mutual promises and benefits to be derived by the parties, they do hereby agree to the following:

1. Assignor entered into a contract dated _____ with _____ , a copy of which is attached to this and incorporated.

2. Assignor hereby assigns all rights, interests, burdens, and benefits described in the contract to Assignee.

3. Assignor warrants that the contract is still in full effect and has not been modified except as indicated in writing. Assignor agrees to indemnify and hold harmless the Assignee from all claims resulting from Assignor's failure to perform under the contract prior to the date of assignment.

4. Assignee agrees to perform all the duties and obligations called for under the contract. Assignee agrees to indemnify and hold the Assignor harmless from all claims which may result from Assignee's failure to perform under this contract.

5. This contract binds the parties and all successors.

The parties have signed this agreement on the date first above written.

_____   _____
Witness   Signature

_____
Witness

_____   _____
Witness   Signature

_____
Witness

Termination of Contract

THIS AGREEMENT, entered into this the _3rd_ day of _August_ , 199 _6_ , by and between _Charles Jones_ (_Jones_), whose address is _147 W. Bay Street_ , city of _St. Petersburg Beach_ , state of _Florida_ , and _New Press_ (_New_), whose address is _832 Century Blvd._ , city of _St. Petersburg Beach_ , state of _Florida_ .

FOR AND IN CONSIDERATION OF the mutual promises and benefits to be derived by the parties, they do hereby agree to the following:

1. The parties entered into a contract dated _August 3, 1996_ , a copy of which is attached.
2. The parties agree to terminate and cancel this contract effective this date.
3. The parties mutually release each other of any and all obligations arising out of the contract as though it were never created.
4. This termination extends to all successors and assigns and includes any modifications.

The parties have signed this agreement on the date written above.

Kathleen Shuman
Witness

Charles Jones
Signature

Sarah Barnett
Witness

Greg Taylor
Witness

Mark Barts, New Press
Signature

Chris Johnson
Witness

Termination of Contract

THIS AGREEMENT, entered into this the _____ day of
_____ , 199 ___ , by and between _____ (_____),
whose address is _____ , city of _____ , state of
_____ , and _____ (_____), whose address is
_____ , city of _____ , state of _____ .

FOR AND IN CONSIDERATION OF the mutual promises and benefits
to be derived by the parties, they do hereby agree to the
following:

1. The parties entered into a contract dated _____ , a
   copy of which is attached.
2. The parties agree to terminate and cancel this contract
   effective this date.
3. The parties mutually release each other of any and all
   obligations arising out of the contract as though it were
   never created.
4. This termination extends to all successors and assigns and
   includes any modifications.

The parties have signed this agreement on the date written
above.

_____   _____
Witness   Signature

_____
Witness

_____   _____
Witness   Signature

_____
Witness

Notification of Assignment

Date: *April 4, 1996*
To: *Charles Jones*
From: *Brown Printing*
Subject: *Assignment of Printing Contract
of June 8, 1995*

Please be advised that on *April 4* , 199 *6* , all rights and interest of *Brown Printing* of *421 E. 2nd Avenue* , city of *St. Petersburg Beach* , state of *Florida* , have been assigned to *New Press* of *832 Century Blvd.* , city of *St. Petersburg Beach* , state of *Florida* .

Sean Brown
Signature

Notification of Assignment

Date: _____

To: _____

From: _____

Subject: _____

(describe contract and date)

_____

Please be advised that on _____ , 199 ___ , all rights and interest of _____ of _____ , city of _____ , state of _____ have been assigned to _____ of _____ , city of _____ , state of _____ .

_____
Signature

Consent to Assignment of Contract

Date: *April 5, 1996*
To: *Brown Printing*
From: *Charles Jones*
Subject: *Printing Contract of June 8, 1995*

In accordance with the above named contract, I consent to the assignment of all rights and obligations thereunder to *New Press* of *832 Century Blvd.* , city of *St. Petersburg Beach* , state of *Florida* .

Charles Jones
Signature

Consent to Assignment of Contract

```
Date:      _____
To:        _____
From:      _____
Subject: _____
           (describe contract and date
           _____
```

In accordance with the above named contract, I consent to the assignment of all rights and obligations thereunder to _____ of _____ , city of _____ , state of _____

_____
Signature

Notice of Breach of Contract

Date: _December 14, 1996_
To: _New Press_
From: _Charles Jones_
Subject: _Printing Contract_

This notice is to inform you that as of _December 14_ , 199 _6_ , you are in breach of contract for the following reasons: _Delivery of the newsletter is six (6) days later than called for in the contract. This delay jeopardizes prompt delivery to clients._

Please be advised that the breach of contract must be corrected within _five (5)_ days of this notice or additional action will be taken to protect rights under the contract.

Charles Jones
Signature

Notice of Breach of Contract

Date: _____

To: _____

From: _____

Subject: _____

This notice is to inform you that as of _____ , 199 ___ , you are in breach of contract for the following reasons:

_____

_____

_____

_____

_____

Please be advised that the breach of contract must be corrected within _____ days of this notice or additional action will be taken to protect rights under the contract.

_____
Signature

General Release

THE UNDERSIGNED, for good and valuable consideration, forever releases, discharges, acquits, and forgives _New Press_ of _832 Century Blvd._ , city of _St. Petersburg Beach_ , state of _Florida_ , from any and all claims, actions, suits, demands, agreements, liabilities, and proceedings of every nature and description both at law and in equity arising from the beginning of time to the date of these presents, including but not limited to an incident or claim that arose out of: _The printing contract between Brown Printing and Charles Jones dated June 8, 1995 and subsequent assignment to New Press on April 4, 1996._

THIS RELEASE shall be governed under the laws of the state of Florida and shall be binding upon and inure to the benefit of the parties, their successors, assigns, and personal representatives.

Signed under seal this _3rd_ day of _August_ , 199 _6_ .

Sarah Barnett
Witness

Charles Jones
Signature

Chris Johnson
Witness

General Release

THE UNDERSIGNED, for good and valuable consideration, forever releases, discharges, acquits, and forgives _____ of _____ , city of _____ , state of _____ , from any and all claims, actions, suits, demands, agreements, liabilities, and proceedings of every nature and description both at law and in equity arising from the beginning of time to the date of these presents, including but not limited to an incident or claim that arose out of: _____

_____
_____
_____
_____
_____
_____
_____

THIS RELEASE shall be governed under the laws of the state of _____ and shall be binding upon and inure to the benefit of the parties, their successors, assigns, and personal representatives.

Signed under seal this _____ day of _____ , 199 ___ .

_____   _____
Witness   Signature

_____
Witness

Specific Release

THE UNDERSIGNED, for good and valuable consideration, hereby jointly and severally forever releases, discharges, and acquits _New Press_ of _832 Century Blvd._ , city of _St. Petersburg Beach_ , state of _Florida_ , from any and all contracts, claims, suits, actions, or liabilities both in law and in equity specifically arising from, relating to otherwise described as, and limited to: _The printing contract between New Press and Charles Jones dated June 8, 1995._

THIS RELEASE applies only to the foregoing matters and extends to no other debt, account, agreement, obligations, cause of action, liability, or undertaking by and between the parties, which, if existing, shall survive this release and remain in full force and effect and undisturbed by this specific release.

THIS RELEASE shall be governed by the laws of the state of _Florida_ and shall be binding upon and inure to the benefit of the parties, their successors, assigns, and personal representatives.

Signed under seal this _3rd_ day of _August_ , 199 _6_ .

Chris Johnson
Witness

Charles Jones
Signature

Greg Taylor
Witness

Mary Smith
Signature

Specific Release

THE UNDERSIGNED, for good and valuable consideration, hereby jointly and severally forever releases, discharges, and acquits _____ of _____ , city of _____ , state of _____ , from any and all contracts, claims, suits, actions, or liabilities both in law and in equity specifically arising from, relating to otherwise described as, and limited to: _____

_____
_____
_____
_____
_____
_____

THIS RELEASE applies only to the foregoing matters and extends to no other debt, account, agreement, obligations, cause of action, liability, or undertaking by and between the parties, which, if existing, shall survive this release and remain in full force and effect and undisturbed by this specific release.

THIS RELEASE shall be governed by the laws of the state of _____ and shall be binding upon and inure to the benefit of the parties, their successors, assigns, and personal representatives.

Signed under seal this _____ day of _____ , 199 ___ .

_____   _____
Witness   Signature

_____   _____
Witness   Signature

Mutual Release

THIS AGREEMENT, entered into this _3rd_ day of _August_ , 199 _5_ , by and between _New Press_ (_New_) of _832 Century Blvd._ , city of _St. Petersburg Beach_ , state of _Florida_ , and _Charles Jones_ (_Jones_) of _147 W. Bay Street_ , city of _St. Petersburg Beach_ , state of _Florida_ .

FOR AND IN CONSIDERATION of the mutual promises and benefits to be derived by the parties, they do hereby completely, mutually, and reciprocally release, discharge, acquit, and forgive each other from all claims, contracts, actions, suits, demands, agreements, liabilities, and proceedings of every nature and description both at law and in equity that either party has or may have against the other, arising from the beginning of time to this date, including but not limited to any claim arising from: _The printing contract between New Press and Charles Jones dated June 8, 1995._

THIS RELEASE shall be governed by the laws of the state of _Florida_ and shall be binding upon and inure to the benefits of the parties, their successors, assigns, and personal representatives.

Signed under seal on the date first above written.

Sarah Barnett
Witness

Mark Barts
Mark Barts, President, New Press

Chris Johnson
Witness

Charles Jones
Charles Jones

Mutual Release

THIS AGREEMENT, entered into this _____ day of _____ ,
199 ___ , by and between _____ (_____) of _____ ,
city of _____ , state of _____ , and _____
(_____) of _____ , city of _____ , state of
_____ .

FOR AND IN CONSIDERATION, of the mutual promises and benefits
to be derived by the parties, they do hereby completely, mutually
and reciprocally release, discharge, acquit and forgive each other
from all claims, contracts, actions, suits, demands, agreements,
liabilities, and proceedings of every nature and description both
at law and in equity that either party has or may have against the
other, arising from the beginning of time to this date, including
but not limited to any claim arising from: _____

_____

_____

_____

_____

_____

_____

THIS RELEASE shall be governed by the laws of the state of
_____ and shall be binding and inure to the benefits of the
parties, their successors, assigns and personal representatives.
Signed under seal on the date first above written.

_____   _____
Witness   Signature

_____   _____
Witness   Signature

Covenant Not to Sue

THE UNDERSIGNED, being the holder of an actual, existing, asserted or prospective claim against _New Press_ of _832 Century Blvd._ , city of _St. Petersburg Beach_ , state of _Florida_ arising from or relative to: _That certain printing contract dated June 8, 1995 and subsequently assigned from Brown Printing to New Press_ , do hereby covenant in exchange for good and valuable consideration, that I/we shall not commence, maintain, or prosecute any suit thereon against said party whether at law or in equity. Nothing herein shall constitute a release of this or any other party from any duties or obligations, and I/we expressly reserve all rights against any third parties.

The payment of any consideration hereunder shall not constitute an admission of liability by any party. There are no promises or inducements except as herein contained.

This covenant shall be governed under the laws of the state of _Florida_ and shall be binding upon and inure to the benefit of the parties, their successors, assigns, and personal representatives.

Signed under seal this _3rd_ day of _August_ , 199 _6_ .

Sarah Barnett   _Charles Jones_
Witness   Charlie Jones

Chris Johnson
Witness

Covenant Not to Sue

THE UNDERSIGNED, being the holder of an actual, existing, asserted, or prospective claim against _____ of _____ , city of _____ , state of _____ , arising from or relative to: _____

_____

_____

_____

_____

_____

do hereby covenant in exchange for good and valuable consideration, that I/we shall not commence, maintain, or prosecute any suit thereon against said party whether at law or in equity. Nothing herein shall constitute a release of this or any other party from any duties or obligations, and I/we expressly reserve all rights against any third parties.

The payment of any consideration hereunder shall not constitute an admission of liability by any party. There are no promises or inducements except as herein contained.

This covenant shall be governed under the laws of the state of _____ and shall be binding upon and inure to the benefit of the parties, their successors, assigns, and personal representatives.

Signed under seal this _____ day of _____ , 199 ___ .

_____   _____
Witness   Signature

_____   _____
Witness   Signature

Guaranty of Contract

THE UNDERSIGNED GUARANTOR, for good and valuable consideration, does hereby guaranty to _Charles Jones_ of _147 Bay Street_ , city of _St. Petersburg Beach_ , state of _Florida_ , the full, prompt, and complete performance by _New Press_ of _832 Century Blvd._ , city of _St. Petersburg Beach_ , state of _Florida_ of all the terms, conditions, and covenants of a contract between them dated _June 8_ , 199 _5_ , a copy of which is attached and incorporated by reference.

THIS GUARANTY shall continue until all the terms and conditions of said contract have been fully performed. The Guarantor shall not be released of any obligation or liability hereunder so long as there is any claim or right of claim arising out of said contract. In the event of any claimed breach of contract, the Guarantor shall be afforded full right to perform said obligations thereunder. There shall be no modification of said contract without the assent of the Guarantor. This Guaranty shall be unlimited as to duration or amount.

THIS GUARANTY shall be governed under the laws of the state of _Florida_ and shall be binding upon and inure to the benefit of the parties, their successors, assigns, and personal representatives.

Signed under seal this _4th_ day of _April_ , 199 _6_ .

Chris Johnson
Witness

Kathleen Shuman
Witness

Sean Brown
Sean Brown, Brown Printing

Guaranty of Contract

THE UNDERSIGNED GUARANTOR, for good and valuable consideration, does hereby guaranty to _____ of _____ , city of _____ , state of _____ , the full, prompt, and complete performance by _____ of _____ , city of _____ , state of _____ , of all the terms, conditions, and covenants of a contract between them dated _____ , 199 ___ , a copy of which is attached and incorporated by reference.

THIS GUARANTY shall continue until all the terms and conditions of said contract have been fully performed. The Guarantor shall not be released of any obligation or liability hereunder so long as there is any claim or right of claim arising out of said contract. In the event of any claimed breach of contract, the Guarantor shall be afforded full right to perform said obligations thereunder. There shall be no modification of said contract without the assent of the Guarantor. This Guaranty shall be unlimited as to duration or amount.

THIS GUARANTY shall be governed under the laws of the state of _____ and shall be binding upon and inure to the benefit of the parties, their successors, assigns, and personal representatives.

Signed under seal this _____ day of _____ , 199 ___ .

_____   _____
Witness   Signature

_____   _____
Witness   Signature

Chapter 2
Employment Documents

The world is changing, and one of the areas of law feeling the effects fastest is employment.

Perhaps it is a sign of the times. Perhaps it is because so many companies are downsizing. Whatever the reason, lawsuits between employers and employees are on the rise.

The entrepreneur of the 1990s must be prepared to protect himself or herself from the intrusion of government regulation and mounting employee unrest. To do this, you must document what you do and why you do it. No longer is it safe to assume that it is your business and you can jolly well do what you want. An employer adopting such an attitude will quickly learn that such is not the case. Your business is governed by a morass of legal regulation, most of which is designed to protect everyone but you. Maybe someday the rights of the creators of commerce will be recognized once again, but until they are, your best offense and defense will be documentation.

Employment Contract

THIS AGREEMENT, entered into this the _1st_ day of _February_ , 199 _6_ , by and between _Frank's Computer Service_ (_Franks_), employer, and _Judy Stanley_ (_Stanley_) of _407 Care Street_ , city of _Dallas_ , state of _Texas_ , employee.

FOR AND IN CONSIDERATION of the mutual promises and benefits to be derived by the parties, they do hereby agree to the following:

1. The employee is being hired as a _Service Technician_ to perform the following general duties: _repair and service computers and copiers._
    The employee also agrees to perform additional duties incidental to the general job description.

2. Hours of employment: _9:00 A.M. to 5:00 P.M._
    Number of hours per week: _40_
    Beginning date of employment: _February 1, 1996_
    Ending date of employment: _Until termination with or without cause._

3. The employee shall be paid or receive
    Weekly salary: _$750.00_
    Overtime rate: _time and one-half_
    Sick pay or leave: _three days per year paid._
    Vacation days: _Two weeks per year starting after twelve months of work._
    Bonus: _None_
    Retirement benefits: _None_
    Insurance benefits: _Company paid (see attached policy)_

4. The employee agrees to abide by all rules and regulations of the employer in existence at the time of employment and which are from time to time added.

5. This agreement may be terminated without notice by either party.

6. The employee acknowledges that in the course of employment he/she may become aware of certain information about the employer's operations or clients that is considered proprietary. The employee agrees not to disclose such information or use the information in any manner that might be harmful to the employer's business.
7. No modification or amendments shall be made to this contract unless in writing and signed by all parties.
8. Time is of the essence.
9. This contract is governed by the laws of the state of _Texas_ . Should any disagreement arise between the parties as it relates to employment, each party shall be responsible for their own attorneys' fees and court costs.

_____
Witness

Judy Stanley
Judy Stanley

_____
Witness

Frank's Computer Service
By _John Frank_
John Frank, President

Employment Contract

THIS AGREEMENT, entered into this the _____ day of
_____ , 199 ___ , by and between _____ (_____),
employer, and _____ (_____) of _____ , city of
_____ , state of _____ , employee.

FOR AND IN CONSIDERATION of the mutual promises and benefits
to be derived by the parties, they do hereby agree to the
following:

1. The employee is being hired as a _____ to perform the
    following general duties: _____
    _____
    _____
    _____
    _____

    The employee also agrees to perform additional duties
    incidental to the general job description.

2. Hours of employment: _____ to _____
    Number of hours per week: _____
    Beginning date of employment: _____
    Ending date of employment: _____

3. The employee shall be paid or receive
    Weekly salary: _____
    Overtime rate: _____
    Sick pay or leave: _____
    Vacation days: _____
    Bonus: _____
    Retirement benefits: _____
    Insurance benefits: _____

4. The employee agrees to abide by all rules and regulations
    of the employer in existence at the time of employment and
    which are from time to time added.

5. This agreement may be terminated without notice by either
    party.

6. The employee acknowledges that in the course of employment
    he/she may become aware of certain information about the
    employer's operations or clients that is considered
    proprietary. The employee agrees not to disclose such
    information or use the information in any manner that
    might be harmful to the employer's business.

7. No modification or amendments shall be made to this contract unless in writing and signed by all parties.
8. Time is of the essence.
9. This contract is governed by the laws of the state of _____ . Should any disagreement arise between the parties as it relates to employment, each party shall be responsible for their own attorneys' fees and court costs.

_____   _____

Witness   Signature of Employee

_____   _____

Witness   Signature of Employer
                                           By _____
                                           Authorized Signature

Independent Contractor Agreement

THIS AGREEMENT, entered into this the _14th_ day of _November_, 199 _6_, by and between _Kill Bugs, Inc._ (Owner) of _24 E. Robinson Street_, city of _Green Bay_, state of _Wisconsin_, and _Carl Sands_ (Contractor) of _872 Live Oak Circle_, city of _Green Bay_, state of _Wisconsin_.

FOR AND IN CONSIDERATION OF the mutual promises and benefits of the parties, they do hereby agree to the following:

1. The Owner agrees to hire the Contractor to perform the following: _Outside service technician_
2. The Owner agrees to pay the Contractor the following: _Ten dollars ($10.00) per call_.
3. The Owner acknowledges that the Contractor is free to set his own work schedule related to the work performed. However, the parties have agreed to the following general time period: _8:30 A.M. to 5:30 P.M. Monday through Friday_.
4. The Contractor agrees to complete the work to be performed in a manner generally acceptable to the industry in which he is being employed. If the parties have agreed to any specification with regard to the job, they have attached said specification as an addendum to this Agreement.
5. The Contractor agrees to indemnify and hold the Owner harmless from any claim or liability arising from the work provided by the Contractor.
6. Any changes or additions to this contract shall be in writing and signed by all parties.
7. Time is of the essence.
8. This contract shall be governed by the laws of the state of _Wisconsin_.

_____   _Kill Bugs, Inc._
Witness   Name of Owner
                              Betty Taylor
                              Signature of Owner

_____   Carl Sands
Witness   Name of Contractor
                              Carl Sands
                              Signature of Contractor

Independent Contractor Agreement

THIS AGREEMENT, entered into this the _____ day of _____ , 199 ___ , by and between _____ (Owner) of _____ , city of _____ , state of _____ , and _____ (Contractor) of _____ , city of _____ , state of _____ .

FOR AND IN CONSIDERATION OF the mutual promises and benefits of the parties, they do hereby agree to the following:

1. The Owner agrees to hire the Contractor to perform the following: _____
   _____
   _____

2. The Owner agrees to pay the Contractor the following: _____
   _____

3. The Owner acknowledges that the Contractor is free to set his own work schedule related to the work performed. However, the parties have agreed to the following general time period: _____
   _____

4. The Contractor agrees to complete the work to be performed in a manner generally acceptable to the industry in which he is being employed. If the parties have agreed to any specification with regard to the job, they have attached said specification as an addendum to this Agreement.

5. The Contractor agrees to indemnify and hold the Owner harmless from any claim or liability arising from the work provided by the Contractor.

6. Any changes or additions to this contract shall be in writing and signed by all parties.

7. Time is of the essence.

8. This contract shall be governed by the laws of the state of _____ .

_____   _____
Witness   Name of Owner

                                    _____
                                    Signature of Owner

_____   _____
Witness   Name of Contractor

                                    _____
                                    Signature of Contractor

Job Application Waiver

To: *Frank's Computer Service*
From: *Judy Stanley*
Date: *December 1, 1995*

I certify that all of the information given to you on my application for employment is true and correct. I understand that the falsification of any information is grounds for refusal to hire, and, if I am hired, grounds for immediate termination.

I authorize you to inquire into my background and check any reference on my behalf. I authorize any individual or organization to release to you any information concerning my previous employment, specifically releasing such parties from liability for any damage caused by giving you any information.

_____   *Judy Stanley*
Witness   Signature of Applicant

_____   *Frank Adams*
Witness   Signature of Company
                                    Representative

Job Application Waiver

To: _____

From: _____

Date: _____

    I certify that all of the information given to you on my application for employment is true and correct. I understand that the falsification of any information is grounds for refusal to hire, and, if I am hired, grounds for immediate termination.

    I authorize you to inquire into my background and check any reference on my behalf. I authorize any individual or organization to release to you any information concerning my previous employment, specifically releasing such parties from liability for any damage caused by giving you any information.

_____   _____

Witness   Signature of Applicant

_____   _____

Witness   Signature of Company
                            Representative

Temporary Employment Agreement

To: *Frank's Computer Service*
From: *Judy Stanley*
Date: *February 1, 1995*

I acknowledge that I am being employed temporarily and that such employment does not give me any rights or consideration for full-time employment.

I understand that I may be terminated at any time without notice. I also understand that I am not entitled to participate in any company benefit plan, including, but not limited to, insurance, vacations, or retirement programs.

_____	*Judy Stanley*
Witness	Signature of Employee
_____	*Frank Adams*
Witness	Signature of Company
	Representative

Temporary Employment Agreement

To: _____
From: _____
Date: _____

    I acknowledge that I am being employed temporarily and that such employment does not give me any rights or consideration for full-time employment.

    I understand that I may be terminated at any time without notice. I also understand that I am not entitled to participate in any company benefit plan, including, but not limited to, insurance, vacations, or retirement programs.

_____   _____
Witness   Signature of Employee

_____   _____
Witness   Signature of Company
                                  Representative

Employee Warning Notice

To: *Judy Stanley*
From: *Frank's Computer Service*
Date: *June 7, 1995*

Please be advised that the company has determined that your work performance is unsatisfactory for the following reasons: *You have been advised on four occasions about being late for work or leaving early.*

This notice is being given to you with the understanding that we expect immediate correction or you may be dismissed.

If you have any questions about this notice or if we can assist you with the problem, please let us know.

Frank Adams
Company Representative Signature

I acknowledge that I have received a copy of this notice and understand the seriousness of its nature.

Judy Stanley
Employee Signature

Employee Warning Notice

To: _____
From: _____
Date: _____

    Please be advised that the company has determined that your work performance is unsatisfactory for the following reasons:_____
_____
_____
_____
_____

    This notice is being given to you with the understanding that we expect immediate correction or you may be dismissed.
    If you have any questions about this notice or if we can assist you with the problem, please let us know.

_____
Company Representative Signature

    I acknowledge that I have received a copy of this notice and understand the seriousness of its nature.

_____
Employee Signature

Final Warning before Termination

To: _Judy Stanley_
From: _Frank's Computer Service_
Date: _November 9, 1995_

We have previously notified you of various problems in your employment, including: _Arriving late, leaving early, taking extra unexcused sick days._

At the present time, we have not seen satisfactory improvement in these areas and have determined that any continued failure to perform according to the standards of this company shall result in immediate termination without further notice.

Please take immediate action to correct the situation and advise us if we can assist in any way.

Frank Adams
Company Representative

I acknowledge that I have received and understand this final notice.

Judy Stanley
Signature of Employee

Final Warning before Termination

To: _____
From: _____
Date: _____

   We have previously notified you of various problems in your
employment, including: _____
_____
_____
_____
_____

   At the present time, we have not seen satisfactory improvement
in these areas and have determined that any continued failure to
perform according to the standards of this company shall result
in immediate termination without further notice.
   Please take immediate action to correct the situation and
advise us if we can assist in any way.

                              _____
                              Company Representative

   I acknowledge that I have received and understand this final
notice.

                              _____
                              Signature of Employee

Notice of Dismissal

To: _Judy Stanley_
From: _Frank's Computer Service_
Date: _December 30, 1995_

We regret to inform you that your employment has been terminated effective _December 30_ , 199 _5_ , for the following reasons: _Continuing to arrive late for work after numerous warnings._
Your final check along with a statement of account will be sent to you by _January 7_ , 199 _6_ . According to our medical insurance policy, your benefits have also ended with your employment, and we encourage you to quickly look for alternatives. Under a federal law known as COBRA you are entitled to continue your current health benefits provided by this company for a certain period of time at your expense. If you desire to do so, please make immediate arrangements with the company.
We regret that this action became necessary and wish you the best in the future.

Frank Adams
Company Representative

Judy Stanley
Employee

Notice of Dismissal

To: _____
From: _____
Date: _____

    We regret to inform you that your employment has been terminated effective _____ , 199 ___ , for the following reasons: _____

_____

_____

_____

_____

    Your final check along with a statement of account will be sent to you by _____ , 199 ___. According to our medical insurance policy, your benefits have also ended with your employment, and we encourage you to quickly look for alternatives. Under a federal law known as COBRA you are entitled to continue your current health benefits provided by this company for a certain period of time at your expense. If you desire to do so, please make immediate arrangements with the company.

    We regret that this action became necessary and wish you the best in the future.

_____
Company Representative

_____
Signature of Employee

Employee Noncompete and Confidentiality Agreement

THIS AGREEMENT, entered into this the _8th_ day of _June_ , 199 _5_ , by and between _Frank's Computer Service_ , Employer, whose address is _520 Oak Street_ , city of _Longhorn_ , state of _Texas_ , and _Judy Stanley_ , Employee, whose address is _407 Care Street_ , city of _Dallas_ , state of _Texas_ .

FOR AND IN CONSIDERATION of the mutual promises and benefits to be derived by the parties, they do hereby agree to the following:

1. The Employee agrees to not directly or indirectly compete with the Employer or its affiliates, successors, or assigns during the term of employment and for a period of two (2) years following termination.

2. For the purposes of this agreement, "compete" shall include, but not be limited to, owning, managing, operating, consulting, or being employed by a business substantially similar to the business of the company during the term of employment, and, after employment, engaging in any of these activities within a _twenty-five_ (_25_) mile radius of the former employer.

3. This noncompete agreement shall, except where indicated, extend only to the geographic areas where the company generally conducts business and to existing customers or accounts no matter where they are located.

4. The Employee agrees to keep all business secrets of the Employer confidential both during and after employment. For purposes of this agreement, business secrets shall include but not be limited to information about the Employer, clients or customers, finances of the company, research and development, manufacturing processes or any other business or technical information.

5. Employee agrees not to remove from the Employer's premises any copies, computer disks, printouts or other information about the Employer's business, customers, clients, or accounts.

6. The Employee acknowledges that the information contained in the previously mentioned documents directly affects the income and value of the company, and that it may be difficult or even impossible to determine the damage that could result from their loss. Consequently, the parties agree that injunctive relief shall be awarded in the event that a potential breach of this agreement is imminent.

7. If any conflict shall arise between the parties, the law shall be interpreted according to the laws of the state of _Texas_ . Venue shall be _Dallas County_ .

8. In any action between the parties, the prevailing party shall be entitled to attorneys' fees and costs.

In witness whereof, the parties set their hands on this the day first above written.

Sarah Barrett
Witness

Judy Stanley
Signature of Employee

Chris Johnson
Witness

Frank Adams
Signature of Employer

Employee Noncompete and Confidentiality Agreement

THIS AGREEMENT, entered into this the _____ day of _____, 199 ___ , by and between _____ , Employer, whose address is _____ , city of _____ , state of _____ , and _____ , Employee, whose address is _____ , city of _____ , state of _____ .

FOR AND IN CONSIDERATION of the mutual promises and benefits to be derived by the parties, they do hereby agree to the following:

1. The Employee agrees to not directly or indirectly compete with the Employer or its affiliates, successors, or assigns during the term of employment and for a period of _____ years following termination.

2. For the purposes of this agreement, "compete" shall include, but not be limited to, owning, managing, operating, consulting or being employed by a business substantially similar to the business of the company during the term of employment, and, after employment engaging in any of these activities within a _____ (_____) mile radius of the former employer.

3. This noncompete agreement shall, except where indicated, extend only to the geographic areas where the company generally conducts business and to existing customers or accounts no matter where they are located.

4. The Employee agrees to keep all business secrets of the Employer confidential both during and after employment. For purposes of this agreement, business secrets shall include but not be limited to information about the Employer, clients or customers, finances of the company, research and development, manufacturing processes, or any other business or technical information.

5. The Employee agrees not to remove from the Employer's premises any copies, computer disks, printouts, or other information about the Employer's business, customers, clients, or accounts.

6. The Employee acknowledges that the information contained in the previously mentioned documents directly affects the income and value of the company, and that it may be difficult or even impossible to determine the damage that could result from their loss. Consequently, the parties agree that injunctive relief shall be awarded in the event that a potential breach of this agreement is imminent.

7. If any conflict shall arise between the parties, the law shall be interpreted according to the laws of the state of _____ . Venue shall be _____ .

8. In any action between the parties, the prevailing party
    shall be entitled to attorneys' fees and costs.

In witness whereof, the parties set their hands on this the
day first above written.

_____   _____
Witness   Signature of Employee

_____   _____
Witness   Signature of Employer

Confidentiality and Trade Secret Agreement

AGREEMENT by and between *Software Creations, Inc.* (Company) and *Stewart Jones* (Undersigned).

Whereas, the Company agrees to allow the Undersigned access to certain confidential information, trade secrets, or proprietary information relating to the affairs of the Company only for purposes of: *conducting his employment* , and,

Whereas, the Undersigned may review, examine, inspect, have access to, or obtain such information only for the purposes of his employment, and to otherwise hold such disclosed information confidential pursuant to the terms of this agreement.

BE IT ACKNOWLEDGED, that the Company has or shall furnish to the Undersigned certain confidential information, described on the attached list, and the Company may further allow the Undersigned the right to inspect the business of the Company and/or interview suppliers, employees, or representatives of the Company, only on the following conditions:

1. The Undersigned agrees to hold all disclosed confidential or proprietary information or trade secrets ("information") in trust and confidence and agrees that it shall be used only for the contemplated purpose, and shall not be used for any other purpose nor disclosed to any third party without the written consent of the Company.

2. No copies or abstracts will be made or retained of any written information supplied. Upon demand by the Company, all information, including written notes, photographs, or memoranda, shall be returned to the Company.

3. The disclosed information shall not be disclosed to any employee, consultant, or third party unless said party agrees to execute and be bound by the terms of this agreement.

4. It is understood that the Undersigned shall have no obligation to hold confidential any information that is known by the Undersigned or generally known within the industry prior to the date of this agreement, or that shall become common knowledge within the industry thereafter, as said information shall not be deemed protected under this agreement.

5. The Undersigned acknowledges the information disclosed herein as proprietary and trade secrets, and in the event of any breach, the Company shall be entitled to injunctive relief as a cumulative and not necessarily successive remedy without need to post bond.
6. This agreement shall be binding upon and inure to the benefit of the parties, their successors, assigns, and personal representatives.

Signed under seal this _12th_ day of _November_ , 199 _6_ .
In the presence of:

	Software Creations, Inc.
Greg Taylor	_Brian Jones, President_
Witness	Company
Sarah Barrett	_Stewart Jones_
Witness	Undersigned

Confidentiality and Trade Secret Agreement

AGREEMENT by and between _____ (Company) and _____ (Undersigned).

Whereas, the Company agrees to allow the Undersigned access to certain confidential information, trade secrets, or proprietary information relating to the affairs of the Company only for purposes of: _____ , and

Whereas, the Undersigned may review, examine, inspect, have access to, or obtain such information only for the purposes described above, and to otherwise hold such disclosed information confidential pursuant to the terms of this agreement.

BE IT ACKNOWLEDGED, that the Company has or shall furnish to the Undersigned certain confidential information, described on the attached list, and the Company may further allow the Undersigned the right to inspect the business of the Company and/or interview suppliers, employees, or representatives of the Company, only on the following conditions:

1. The Undersigned agrees to hold all disclosed confidential or proprietary information or trade secrets ("information") in trust and confidence and agrees that it shall be used only for the contemplated purpose, and shall not be used for any other purpose nor disclosed to any third party without the written consent of the Company.

2. No copies or abstracts will be made or retained of any written information supplied. Upon demand by the Company, all information, including written notes, photographs, or memoranda, shall be returned to the Company.

3. The disclosed information shall not be disclosed to any employee, consultant, or third party unless said party agrees to execute and be bound by the terms of this agreement.

4. It is understood that the Undersigned shall have no obligation to hold confidential any information that is known by the Undersigned or generally known within the industry prior to the date of this agreement, or that shall become common knowledge within the industry thereafter, as said information shall not be deemed protected under this agreement.

5. The Undersigned acknowledges the information disclosed herein as proprietary and trade secrets, and in the event of any breach, the Company shall be entitled to injunctive relief as a cumulative and not necessarily successive remedy without need to post bond.

6. This agreement shall be binding upon and inure to the benefit of the parties, their successors, assigns, and personal representatives.

Signed under seal this _____ day of _____ , 199 ___ .

In the presence of:

_____   _____
Witness   Company

_____   _____
Witness   Undersigned

Chapter 3
Power of Attorney

It is amazing that such a simple document can convey so much power. A *general power of attorney*, signed by you, conveys to an authorized person the right to become you in the eyes of the law.

For the period of time you grant someone your general power of attorney, he or she can sign contracts binding you, write checks on your account, and speak for you in any legal matter. True, the person is bound to act in your best interest, but if he or she does something you don't like, your recourse is against the person, not against the act. In other words, if a person to whom you have given a general power of attorney sells your home and spends the money, you probably won't be able to void the home sale. Your recourse will be to collect from the individual to whom you gave your power of attorney. Unfortunately, by then, the individual may be long gone.

If this tale of woe makes you leery of using a power of attorney—good! Caution is wise. Being forewarned, let me now tell you how to use the power of attorney effectively.

The power of attorney form conveys to another person the right to act on your behalf. This person becomes your *attorney-in-fact*. This has nothing to do with an attorney-at-law, and a person does not need to have a law degree to be an attorney-in-fact.

There are different types of attorney-in-fact authorizations and, as you might expect, a different form for each.

Note: I would highly recommend that all POAs be notarized so that they may be recorded if necessary. Call your local records office and ask exactly how many witnesses and/or notaries are necessary. Additionally, some courthouses now require special formats for recorded forms, so ask in advance.

This form is the broadest of all the POA forms because it conveys unlimited powers to your appointed attorney-in-fact. Once appointed, the person can act on your behalf for all legal purposes. Occasionally, someone representing another party in a transaction will require specific acts to be spelled out in the document before he or she will accept the POA. This has occasionally happened to me when I have worked with a lender's attorneys. They wanted specific language in the POA regarding a specific piece of property being conveyed. By being overly cautious, the attorneys became an obstacle to the transaction. In one case, it was easy to get the POA to conform the way they wanted, and I complied in order to move things along. In another instance, it would have been impossible to get the POA changed in time, and I held ground, citing chapter and verse. In this case, they gave ground. Since this is a good example of the way law is practiced, I would suggest that you be prepared for modifications in your forms when they become necessary.

The General Power of Attorney I have included in this book has boxes (❏) throughout the form for you to check. I have added these because they give additional proof of your specific intent and give more credence to your desire. Obviously, you need to check the appropriate boxes.

General Power of Attorney

Debi Cade , of _347 W. Reynolds_ , city of _Sanford_ , state of _Florida_ , hereby grants a general power of attorney to _Donna Pierce_, of _342 Storey Lane_ , city of _Lansing_ , state of _Michigan_ , to act as my attorney-in-fact.

(Check all appropriate boxes below.)

In granting this general power of attorney, I am authorizing my attorney-in-fact full authority to do and undertake all acts on my behalf that I could do personally, including but not limited to ❏ sell, deed, buy, trade, lease, mortgage, assign, rent, or dispose of my present or future real or personal property; ❏ the right to execute and perform any contracts in my name; ❏ the right to deposit, endorse, and withdraw funds to and from my bank accounts, depositories, or safe deposit boxes; ❏ the right to borrow, lend, or invest any funds; ❏ the right to initiate, defend, commence, or settle legal actions on my behalf; ❏ the right to vote any shares or beneficial interest I may have; ❏ the right to obtain any accountant, attorney, or other adviser deemed necessary to protect my interest generally or relative to any foregoing unlimited power.

My attorney-in-fact hereby agrees to accept this appointment subject to terms and conditions and to act and perform her duties in a fiduciary capacity consistent with my best wishes as she in her best discretion deems advisable, and I am affirming and ratifying all acts she so undertakes.

This power of attorney is subject to revocation by me at any time and shall be automatically revoked upon my death, provided that any person relying on this power of attorney before or after my death shall have the full right to accept the authority of my attorney-in-fact until receipt of actual notice of revocation.

The undersigned set their hand and seal on this the _5th_ day of _August_ , 199 _5_ .

Kathleen Shuman   _Debi Cade_
Witness   Grantor

Sarah Barrett
Witness

Greg Taylor   _Donna Pierce_
Witness   Attorney-in-fact

Chris Johnson
Witness

State of _Florida_
County of _Seminole_

The foregoing instrument was acknowledged before me this _4th_ day of _August_ , 199 _5_ , by _Debi Cade_ , who is personally known to me or who produced _Florida Driver's License_ as identification.

Jonathan Edwards
Notary Public, State of _Florida_
Jonathan Edwards
Printed Notary Name

My Commission Expires: _October 12, 1997_

General Power of Attorney

_____ , of _____ ,
(Name of Person Giving Power)
city of _____ , state of _____ , hereby grants a
general power of attorney to _____ , of _____ , city of
_____ , state of _____ , to act as my attorney-in-fact.
(Check all appropriate boxes below.)

In granting this general power of attorney, I am authorizing
my attorney-in-fact full authority to do and undertake all acts
on my behalf that I could do personally, including but not
limited to ❏ sell, deed, buy, trade, lease, mortgage, assign,
rent, or dispose of my present or future real or personal
property; ❏ the right to execute and perform any contracts in my
name; ❏ the right to deposit, endorse, and withdraw funds to and
from my bank accounts, depositories, or safe deposit boxes; ❏ the
right to borrow, lend, or invest any funds; ❏ the right to
initiate, defend, commence, or settle legal actions on my behalf;
❏ the right to vote any shares or beneficial interest I may have;
❏ the right to obtain any accountant, attorney, or other adviser
deemed necessary to protect my interest generally or relative to
any foregoing unlimited power.

My attorney-in-fact hereby agrees to accept this appointment
subject to terms and conditions and to act and perform his duties
in a fiduciary capacity consistent with my best wishes as he in
his best discretion deems advisable, and I am affirming and
ratifying all acts he so undertakes.

This power of attorney is subject to revocation by me at any
time and shall be automatically revoked upon my death, provided
that any person relying on this power of attorney before or after
my death shall have the full right to accept the authority of my
attorney-in-fact until receipt of actual notice of revocation.

The undersigned set their hand and seal on this the _____
day of _____ , 199 ___ .

_____   _____
Witness   Grantor

_____
Witness

_____   _____
Witness   Attorney-in-Fact

_____
Witness

State of _____
County of _____

The foregoing instrument was acknowledged before me this
_____ day of _____ , 199 ___, by _____ , who is
personally known to me or who produced _____ as
identification.

_____

Notary Public, State of _____

_____

Printed Notary Name

My Commission Expires: _____

Special Power of Attorney

Debi Cade , of _347 W. Reynolds_ , city of _Sanford_ , state of _Florida_ , hereby grants a special power of attorney to _Donna Pierce_ , of _342 Storey Lane_ , city of _Lansing_ , state of _Michigan_ , to act as my attorney-in-fact.

My attorney-in-fact shall have the full power and authority to undertake and perform the following acts on my behalf as though I had done so personally: _Sign all documents related to the transfer and closing of my home at 778 Jupiter Court, Lansing, Michigan._

The authority granted shall include all incidental acts which may reasonably need to be performed to carry out the authority being granted.

My attorney-in-fact agrees to accept this appointment and agrees to act and perform in a fiduciary capacity consistent with my best interests, and I affirm and ratify all acts undertaken.

This power of attorney can be revoked by me at any time and shall be automatically revoked upon my death. It is provided that any person relying on this power of attorney before or after my death shall have the authority to accept my attorney-in-fact in accordance with the powers granted until receipt of actual notice of revocation.

The undersigned set their hand and seal on this the _4th_ day of _August_ , 199 _5_ .

Kathleen Shuman
Witness

Debi Cade
Grantor

Sarah Barrett
Witness

Greg Taylor
Witness

Donna   Pierce
Attorney-in-Fact

Chris Johnson
Witness

State of _Florida_
County of _Seminole_

The foregoing instrument was acknowledged before me this _4th_ day of _August, 1995_ , by _Debi Cade_ , who is personally known to me or who produced _Florida Driver's License_ as identification.

> _Jonathan Edward_
> Notary Public, State of _Florida_
> Jonathan Edwards
> Printed Notary Name

My Commission Expires: _October 12, 1997_

Special Power of Attorney

_____ , of _____ ,

(Name of Person Giving Power)

city of _____ , state of _____ , hereby grants a special power of attorney to _____ , of _____ , city of _____ , state of _____ , to act as my attorney-in-fact.

My attorney-in-fact shall have the full power and authority to undertake and perform the following acts on my behalf as though I had done so personally: _____

_____

_____

_____

_____

_____

The authority granted shall include all incidental acts which may reasonably need to be performed to carry out the authority being granted.

My attorney-in-fact agrees to accept this appointment and agrees to act and perform in a fiduciary capacity consistent with my best interests, and I affirm and ratify all acts undertaken.

This power of attorney can be revoked by me at any time and shall be automatically revoked upon my death. It is provided that any person relying on this power of attorney before or after my death shall have the authority to accept my attorney-in-fact in accordance with the powers granted until receipt of actual notice of revocation.

The undersigned set their hand and seal on this the _____ day of _____ , 199 ___ .

_____   _____

Witness   Grantor

_____

Witness

_____   _____

Witness   Attorney-in-Fact

_____

Witness

State of _____
County of _____

The foregoing instrument was acknowledged before me this
_____ day of _____ , 199 ___ , by _____ , who is
personally known to me or who produced _____ as
identification.

                                    _____
                                    Notary Public, State of _____

                                    _____
                                    Printed Notary Name

My Commission Expires: _____

Revocation of Power of Attorney

Debi Cade , of _347 W. Reynolds_ , city of _Sanford_ , state of _Florida_ , does hereby revoke the Power of Attorney granted to _Donna Pierce_ , of _342 Storey Lane_ , city of _Lansing_ , state of _Michigan_ , on the _4th_ day of _August_ , 199 _5_ .

This revocation and termination of all duties and authority granted under the power of attorney dated _August 4, 1995_ shall take effect immediately.

The undersigned sets their hand and seal on this the _12th_ day of _September_ , 199 _5_ .

Greg Taylor   _Debi Cade_
Witness   Grantor

Chris Johnson
Witness

State of _Florida_
County of _Seminole_

The foregoing instrument was acknowledged before me this _12th_ day of _September_ , 199_5_, by _Debi Cade_ , who is personally known to me or who produced _Florida Driver's License_ as identification.

Jonathan Edwards
Notary Public, state of _Florida_
Jonathan Edwards
Printed Notary Name

My Commission Expires: _October 12, 1997_

I, _Donna Pierce_ , hereby acknowledge receipt of termination.

Donna Pierce
Attorney-in-Fact

Revocation of Power of Attorney

_____ , of _____ , city of _____ ,
(Name of Revoking Party)
state of _____ , does hereby revoke the Power of Attorney
granted to _____ , of _____ , city of _____ ,
state of _____ , on the _____ day of _____ ,
199 ___ .

This revocation and termination of all duties and authority
granted under the power of attorney dated _____ shall take
effect immediately.

The undersigned sets their hand and seal on this the
_____ day of _____ , 199 ___ .

_____   _____
Witness   Grantor

_____
Witness

State of _____
County of _____

The foregoing instrument was acknowledged before me this
_____ day of _____ , 199 ___ , by _____ , who is
personally known to me or who produced _____ as
identification.

                              _____
                              Notary Public, state of _____
                              _____
                              Printed Notary Name

My Commission Expires: _____

I, _____ , hereby acknowledge receipt of termination.
    Attorney-in-Fact

                              _____
                              Attorney-in-Fact

Chapter 4
Loan Agreements and Guarantees

There are many opportunities to use promissory notes in business. Some you will sign; others will be signed by your customers, employees, and people you lend money to for one reason or another.

A couple of important observations are called for. First, when you lend money to people you know, there is a tendency not to use a promissory note. After all, you know them, right? Wrong! Not using a promissory note is a big mistake. It isn't so much that you need the piece of paper in order to collect; it is that writing it down shows that you are serious about the loan. It also allows you to ask important questions like, "When are you going to pay this back?" and "How much interest you will pay?"

The second thing the promissory note will do is help people's memory. Without a note, people tend to forget that you loaned them money, and when you finally are forced to ask for repayment, you wind up looking like the bad guy.

I also want you to know that not all promissory notes are the same. When someone says to you, "This is just a standard note," beware. The question you should ask is, "Whose standard?"

You will find that there are in fact "plain vanilla" notes where you simply promise to repay, and there are also others in which you pledge assets, waive rights, and personally guarantee corporate obligations. While some of these more onerous notes may seem a bit unfair, let me remind you that your signature will show that you agreed.

When you understand these differing points concerning promissory notes, you will see that there are some you will be willing to sign as the maker and some you will want to sign only if you are the lender.

A guarantee is a form you don't really want to sign, but you probably will have to sign at some point. The guarantee is used by a lender to give it additional security on a loan. Since the S&L crisis of the late 1980s, lenders are even more concerned about security. Consequently, if you obtain a business loan for your corporation, you are likely to be asked to guarantee it personally. Depending on your company's net worth and your personal net worth, your spouse may also be asked to sign the guarantee. You might as well start thinking about it because sooner or later you will be asked the question, and how you respond may well determine the decision on your loan.

As with most legal documents, there are simple versions and there are extremely complicated ones. In the case of guarantees, the lender typically attempts to include everything you and your spouse have or may have in the future. I've seen bank guarantees that run six or seven pages of very small type. Amazingly, a bank officer dropped one of these on me at a closing with the classic phrase, "Oh, it's just one of our standard forms." Don't you believe it for a minute. There is nothing standard about guaranteeing the repayment of a loan.

Promissory Demand Note

October 12, 1995 $ _5,000.00_

    FOR VALUE RECEIVED, the undersigned promises to pay _Brad Loan_ , whose address is _187 Sycamore Street_ , city of _Plant_ , state of _Florida_ , the principal amount of _Five Thousand and no/100 dollars_ ($ _5,000.00_) plus interest at the annual rate of _ten_ percent (_10_ %) on any unpaid balance.

    THIS NOTE is immediately due and payable in full, including interest, upon written demand of the noteholder to the borrower.

    THE NOTE is not assumable without the written consent of the borrower. The borrower waives presentment, demand, protest, and notice. In the event of any default, the borrower shall be responsible for all reasonable attorneys' fees and costs.

Sarah Barrett   _Jason Sweet_
Witness   Borrower's Signature

Greg Taylor   Jason Sweet
Witness   741 Flower Street
                                   Plant, FL 33566

_____   _____
Witness   Co-Borrower (if any)

_____   _____
Witness   Print Co-Borrower's Name

                                   _____
                                   Address

                                   _____
                                   City, State, Zip

Promissory Demand Note

_____
Date

$ _____
Total Amount

    FOR VALUE RECEIVED, the undersigned promises to pay _____ , whose address is _____ city of _____ , state of _____ , the principal amount of _____ ($ _____) plus interest at the annual rate of _____ percent (___ %) on any unpaid balance.

    THIS NOTE is immediately due and payable in full, including interest, upon written demand of the noteholder to the borrower.

    THE NOTE is not assumable without the written consent of the borrower. The borrower waives presentment, demand, protest, and notice. In the event of any default, the borrower shall be responsible for all reasonable attorneys' fees and costs.

_____
Witness

_____
Borrower's Signature

_____
Witness

_____
Print Borrower's Name

_____
Address

_____
City, State, Zip

_____
Witness

_____
Co-Borrower (if any)

_____
Witness

_____
Print Co-Borrower's Name

_____
Address

_____
City, State, Zip

Promissory Balloon Note

October 12, 1995 $ *5,000.00*

FOR VALUE RECEIVED, the undersigned promises to pay *Brad Loan* , whose address is *187 Sycamore Street* , city of *Plant* , state of *Florida* , the principal amount of *Five Thousand and no/100 dollars* ($ *5,000.00*) plus interest at the annual rate of *ten* percent (*10* %) on any unpaid balance.

THIS NOTE is due and payable in full on or before *October 12* , 199 *6* . All payments received shall apply first to interest and then to principal.

THIS NOTE is not assumable without the written consent of the borrower. The borrower waives presentment, demand, protest, and notice. In the event of any default, the borrower shall be responsible for all reasonable attorneys' fees and costs.

Kathleen Shuman   *Jason Sweet*
Witness   Borrower's Signature

Sarah Barrett   Jason Sweet
Witness   741 Flower Street
                                     Plant, FL 33566

_____   _____
Witness   Co-Borrower (if any)

_____   _____
Witness   Print Co-Borrower's Name

                                     _____
                                     Address

                                     _____
                                     City, State, Zip

Promissory Balloon Note

_____ $ _____

Date   Total Amount

         FOR VALUE RECEIVED, the undersigned promises to pay _____ , whose address is _____ , city of _____ , state of _____ , the principal amount of _____ ($ _____) plus interest at the annual rate of _____ percent (___ %) on any unpaid balance.

         THIS NOTE is due and payable in full on or before _____ , 199 ___ . All payments received shall apply first to interest and then to principal.

         THIS NOTE is not assumable without the written consent of the borrower. The borrower waives presentment, demand, protest, and notice. In the event of any default, the borrower shall be responsible for all reasonable attorneys' fees and costs.

_____   _____

Witness   Borrower's Signature

_____   _____

Witness   Print Borrower's Name

                                            _____

                                            Address

                                            _____

                                            City, State, Zip

_____   _____

Witness   Co-Borrower (if any)

_____   _____

Witness   Print Co-Borrower's Name

                                            _____

                                            Address

                                            _____

                                            City, State, Zip

Promissory Installment Note

October 12, 1995 $ _5,000.00_

   FOR VALUE RECEIVED, the undersigned promises to pay _Brad Loan_ , whose address is _187 Sycamore Street_ , city of _Plant_ , state of _Florida_ , the principal amount of _Five Thousand and no/100 dollars_ ($ _5,000.00_) plus interest at the annual rate of _ten_ percent (_10_ %) on any unpaid balance.

   Payments are payable to the noteholder in equal consecutive _monthly_ payments of _$439.58_ , including interest and continuing until paid in full. The final due date is _October 12_ , 199 _6_ , unless paid off sooner. All payments shall be applied first to interest earned then to principal.

   In the event of default under this note by the failure to make a payment within _five_ (_5_) business days of its due date, or upon death, bankruptcy, or insolvency of the maker, the entire amount then owing shall be due upon demand.

   THIS NOTE is not assumable without the written consent of the borrower. The borrower waives presentment, demand, protest, and notice. In the event of any default, the borrower shall be responsible for all reasonable attorneys' fees and costs.

   This contract shall be governed under the laws of the state of _Florida_ . Time is of the essence as to each and every promissory.

Kathleen Shuman	_Jason Sweet_
Witness	Borrower's Signature
Sarah Barrett	Jason Sweet
Witness	741 Flower Street
	Plant, FL 33566
_____	_____
Witness	Co-Borrower (if any)
_____	_____
Witness	Print Co-Borrower's Name
	_____
	Address
	_____
	City, State, Zip

Promissory Installment Note

_____ $ _____
Date   Total Amount

    FOR VALUE RECEIVED, the undersigned promises to pay _____ ,
whose address is _____ , city of _____ , state of
_____ , the principal amount of _____ ($_____)
plus interest at the annual rate of _____ percent (___ %)
on any unpaid balance.

    Payments are payable to the noteholder in equal consecutive
_____ payments of $ _____ , including
(monthly, quarterly, annual)
interest and continuing until paid in full. The final due date is
_____ , 199 ___ , unless paid off sooner. All payments shall
be applied first to interest earned and then to principal.

    In the event of default under this note by the failure to make
a payment within _____ (___) business days of its due
date, or upon death, bankruptcy, or insolvency of the maker, the
entire amount then owing shall be due upon demand.

    THIS NOTE is not assumable without the written consent of the
borrower. The borrower waives presentment, demand, protest, and
notice. In the event of any default, the borrower shall be
responsible for all reasonable attorneys' fees and costs.

    This contract shall be governed under the laws of the state of
_____ . Time is of the essence as to each and every
promissory.

_____   _____
Witness   Borrower's Signature

_____   _____
Witness   Print Borrower's Name

                                     _____
                                     Address

                                     _____
                                     City, State, Zip

_____   _____
Witness   Co-Borrower (if any)

_____   _____
Witness   Print Co-Borrower's Name

                                     _____
                                     Address

                                     _____
                                     City, State, Zip

Payment in Full Receipt

    THE UNDERSIGNED hereby acknowledges receipt of $ _5,000.00_ paid by _Jason Sweet_ of _711 Flower Street_ , city of _Plant_ , state of _Florida_ .

    This payment is made in full satisfaction of the following described debt: _Promissory Note dated October 12, 1995._

September 1, 1996
Date

Brad Loan
Signature

Payment in Full Receipt

THE UNDERSIGNED hereby acknowledges receipt of $ _____ paid by _____ of _____ , city of _____ , state of _____ .

    This payment is made in full satisfaction of the following described debt: _____

_____

_____

_____

_____

_____

_____

_____   _____

Date   Signature

Payment Receipt

THE UNDERSIGNED hereby acknowledges receipt of $ _1,000_ paid
by _Jason Sweet_ of _741 Flower Street_ , city of _Plant_ , state
of _Florida_ .

This payment shall be credited to the following account:
Promissory Note dated October 12, 1995.

February 15, 1996
Date

Brad Loan
Signature

Payment Receipt

THE UNDERSIGNED hereby acknowledges receipt of $ _____
paid by _____ of _____ , city of _____ , state of
_____ .

This payment shall be credited to the following account: _____

_____
_____
_____
_____
_____
_____

_____   _____
Date   Signature

Security Agreement

THE UNDERSIGNED for good and valuable consideration grant to _Brad Loan_ of _187 Sycamore Street_ , city of _Plant City_ , state of _Florida_ , a security agreement on the following described property:

1. _A 1994 Brunswick Pool Table._
2. _A 1991 Sea Ray 20' Boat & Trailer._

The purpose of this document is to convey a security interest in the described property pursuant to Article 9 of the Uniform Commercial Code.

The security interest is granted to secure the payment of that certain debt obligation between the parties in the amount of _Five Thousand and no/100 dollars_ ($ _5,000.00_) and evidenced by a promissory note dated _October 12, 1995_ as attached to this document and incorporated.

The undersigned acknowledge and warrant:

1. They are the sole owners of the described property, and it is free and clear of any other lien or encumbrances.
2. The undersigned have full authority to convey this interest.
3. They agree to sign any agreements necessary to ultimately perfect a security interest in the property listed.
4. The collateral will remain at its current location of _187 Sycamore Street_ , city of _Plant City_ , state of _Florida._
5. The undersigned ❑ shall ❑ shall not maintain full insurance replacement coverage against the property.
6. Upon default of any payment or performance of the undersigned's obligation secured by this agreement, then the secured party may declare all obligations immediately due and payable and have all remedies of a secured party under the Uniform Commercial Code.

7. This security agreement shall be in default upon the death, insolvency, or bankruptcy of the maker under this agreement.
8. Upon default, the undersigned shall pay all reasonable attorneys' fees and cost necessary to enforce collection under this agreement.

Kathleen Shuman
Witness

Greg Taylor
Witness

Jason Sweet
Undersigned Debtor's Signature

Jason Sweet
711 Flower Street
Plant City, FL 33566

State of _Florida_
County of _Seminole_

Sworn to and subscribed before me this _12th_ day of _October_ , 199 _5_ , by _Jason Sweet_ , who is personally known to me or who produced _Florida Driver's License_ as identification.

Caroline Smith
Notary Public, state of _Florida_
Caroline Smith
Notary's Printed Name

My Commission Expires: _October 12, 1997_

Security Agreement

THE UNDERSIGNED for good and valuable consideration grant to
_____ of _____ , city of _____ , state of
_____ , a security agreement on the following described
property: _____
_____
_____
_____
_____

The purpose of this document is to convey a security interest
in the described property pursuant to Article 9 of the Uniform
Commercial Code.

The security interest is granted to secure the payment of that
certain debt obligation between the parties in the amount of
_____ ($ _____) and evidenced by a promissory note
dated _____ as attached to this document and incorporated.

The undersigned acknowledge and warrant:

1. They are the sole owners of the described property, and it
   is free and clear of any other lien or encumbrances.
2. The undersigned have full authority to convey this interest.
3. They agree to sign any agreements necessary to ultimately
   perfect a security interest in the property listed.
4. The collateral will remain at its current location of
   _____ , city of _____ , state of _____ .
5. The undersigned ❑ shall ❑ shall not maintain full
   insurance replacement coverage against the property.
6. Upon default of any payment or performance of the
   undersigned's obligation secured by this agreement, then
   the secured party may declare all obligations immediately
   due and payable and have all remedies of a secured party
   under the Uniform Commercial Code.
7. This security agreement shall be in default upon the death,
   insolvency, or bankruptcy of the maker under this agreement.
8. Upon default, the undersigned shall pay all reasonable
   attorneys' fees and costs necessary to enforce collection
   under this agreement.

_____   _____
Witness   Undersigned Debtor's Signature

_____   _____
Witness   Printed Name

                                 _____
                                 Address

                                 _____
                                 City, State, Zip

State of _____
County of _____

Sworn to and subscribed before me this _____ day of _____,
199 ___ , by _____ , who is personally known to me or who
produced _____ as identification.

_____
Notary Public, state of _____

_____
Notary's Printed Name

My Commission Expires: _____

Pledge of Personal Property

FOR GOOD AND VALUABLE CONSIDERATION, the undersigned (Pledgor) of _741 Flower St._ , city of _Plant City_ , state of _Florida_ , deposits, delivers to, and pledges with _Brad Loan_ (Pledgee) of _187 Sycamore St._ , city of _Plant City_ , state of _Florida_ , as collateral security to secure the payment of the following described debt owing Pledgee: _Five Thousand Dollars_

The collateral consisting of the following personal property (collateral):

1. _1994 Brunswick Pool Table_
2. _1991 Sea Ray 20' Boat & Trailer_

It is further agreed that:

1. Pledgee may assign or transfer said debt and the pledged collateral hereunder to any third party.
2. The Pledgor shall pay any and all insurance it elects to maintain or the Pledgee reasonably requires on the pledged collateral and shall pay any personal property, excise, or other tax or levy.
3. Pledgee shall have no liability for loss, destruction, or casualty to the collateral unless caused by its own negligence or the negligence of any assignee.
4. The Pledgor warrants that it has good title to the pledge collateral and full authority to pledge same, and that said collateral is free of any adverse lien, encumbrance, or adverse claim.
5. Upon default of payment of the debt or breach of this pledge agreement, the Pledgee or holder shall have full rights to foreclose on the pledged collateral and exercise its rights as a secured party pursuant to Article 9 of the Uniform Commercial Code, said rights being cumulative with any other rights the Pledgee or holder may have against the Pledgor.

Pledgor understands that upon foreclosure the pledged property may be sold at public auction or private sale. The Pledgor shall be provided reasonable notice of any said intended public or private sale, and the Pledgor shall have full rights to redeem said collateral at any time prior to said sale upon payment of the balance due hereunder together with accrued fees and expense of collection. In the event the collateral shall be sold for less than the amount then owing, the Pledgor shall be liable for any deficiency.

Upon payment of the obligation for which the collateral is pledged, the property shall be returned to the Pledgor and this pledge agreement shall be terminated.

This pledge agreement shall be binding upon and inure to the benefit of the parties, their successors, assigns, and personal representatives.

Upon default the Pledgor shall pay all reasonable attorneys' fees and costs of collection.

Signed under seal this _8th_ day of _August, 1995_ .

Chris Johnson
Witness

Jason Sweet
Pledgor

Greg Taylor
Witness

Brad Loan
Pledgee

State of _____
County of _____

Sworn to and subscribed before me this _____ day of _____ , 199 ___ , by _____ who is personally known to me or who produced _____ as identification.

_____
Notary Public, state of _____

_____
Notary's Printed Name

My Commission Expires: _____

Pledge of Personal Property

FOR GOOD AND VALUABLE CONSIDERATION, the undersigned (Pledgor) of _____ , city of _____ , state of _____ , deposits, delivers to, and pledges with _____ (Pledgee) of _____ , city of _____ , state of _____ , as collateral security to secure the payment of the following described debt owing Pledgee: _____

_____
_____
_____
_____
_____
_____

The collateral consisting of the following personal property (collateral):

_____
_____
_____
_____
_____

It is further agreed that:

1. Pledgee may assign or transfer said debt and the pledged collateral hereunder to any third party.

2. The Pledgor shall pay any and all insurance it elects to maintain or the Pledgee reasonably requires on the pledged collateral and shall pay any personal property, excise, or other tax or levy.

3. Pledgee shall have no liability for loss, destruction, or casualty to the collateral unless caused by its own negligence, or the negligence of any assignee.

4. The Pledgor warrants that it has good title to the pledge collateral and full authority to pledge same, and that said collateral is free of any adverse lien, encumbrance, or adverse claim.

5. Upon default of payment of the debt or breach of this pledge agreement, the Pledgee or holder shall have full rights to foreclose on the pledged collateral and exercise its rights as a secured party pursuant to Article 9 of the Uniform Commercial Code, said rights being cumulative with any other rights the Pledgee or holder may have against the Pledgor.

Pledgor understands that upon foreclosure the pledged property may be sold at public auction or private sale. The Pledgor shall be provided reasonable notice of any said intended public or private sale, and the Pledgor shall have full rights to redeem said collateral at any time prior to said sale upon payment of the balance due hereunder together with accrued fees and expense of collection. In the event the collateral shall be sold for less than the amount then owing, the Pledgor shall be liable for any deficiency.

Upon payment of the obligation for which the collateral is pledged, the property shall be returned to the Pledgor and this pledge agreement shall be terminated.

This pledge agreement shall be binding upon and inure to the benefit of the parties, their successors, assigns, and personal representatives.

Upon default the Pledgor shall pay all reasonable attorneys' fees and costs of collection.

Signed under seal this _____ day of _____ , 199 ___.

_____   _____
Witness   Pledgor

_____   _____
Witness   Pledgee

State of _____
County of _____

Sworn to and subscribed before me this _____ day of _____ , 199 ___ , by _____ who is personally known to me or who produced as identification.

                              _____
                              Notary Public, state of _____

                              _____
                              Notary's Printed Name

My Commission Expires: _____

Pledge of Shares of Stock

FOR GOOD AND VALUABLE CONSIDERATION, the undersigned (Pledgor) hereby deposits, delivers to, and pledges with _Brad Loan_ (Pledgee) of _187 Sycamore St._ , city of _Plant_ , state of _Florida_ , as collateral security to secure the payment of the following described debt owing Pledgee: _Five Thousand and no/100 Dollars ($5,000)_

The shares of stock, described as _200_ shares of stock of _Able_ (Corporation), represented as stock certificate number(s) _1002_ .

It is further agreed that:

1. Pledgee may assign or transfer said debt and the collateral pledged hereunder to any third party.
2. In the event a stock dividend or further issue of stock in the Corporation is issued to Pledgor, Pledgor shall pledge said shares as additional collateral for the debt.
3. Pledgor shall have full rights to vote said shares and shall be entitled to all dividend income, except that stock dividends shall also be pledged.
4. Pledgor shall not issue any proxy or assignment of rights to the pledged shares.
5. Pledgor warrants and represents that it has good title to the shares being pledged, they are free from liens and encumbrances or prior pledge, and the Pledgor has full authority to transfer said shares as collateral security.
6. Upon default of payment of the debt or breach of this pledge agreement, the Pledgee or holder shall have full rights to foreclose on the pledged shares and exercise its rights as a secured party pursuant to Article 9 of the Uniform Commercial Code, said rights being cumulative with any other rights the Pledgee or holder may have against the Pledgor.

Pledgor understands that upon foreclosure the pledged shares may be sold at public auction or private sale. The Pledgor shall be provided reasonable notice of said intended public or private sale, and the Pledgor shall have full rights to redeem said shares at any time prior to said sale upon payment of the balance due hereunder and accrued costs of collection. In the event the shares shall be sold for less than the amount then owing, the Pledgor shall be liable for any deficiency.

Upon payment of the obligation for which the shares are pledged, the shares shall be returned to the Pledgor and this pledge agreement shall be terminated.

This pledge agreement shall be binding upon and inure to the benefit of the parties, their successors, assigns, and personal representatives.

Upon default the Pledgor shall pay all reasonable attorneys' fees and costs of collection.

Signed under seal this _8th_ day of _August_ , 199 _5_ .

Sarah Barrett	_Jason Sweet_
Witness	Pledgor
Greg Taylor	_Brad Loan_
Witness	Pledgee

Pledge of Shares of Stock

FOR GOOD AND VALUABLE CONSIDERATION, the undersigned (Pledgor) hereby deposits, delivers to, and pledges with _____ (Pledgee) of _____ , city of _____ , state of _____ , as collateral security to secure the payment of the following described debt owing Pledgee: _____

_____

_____

_____

_____

_____

_____

The shares of stock, described as _____ shares of stock of _____ (Corporation), represented as stock certificate number(s) _____ .

It is further agreed that:

1. Pledgee may assign or transfer said debt and the collateral pledged hereunder to any third party.

2. In the event a stock dividend or further issue of stock in the Corporation is issued to Pledgor, Pledgor shall pledge said shares as additional collateral for the debt.

3. Pledgor shall have full rights to vote said shares and shall be entitled to all dividend income, except that stock dividends shall also be pledged.

4. Pledgor shall not issue any proxy or assignment of rights to the pledged shares.

5. Pledgor warrants and represents that it has good title to the shares being pledged, they are free from liens and encumbrances or prior pledge, and the Pledgor has full authority to transfer said shares as collateral security.

6. Upon default of payment of the debt or breach of this pledge agreement, the Pledgee or holder shall have full rights to foreclose on the pledged shares and exercise its rights as a secured party pursuant to Article 9 of the Uniform Commercial Code, said rights being cumulative with any other rights the Pledgee or holder may have against the Pledgor.

Pledgor understands that upon foreclosure the pledged shares may be sold at public auction or private sale. The Pledgor shall be provided reasonable notice of said intended public or private sale, and the Pledgor shall have full rights to redeem said shares at any time prior to said sale upon payment of the balance due hereunder and accrued costs of collection. In the event the shares shall be sold for less than the amount then owing, the Pledgor shall be liable for any deficiency.

Upon payment of the obligation for which the shares are pledged, the shares shall be returned to the Pledgor and this pledge agreement shall be terminated.

This pledge agreement shall be binding upon and inure to the benefit of the parties, their successors, assigns, and personal representatives.

Upon default the Pledgor shall pay all reasonable attorneys' fees and costs of collection.

Signed under seal this _____ day of _____ , 199 ___ .

_____   _____
Witness   Pledgor

_____   _____
Witness   Pledgee

Unlimited Guaranty

FOR VALUE RECEIVED, and as an inducement for _Brad Loan_ (Creditor) of _187 Sycamore St._ , city of _Plant City_ , state of _Florida_ , to extend credit to _Jason Sweet_ (Borrower) of _741 Flower St._ , city of _Plant City_ , state of _Florida_ , the undersigned unconditionally guarantees to Creditor the prompt and full payment of all sums now or hereinafter due Creditor from Borrower.

The undersigned agrees to remain fully bound to this guaranty notwithstanding any extension, forbearance, modification, or waiver, or release, discharge, or substitution of any party, collateral, or security for the debt, and the undersigned consents to and waives all notice of same. In the event of default, the Creditor may seek payment directly from the undersigned without need to proceed first against the Borrower. The undersigned waives all suretyship defenses generally.

In the event enforcement of this guaranty shall become necessary, Guarantor agrees to pay all costs associated with enforcement and collection, including all reasonable attorneys' fees.

This guaranty is unlimited as to amount or duration. Guarantor hereto may terminate his obligations as to future credit extended after delivery of notice of guaranty termination to the Creditor by certified mail, return receipt. Notice of termination shall not discharge Guarantor's obligations as to debts incurred prior to the date of termination.

This guaranty shall be governed by the laws of the state of _Florida_ and shall be binding upon and inure to the benefit of the parties, their successors, assigns, and personal representatives.

Signed under seal this _8th_ day of _August_ , 199 _5_ .

Kathleen Shuman
Witness

Bob Reynolds
Witness

Brenda Sweet
Guarantor

Brenda Sweet
21 Bose St.
Plant City, FL 33566

Unlimited Guaranty

FOR VALUE RECEIVED, and as an inducement for _____
(Creditor) of _____ , city of _____ , state of
_____ , to extend credit to _____ (Borrower) of
_____ , city of _____ , state of _____ , the
undersigned unconditionally guarantees to Creditor the prompt and
full payment of all sums now or hereinafter due Creditor from
Borrower.

The undersigned agrees to remain fully bound to this guaranty
notwithstanding any extension, forbearance, modification, or
waiver, or release, discharge, or substitution of any party,
collateral, or security for the debt, and the undersigned
consents to and waives all notice of same. In the event of
default, the Creditor may seek payment directly from the
undersigned without need to proceed first against the Borrower.
The undersigned waives all suretyship defenses generally.

In the event enforcement of this guaranty shall become
necessary, Guarantor agrees to pay all costs associated with
enforcement and collection, including all reasonable attorneys'
fees.

This guaranty is unlimited as to amount or duration. Guarantor
hereto may terminate his obligations as to future credit extended
after delivery of notice of guaranty termination to the Creditor
by certified mail, return receipt. Notice of termination shall
not discharge Guarantor's obligations as to debts incurred prior
to the date of termination.

This guaranty shall be governed by the laws of the state of
_____ and shall be binding upon and inure to the benefit of
the parties, their successors, assigns, and personal
representatives.

Signed under seal this _____ day of _____ , 199 ___ .

_____
Witness

_____
Witness

_____
Guarantor

_____
Address

_____
City, State, Zip

Limited Guaranty

FOR VALUE RECEIVED, and as an inducement for _Brad Loan_ (Creditor) of _187 Sycamore St._ , city of _Plant City_ , state of _Florida_ , to extend credit to _Jason Sweet_ (Borrower) of _741 Flower St._ , city of _Plant City_ , state of _Florida_ , the undersigned unconditionally guarantees to Creditor the prompt and punctual payment of certain sums now or hereinafter due Creditor from Borrower, provided that the liability of the Guarantor hereunder shall be limited to the sum of _Three thousand and no/100 dollars_ ($ _3,000.00_) as a maximum liability and Guarantor shall not be liable under this guaranty for any greater or further amount.

The undersigned Guarantor agrees to remain fully bound on this guaranty, notwithstanding any extension, forbearance, indulgence, or waiver, or release or discharge or substitution of any party or collateral or security for the debt. In the event of default, Creditor may seek payment directly from the undersigned without need to proceed first against Borrower. Guarantor further waives all suretyship defenses consistent with this limited guaranty.

In the event enforcement of this guaranty shall become necessary, Guarantor agrees to pay all costs associated with enforcement and collection, including all reasonable attorneys' fees.

Guarantor hereto may terminate his obligations as to future credit extended after delivery of notice of guaranty termination to the Creditor by certified mail, return receipt. Notice of termination shall not discharge Guarantor's obligations as to debts incurred prior to the date of termination.

This guaranty shall be governed by the laws of the state of _Florida_ and shall be binding upon and inure to the benefit of the parties, their successors, assigns, and personal representatives.

Signed under seal this _8th_ day of _August_ , 199 _5_ .

Sarah Barrett
Witness

Greg Taylor
Witness

Brenda Sweet
Guarantor

Brenda Sweet
21 Bose St.
Plant City, FL 33566

Limited Guaranty

FOR VALUE RECEIVED, and as an inducement for _____ (Creditor) of _____ , city of _____ , state of _____ , to extend credit to _____ (Borrower) of _____ , city of _____ , state of _____ , the undersigned unconditionally guarantees to Creditor the prompt and punctual payment of certain sums now or hereinafter due Creditor from Borrower, provided that the liability of the Guarantor hereunder shall be limited to the sum of _____ ($ _____) as a maximum liability and Guarantor shall not be liable under this guarantee for any greater or further amount.

The undersigned Guarantor agrees to remain fully bound on this guaranty, notwithstanding any extension, forbearance, indulgence, or waiver, or release or discharge or substitution of any party or collateral or security for the debt. In the event of default, Creditor may seek payment directly from the undersigned without need to proceed first against borrower. Guarantor further waives all suretyship defenses consistent with this limited guaranty.

In the event enforcement of this guaranty shall become necessary, Guarantor agrees to pay all costs associated with enforcement and collection, including all reasonable attorneys' fees.

This guaranty is unlimited as to amount or duration. Guarantor hereto may terminate his obligations as to future credit extended after delivery of notice of guaranty termination to the Creditor by certified mail, return receipt. Notice of termination shall not discharge Guarantor's obligations as to debts incurred prior to the date of termination.

This guaranty shall be governed by the laws of the state of _____ and shall be binding upon and inure to the benefit of the parties, their successors, assigns, and personal representatives.

Signed under seal this _____ day of _____ , 199 ___ .

_____   _____
Witness   Guarantor

_____   _____
Witness   Address

                                  _____
                                  City, State, Zip

Specific Guaranty

FOR VALUE RECEIVED, and as an inducement for _Brad Loan_ (Creditor) of _187 Sycamore St._ , city of _Plant City_ , state of _Florida_ , to extend credit to _Jason Sweet_ (Borrower) of _741 Flowers St._ , city of _Plant City_ state of _Florida_ , the undersigned unconditionally guarantees to Creditor the prompt and full payment of the following specific debt owed to Creditor from Borrower: _Five Thousand and no/100 Dollars_ ($ _5,000_).

And the undersigned agree to remain bound on this guaranty notwithstanding any extension, renewal, indulgence, forbearance, or waiver, or release, discharge, or substitution of any collateral or security for the debt. In the event of default, Creditor may seek payment directly from the undersigned without need to proceed first against Borrower, and the undersigned waive all suretyship defenses.

The obligations of the undersigned under this guarantee shall be only to the specific debt described and to no other debt or obligation between Borrower and Creditor.

In the event of default, the Guarantor shall be responsible for all attorneys' fees and reasonable costs of collection.

This guaranty shall be governed by the laws of the state of _Florida_ and shall be binding upon and inure to the benefit of the parties, their successors, assigns, and personal representatives.

Signed under seal this _8th_ day of _August_ , 199 _5_ .

Sarah Barrett	_Brenda Sweet_
Witness	Guarantor
Greg Taylor	_Brenda Sweet_
Witness	_21 Bose St._
	Plant City, FL 33566

Specific Guaranty

FOR VALUE RECEIVED, and as an inducement for _____ (Creditor) of _____ , city of _____ , state of _____ , to extend credit to _____ (Borrower) of _____ , city of _____ , state of _____ , the undersigned unconditionally guarantees to Creditor the prompt and full payment of the following specific debt owed to Creditor from Borrower:

_____
_____
_____
_____

And the undersigned agree to remain bound on this guaranty notwithstanding any extension, renewal, indulgence, forbearance, or waiver, or release, discharge, or substitution of any collateral or security for the debt. In the event of default, Creditor may seek payment directly from the undersigned without need to proceed first against Borrower, and the undersigned waive all suretyship defenses.

The obligations of the undersigned under this guarantee shall be only to the specific debt described and to no other debt or obligation between Borrower and Creditor.

In the event of default, the Guarantor shall be responsible for all attorneys' fees and reasonable costs of collection.

This guaranty shall be governed by the laws of the state of _____ and shall be binding upon and inure to the benefit of the parties, their successors, assigns, and personal representatives.

Signed under seal this _____ day of _____ , 199 ___ .

_____   _____
Witness   Guarantor

_____   _____
Witness   Address

                                   _____
                                   City, State, Zip

Guaranty Revocation

Date: _November 1, 1995_
To: _Brad Loan_
From: _Brenda Sweet_
Subject: Revocation of Guaranty for _Jason Sweet_

Effective immediately, the undersigned hereby cancels and revokes the guaranty for _Jason Sweet_ under that certain loan made _August 8_ , 199 _5_ , in the amount of $ _5,000.00_ . This revocation shall likewise extend to any future credit extended by you to the Borrower.

Sincerely,

Brenda Sweet
Guarantor

Brenda Sweet
21 Bose St.
Plant City, FL 33566

SENT CERTIFIED MAIL, RETURN RECEIPT REQUESTED.

Guaranty Revocation

Date: _____

To: _____

From: _____

Subject: Revocation of Guaranty for _____

Effective immediately, the undersigned hereby cancels and revokes the guaranty for _____ under that certain loan made _____ , 199 ___ , in the amount of $ _____ . This revocation shall likewise extend to any future credit extended by you to the Borrower.

Sincerely,

_____

Guarantor

_____

Address

_____

City, State, Zip

SENT CERTIFIED MAIL, RETURN RECEIPT REQUESTED.

Subordination Agreement

FOR GOOD AND VALUABLE CONSIDERATION RECEIVED, the undersigned hereby subordinates any and all claims or other rights to monies currently owed from _Jason Sweet_ (Debtor) of _741 Flower St._ , city of _Plant City_ , state of _Florida_ , to any and all claims as may now or hereinafter be due _Brad Loan_ (Creditor) of _187 Sycamore St._ , city of _Plant City_ , state of _Florida_ , from said Debtor.

The subordination herein shall be unconditional, irrevocable, and unlimited. Irrespective of any rights to priority as may exist, the undersigned shall forebear on collecting any monies due on its claim until all claims due Creditor from Debtor have been fully paid.

This guaranty shall be governed by the laws of the state of _Florida_ and shall be binding upon and inure to the benefit of the parties, their successors, assigns, and personal representatives.

Signed under seal this _8th_ day of _August_ , 199 _5_ .

Greg Taylor
Witness

Susan Smith
Witness

Sam Bellows, V.P.
First Financial
487 Wymon Ave.
Plant City, FL 33566

Subordination Agreement

FOR GOOD AND VALUABLE CONSIDERATION RECEIVED, the undersigned hereby subordinates any and all claims or other rights to monies currently owed from _____ (Debtor) of _____ , city of _____ , state of _____ , to any and all claims as may now or hereinafter be due _____ (Creditor) of _____ , city of _____ , state of _____ , from said Debtor.

The subordination herein shall be unconditional, irrevocable, and unlimited. Irrespective of any rights to priority as may exist, the undersigned shall forebear on collecting any monies due on its claim until all claims due Creditor from Debtor have been fully paid.

This guaranty shall be governed by the laws of the state of and shall be binding upon and inure to the benefit of the parties, their successors, assigns, and personal representatives.

Signed under seal this _____ day of _____ , 199 ___ .

_____
Witness

_____
Witness

_____
Lender

_____
Address

_____
City, State, Zip

Agreement to Assume Obligation

THIS AGREEMENT, entered into by and between _Brad Loan_ (Creditor) of _187 Sycamore St._ , city of _Plant City_ , state of _Florida_ , and _Jason Sweet_ (Borrower) of _741 Flowers St._ , city of _Plant City_ , state of _Florida_ ,and, _Steve Lot_ (Undersigned) of _22 Bryan St._ , city of _Plant City_ , state of _Florida_ .

FOR GOOD AND VALUABLE CONSIDERATION, the parties hereby agree to the following:

1. Both the Borrower and the Creditor confirm that Borrower presently owes Creditor the sum of $ _5,000.00_ (Debt), which sum is fully due and payable.

2. The undersigned unconditionally and irrevocably agrees to assume and fully pay said Debt and otherwise guarantee to Creditor the prompt payment of said Debt on the terms below, and to fully indemnify and save harmless Creditor from any loss thereto.

3. Said Debt shall be promptly paid in the manner following: _Five hundred dollars per month until paid._

4. This shall not constitute a release or discharge of the obligations of Borrower to Creditor for the payment of said Debt, provided that so long as the undersigned shall promptly pay the Debt in the manner above described, Creditor shall forebear in commencing collection actions against Borrower. In the event of default of payment, Creditor shall have full rights, jointly and severally, against both Borrower and/or the undersigned for any balance then owing. This Agreement extends only to the above debt and to no other or greater obligation.

5. This Agreement shall be governed under the laws of the state of _Florida_ and shall be binding upon and inure to the benefit of the parties, their successors, assigns, and personal representatives.

Signed under seal this _8th_ day of _August_ , 199 _5_ .

Kathleen Shuman	_Steve Lot_
Witness	Undersigned
Sarah Barrett	_Brad Loan_
Witness	Creditor
Greg Taylor	_Jason Sweet_
Witness	Borrower

Agreement to Assume Obligation

THIS AGREEMENT, entered into by and between _____ (Creditor) of _____ , city of _____ , state of _____ , and _____ (Borrower) of _____ , city of _____ , state of _____ , and _____ (Undersigned) of _____ , city of _____ , state of _____ .

FOR GOOD AND VALUABLE CONSIDERATION, the parties hereby agree to the following:

1. Both the Borrower and the Creditor confirm that Borrower presently owes Creditor the sum of $ _____ (Debt), which sum is fully due and payable.

2. The undersigned unconditionally and irrevocably agrees to assume and fully pay said Debt and otherwise guarantee to Creditor the prompt payment of said Debt on the terms below, and to fully indemnify and save harmless Creditor from any loss thereto.

3. Said Debt shall be promptly paid in the manner following:

   _____
   _____
   _____
   _____

4. This shall not constitute a release or discharge of the obligations of Borrower to Creditor for the payment of said Debt, provided that so long as the undersigned shall promptly pay the Debt in the manner above described, Creditor shall forebear in commencing collection actions against Borrower. In the event of default of payment, Creditor shall have full rights, jointly and severally, against both Borrower and/or the undersigned for any balance then owing. This Agreement extends only to the above debt and to no other or greater obligation.

5. This Agreement shall be governed under the laws of the state of _____ and shall be binding upon and inure to the benefit of the parties, their successors, assigns, and personal representatives.

Signed under seal this _____ day of _____ , 199 ___ .

_____   _____
Witness   Undersigned

_____   _____
Witness   Creditor

_____   _____
Witness   Borrower

Notice of Default on Promissory Note

Date: _November 12, 1995_
To: _Jason Sweet, Borrower_
     741 Flower St.
     Plant, FL 33566
From: _Brad Loan_

Please be advised that your note dated _August 8_ , 199 _5_ , in the original principal amount of $ _5,000_ is now in default. The following payment(s) have not been received:

Payment Due Date	Amount Due
September 8	_$ 500_
October 8	_$ 500_
Total Arrears	$ _1,000_

In accordance with the terms of your agreement, demand is hereby made for full payment of the entire balance of $ _5,000_ due under the note. If payment is not received within _10_ days, this note shall be forwarded to our attorneys for collection and you shall additionally be liable for all reasonable costs of collection.

Sincerely,

Brad Loan
Creditor

SENT CERTIFIED MAIL, RETURN RECEIPT REQUESTED.

Notice of Default on Promissory Note

Date: _____

To: _____

Borrower

_____

Address

_____

City, State, Zip

From: _____

Creditor

Please be advised that your note dated _____ , 199 ___ , in the original principal amount of $ _____ is now in default.

The following payment(s) have not been received:

Payment Due Date	Amount Due
_____	_____
_____	_____
_____	_____
Total Arrears	$ _____

In accordance with the terms of your agreement, demand is hereby made for full payment of the entire balance of $ _____ due under the note. If payment is not received within _____ days, this note shall be forwarded to our attorneys for collection and you shall additionally be liable for all reasonable costs of collection.

Sincerely,

_____

Creditor

SENT CERTIFIED MAIL, RETURN RECEIPT REQUESTED.

Demand to Guarantors for Payment

Date: *November 12, 1995*
To: *Brenda Sweet, Guarantor*
           21 Bose St.
           Plant, FL 33566
From: *Brad Loan*
Re: Guaranty of *Jason Sweet*

Please be advised that the undersigned is the holder of the
above-referenced guaranty.

Please be advised that payments on said debt are in default.
In accordance with the terms and conditions of your guaranty,
demand is made upon you as a guarantor for full payment on the
outstanding debt now due in the amount of $ *5,000* .

In the event payment on your guaranty is not made within *10*
days from the date above, we shall proceed to enforce our rights
against you under the guaranty and shall additionally hold you
responsible for attorneys' fees and costs of collection as
provided for under your guaranty.

Sincerely,

Brad Loan
Brad Loan

SENT CERTIFIED MAIL, RETURN RECEIPT REQUESTED.

Demand to Guarantors for Payment

Date: _____

To: _____

     Guarantor

     _____

     Address

     _____

     City, State, Zip

From: _____

     Creditor

Re: Guaranty of _____

Please be advised that the undersigned is the holder of the above-referenced guaranty.

Please be advised that payments on said debt are in default. In accordance with the terms and conditions of your guaranty, demand is made upon you as a guarantor for full payment on the outstanding debt now due in the amount of $ _____ .

In the event payment on your guaranty is not made within _____ days from the date above, we shall proceed to enforce our rights against you under the guaranty and shall additionally hold you responsible for attorneys' fees and costs of collection as provided for under your guaranty.

Sincerely,

_____

SENT CERTIFIED MAIL, RETURN RECEIPT REQUESTED.

Chapter 5
Credit and Collections

I wish I could tell you that you won't need these forms, but you will. Collections, and in fact noncollections, are an unfortunate part of doing business.

The forms included in this section will do two things for you: First, they will give you an organized collection process, and second, they will serve notice to the debtor that you are serious about your collections or you wouldn't have these forms.

The key to any collection process is action. Time is on the debtor's side. The longer you wait, the more chance there is of unfavorable things occurring. The customer could move or go bankrupt. Consequently, you want to have a step-by-step process that moves the account along to collection.

Payment Request

To: *J. D. Hardware Store*
From: *DRI Inc.*
Date: *October 2, 1995*
Re: Account Number *4712*

Please be advised that our records indicate that the above-referenced account is outstanding. Our records indicate the following: *Total Due $750.*

Please be advised that we have not received payment to date and would appreciate your sending it by return mail. If full payment has been made, we thank you for your business.

Sincerely,

John Sampson
John Sampson, Company Representative

Payment Request

To: _____
From: _____
Date: _____
Re: Account Number _____

Please be advised that our records indicate that the above-referenced account is outstanding. Our records indicate the following: _____

_____

_____

_____

_____

_____

Please be advised that we have not received payment to date and would appreciate your sending it by return mail. If full payment has been made, we thank you for your business.
Sincerely,

_____
Company Representative

Second Request for Payment

To: _J. D. Hardware Store_
From: _DRI Inc._
Date: _November 1, 1995_
Re: Account Number _4712_

Please be advised that our records indicate the following outstanding balance: _Total Due $750._
    On _October 2. 1995_ , we sent you a request for payment. We have not received it. Please send payment to us by return mail.
    Thank you for your prompt attention to this matter.
    Sincerely,

John Sampson
John Sampson, Company Representative

Second Request for Payment

To: _____
From: _____
Date: _____
Re: Account Number _____

    Please be advised that our records indicate the following
outstanding balance: _____
_____
_____
_____
_____
_____
_____

    On _____ , we sent you a request for payment. We have not
received it. Please send payment to us by return mail.
    Thank you for your prompt attention to this matter.
    Sincerely,

_____
Company Representative

Final Demand for Payment

To: _J. D. Hardware Store_
From: _DRI Inc._
Date: _December 1, 1995_
Re: Account Number _4712_

The above-referenced account is now delinquent in the amount of $ _750_ . We have sent two previous notices of this outstanding balance. **THIS IS YOUR FINAL NOTICE.**

Please be advised that unless we receive full payment on your account within ten (10) days of this notice, we will turn the account over to our attorneys for collection.

To avoid the increased cost to you because of the collection expense, we ask that you pay your account in full immediately. Doing so not only will save you substantial increased cost, it will preserve your credit rating for the future. We ask you to take action today.

Sincerely,

John Sampson
John Sampson, Company Representative

Final Demand for Payment

```
To:         _____
From:       _____
Date:       _____
Re:         Account Number _____
```

The above-referenced account is now delinquent in the amount of $ _____ . We have sent two previous notices of this outstanding balance. **THIS IS YOUR FINAL NOTICE.**

Please be advised that unless we receive full payment on your account within ten (10) days of this notice, we will turn the account over to our attorneys for collection.

To avoid the increased cost to you because of the collection expense, we ask that you pay your account in full immediately. Doing so not only will save you substantial increased cost, it will preserve your credit rating for the future. We ask you to take action today.

Sincerely,

_____
Company Representative

Notice of Assignment of Account for Collection

To: _J. D. Hardware Store_
From: _DRI Inc._
Date: _December 15, 1995_
Re: Account Number _4712_

Please be advised that as of _December 15_ , 199 _5_ , your account has been turned over to _Allied Collection_ of _Longwood, Florida_ for collection.

To discuss payment on the outstanding balance of $ _750_ , you may contact them at (_407_) _333-3700_ .

Sincerely,

John Sampson
John Sampson, Company Representative

Notice of Assignment of Account for Collection

```
To:        _____
From:      _____
Date:      _____
Re:        Account Number _____
```

Please be advised that as of _____ , 199 ___ , your account has been turned over to _____ of _____ for collection.

To discuss payment on the outstanding balance of $ _____ , you may contact them at (___) _____ .

Sincerely,

_____

Company Representative

Notice of Disputed Account

To: _DRI Inc._

From: _J. D. Hardware Store_

Date: _October 30, 1995_

Re: Account Number _4712_

Please be advised that we have received your statement on the above-referenced account. We dispute the account for the following reasons: _The bill included $300 worth of nails not ordered or delivered._

Please adjust our account accordingly or contact _Jake Dolan_ at (_407_) _942-1712_ to discuss the discrepancy.

Sincerely,

Jake Dolan

Jake Dolan, Company Representative

Notice of Disputed Account

To: _____

From: _____

Date: _____

Re: Account Number _____

Please be advised that we have received your statement on the above-referenced account. We dispute the account for the following reasons: _____

_____

_____

_____

_____

_____

_____

Please adjust our account accordingly or contact _____ at (___) _____ to discuss the discrepancy.

Sincerely,

_____

Company Representative

Offer of Account Settlement

To: _DRI, Inc._
From: _J. D. Hardware Store_
Date: _November 30, 1995_
Re: Account Number _4712_

We are in receipt of your statements on the above-referenced account.

We advised you on _October 30_ , 199 _5_ , that we dispute the account for the following reasons: _The bill included $300 for nails not ordered or delivered._

In order to settle the account as soon as possible and without admitting any liability, we will offer payment in full in the amount of $ _450_ . Please indicate your acceptance of this offer by signing this and returning it to us. Payment will be sent immediately.

Sincerely,

Jake Dolan
Jake Dolan, Company Representative

I (we) accept your offer in settlement as payment in full.

John Sampson
John Sampson, Company Representative

Offer of Account Settlement

To: _____
From: _____
Date: _____
Re: Account Number _____

We are in receipt of your statements on the above-referenced account.

We advised you on _____ , 199 ___ , that we dispute the account for the following reasons: _____
_____
_____
_____
_____
_____
_____

In order to settle the account as soon as possible and without admitting any liability, we will offer payment in full in the amount of $ _____ . Please indicate your acceptance of this offer by your signing this and returning it to us. Payment will be sent immediately.

Sincerely,

_____
Company Representative

I (we) accept your offer in settlement as payment in full.

_____
Company Representative

Agreement to Compromise Debt

FOR GOOD AND VALUABLE CONSIDERATION, the undersigned, _DRI, Inc._ (Creditor) of _415 Deacon Blvd._ , city of _Melrose_ , state of _Illinois_ , and _J. D. Hardware Store_ (Debtor) of _682 Haines St._ , city of _Houston_ , state of _Texas_ , compromise and discharge the indebtedness due from Debtor on the following terms and conditions:

1. Debtor and Creditor acknowledge that the present debt due and owing Creditor is in the amount of $ _3,000_ .

2. The parties agree that Creditor shall accept the sum of $ _2,000_ as full and total payment on said debt and in complete discharge, release, satisfaction, and settlement of all monies presently due, provided the sum herein shall be fully and punctually paid in the manner following: _$1,000 cash, $500 per month for the next two months following the execution of this agreement._

3. In the event Debtor defaults on the terms of payment, Creditor shall have full rights to prosecute its claim for the full amount of $ _3,000_ less credits for payments made.

4. In the event of default in payment, Debtor agrees to pay all reasonable attorneys' fees and costs of collection.

5. This agreement shall be governed by the laws of the state of _Illinois_ and shall be binding upon and inure to the benefit of the parties, their successors, assigns, and personal representatives.

Signed under seal this 12th day of _October_ , 199 _5_ .

Greg Taylor	_John Sampson_
Witness	John Sampson, DRI, Inc., Creditor
Chris Johnson	_Jake Dolan_
Witness	Jake Dolan, J. D. Hardware Store, Debtor

Agreement to Compromise Debt

FOR GOOD AND VALUABLE CONSIDERATION, the undersigned
_____ (Creditor) of _____ city of _____ , state of
and _____ (Debtor) of _____ city of _____ , state
of _____ compromise and discharge the indebtedness due from
Debtor on the following terms and conditions:

1. Debtor and Creditor acknowledge that the present debt due
   and owing Creditor is in the amount of $ _____ .

2. The parties agree that Creditor shall accept the sum of
   $ _____ as full and total payment on said debt and in
   complete discharge, release, satisfaction and settlement
   of all monies presently due, provided the sum herein shall
   be fully and punctually paid in the manner following: _____

   _____
   _____
   _____
   _____
   _____
   _____

3. In the event Debtor defaults on the terms of payment,
   Creditor shall have full rights to prosecute its claim for
   the full amount of $ _____ less credits for payments
   made.

4. In the event of default in payment, Debtor agrees to pay
   all reasonable attorneys' fees and costs of collection.

5. This agreement shall be governed by the laws of the state
   of _____ and shall be binding upon and inure to the
   benefit of the parties, their successors, assigns and
   personal representatives.

Signed under seal this _____ day of _____ , 199 ___ .

_____   _____
Witness   Creditor

_____   _____
Witness   Debtor

Notice of Dishonored Check

Date: *October 30, 1995*

To: *J. D. Hardware Store*
           682 Haines St.
           Houston, TX

From: *DRI, Inc.*
           415 Deacon Blvd.
           Melrose, IL

Please be advised that your check number *46* in the amount of $ *1,000* , paid to us on *October 10* , 199 *5* has been refused by your bank because of insufficient funds. We have verified with your bank that there are still insufficient funds to pay the check.

We request that you immediately forward to us a certified check to replace the one dishonored.

Sincerely,

John Sampson
John Sampson, DRI, Inc.

CERTIFIED MAIL, RETURN RECEIPT REQUESTED

Notice of Dishonored Check

Date: _____

To: _____

    _____

    Address

    _____

    City, State, Zip

From: _____

    _____

    Address

    _____

    City, State, Zip

Please be advised that your check number _____ in the amount of $ _____ , paid to us on _____ , 199 ___ , has been refused by your bank because of insufficient funds. We have verified with your bank that there are still insufficient funds to pay the check.

We request that you immediately forward to us a certified check to replace the one dishonored.

Sincerely,

_____

SENT CERTIFIED MAIL, RETURN RECEIPT REQUESTED

Request for Credit Reference

Date: _November 1, 1995_

To: _Super Paints_
           643 Superior St.
           Chicago, IL 60622

From: _DRI, Inc._
           415 Deacon Blvd.
           Melrose Park, IL 60164

Re: _J. D. Hardware Store_

Please be advised that the above-captioned party has recently applied for credit and listed you as a credit reference. In order for us to make our credit decision, would you advise us of your credit experience with this party by providing us the following information:

High credit limit: _$5,000_
Low credit limit: _$1,000_
Terms of sale: _Cash_
How long sold: _Five Years_
Present balance: _None_
Payment history: _Excellent_

Please note other credit information you may believe useful on the reverse side. This information shall, of course, be held in strict confidence.

A stamped return envelope is enclosed for your convenience.

Sincerely,

John Sampson
John Sampson, Company Representative

Request for Credit Reference

```
Date:      _____
To:        _____
           _____
           Address

           _____
           City, State, Zip
From:      _____

           _____
           Address

           _____
           City, State, Zip
Re:        _____
```

Please be advised that the above-captioned party has recently applied for credit and listed you as a credit reference. In order for us to make our credit decision, would you advise us of your credit experience with this party by providing us the following information:

```
High credit limit:    _____
Low credit limit:     _____
Terms of sale:        _____
How long sold:        _____
Present balance:      _____
Payment history:      _____
```

Please note other credit information you may believe useful on the reverse side. This information shall, of course, be held in strict confidence.

A stamped return envelope is enclosed for your convenience.

Sincerely,

_____
Company Representative

Authorization to Release Credit Information

Date: _October 14, 1995_
To: _DRI, Inc., Creditor_
          415 Deacon Blvd.
          Melrose, IL
Re: Account Number _4712_

Please forward to the credit agencies listed below a copy of my credit history with your company.
Thank you for your assistance in this matter.

Jake Dolan
Signature

Jake Dolan, J. D. Hardware Store
682 Haines St.
Houston, TX

_____
Signature of Joint Applicant (if any)

_____
Name of Account

_____
Account Number

Credit Reporting Agencies:
TRW   _100 TRW Blvd., Denver, CO_
Agency   Address

Authorization to Release Credit Information

```
Date:      _____
To:        _____
           Creditor

           _____
           Address

           _____
           City, State, Zip
Re:        Account Number _____
```

Please forward to the credit agencies listed below a copy of my credit history with your company.
Thank you for your assistance in this matter.

_____
Signature

_____
Address

_____
Signature of Joint Applicant (if any)

_____
Name of Account

_____
Account Number

Credit Reporting Agencies:

_____	_____
Agency	Address
_____	_____
_____	_____
_____	_____

Consignment Agreement

THIS AGREEMENT, entered into this _14th_ day of _April_ , 199 _5_ , by and between _Jarod Williams_ (Consignor) of _495 Brooks Circle_ , city of _Webster_ , state of _Florida_ , and _J. D. Hardware Store_ (Merchant) of _682 Haines St._ , city of _Houston_ , state of _Texas_ .

1. Merchant hereby acknowledges receipt of goods as described on the attached schedule. Said goods shall remain the property of Consignor until sold.

2. Merchant agrees to use its best efforts to sell the goods for Consignor for cash and at such prices as shall from time to time be set by Consignor. Merchant agrees to display goods but reserves the right to determine how and where they are to be displayed. Merchant may return goods at any time to Consignor and will upon request make them available to Consignor.

3. Merchant agrees, upon sale, to maintain proceeds due Consignor in trust and deliver such proceeds, less commissions, to Consignor together with an accounting within _15_ days of said sale.

4. Merchant agrees to accept as full payment a commission equal to _30_ % of the gross sales price (exclusive of any sales tax). Merchant is responsible for collecting and paying all appropriate sales tax.

5. Merchant agrees to permit Consignor to enter the premises at reasonable times to examine and inspect the goods and reconcile an accounting of sums due.

6. Merchant acknowledges that title to the goods shall remain with Consignor until goods are sold in the ordinary course of business.

7. Risk of loss of the goods shall be the responsibility of Merchant while said goods are within its possession. Merchant agrees to maintain insurance to cover Consignor's goods from fire and theft.

8. This Agreement may be terminated by either party at will. Upon termination, all unsold goods shall be returned to Consignor together with payment of any monies due.

9. This Agreement is not assignable and shall not be modified except by written modification.
10. This Agreement shall be governed by the laws of the state of _Texas_ and shall be binding upon and inure to the benefit of the parties, their successors, assigns, and personal representatives.

Jarod Williams
Consignor, Jarod Williams

Jake Dolan
Merchant, Jake Dolan, J. D.
   Hardware Store

Consignment Agreement

THIS AGREEMENT, entered into this _____ day of _____ , 199 ___ , by and between _____ (Consignor) of _____ , city of _____ , state of _____ , and _____ (Merchant) of _____ , city of _____ , state of _____ .

1. Merchant hereby acknowledges receipt of goods as described on the attached schedule. Said goods shall remain the property of Consignor until sold.

2. Merchant agrees to use its best efforts to sell the goods for Consignor for cash and at such prices as shall from time to time be set by Consignor. Merchant agrees to display goods but reserves the right to determine how and where they are to be displayed. Merchant may return goods at any time to Consignor and will upon request make them available to Consignor.

3. Merchant agrees, upon sale, to maintain proceeds due Consignor in trust and deliver such proceeds, less commissions, to Consignor together with an accounting within _____ days of said sale.

4. Merchant agrees to accept as full payment a commission equal to ___ % of the gross sales price (exclusive of any sales tax). Merchant is responsible for collecting and paying all appropriate sales tax.

5. Merchant agrees to permit Consignor to enter the premises at reasonable times to examine and inspect the goods and reconcile an accounting of sums due.

6. Merchant acknowledges that title to the goods shall remain with Consignor until goods are sold in the ordinary course of business.

7. Risk of loss of the goods shall be the responsibility of Merchant while said goods are within its possession. Merchant agrees to maintain insurance to cover Consignor's goods from fire and theft.

8. This Agreement may be terminated by either party at will. Upon termination, all unsold goods shall be returned to Consignor together with payment of any monies due.

9. This Agreement is not assignable and shall not be modified except by written modification.

10. This Agreement shall be governed by the laws of the state of _____ and shall be binding upon and inure to the benefit of the parties, their successors, assigns, and personal representatives.

_____
Consignor

_____
Merchant

Offer of Settlement

May 1, 1995

Jake Dolan
682 Haines St.
Houston, TX

Stacy Jones
Tiger Supplies
6700 Dorral St.
Houston, TX

Re: Account Number 672
          Settlement Request

Dear Sir/Madam:

I am writing in reference to the above-stated account, which is presently overdue. I am prepared to make a lump sum payment of $ 2,000 to settle the account in exchange for your assurance that your company will restore a positive credit rating on this account.

If this settlement proposal is acceptable to your company, please have an authorized representative indicate acceptance by signing this letter and returning the original to me. Upon receipt of the letter, I will forward the payment to you immediately.

If you have any questions or would like to discuss this matter further, please feel free to call me at (407) 331-8004 .

Sincerely,

Jake Dolan

As an authorized representative for Tiger Supplies , I hereby accept all the above terms and conditions, including the restoration of a favorable credit rating on the above account.

Stacy Jones
Authorized Representative
Date: May 5, 1995

Offer of Settlement

_____

Date

_____

Your Name

_____

Street Address

_____

City, State, Zip

_____

Credit Manager

_____

Name of Creditor

_____

Street Address

_____

City, State, Zip

Re: Account Number _____
            Settlement Request

Dear Sir/Madam:

I am writing in reference to the above-stated account which is presently overdue. I am prepared to make a lump sum payment of _____ to settle the account in exchange for your assurance that your company will restore a positive credit rating on this account.

If this settlement proposal is acceptable to your company, please have an authorized representative indicate acceptance by signing this letter and returning the original to me. Upon receipt of the letter, I will forward the payment to you immediately.

If you have any questions or would like to discuss this matter further, please feel free to call me at (___) _____ .

Sincerely,

_____

Signature

As an authorized representative for _____ , I hereby accept all the above terms and conditions, including the restoration of a favorable credit rating on the above account.

_____

Authorized Representative
Date: _____

Letter to Remove Information over Seven Years Old

May 1, 1995

Jake Dolan
682 Haines St.
Houston, TX 78237

Easy Credit Bureau
102 Fast St.
Washington, DC 21234

Re: Removal of Outdated Information

Dear Sir/Madam:

My credit report indicates negative information that is more than seven years old. In accordance with the Fair Credit Reporting Act, you are required to delete information that exceeds this time period. Consequently, please delete the following:

Creditor: *DRI, Inc.*
Account Number: *4712*

After correcting this information, please forward to me a copy of my updated credit report.

Thank you for your attention to this matter.

Sincerely,

Jake Dolan
Signature
Social Security Number: *265-93-4217*
Date of Birth: *9/17/44*

Letter to Remove Information over Seven Years Old

_____
Date

_____
Your Name
_____
Address
_____
City, State, Zip

_____
Credit Bureau
_____
Address
_____
City, State, Zip

Re: Removal of Outdated Information

Dear Sir/Madam:
My credit report indicates negative information that is more than seven years old. In accordance with the Fair Credit Reporting Act, you are required to delete information that exceeds this time period. Consequently, please delete the following:

Creditor: _____
Account Number: _____

After correcting this information, please forward to me a copy of my corrected credit report.
Thank you for your prompt attention to this matter.
Sincerely,

_____
Signature
Social Security Number: _____
Date of Birth: _____

Follow-up Letter to Credit Agency

June 3, 1995

Jake Dolan
265-93-4217
682 Haines St.
Houston, TX 78237

Easy Credit Bureau
102 Fast St.
Washington, DC 21234

Re: Account Number: _4721_
          Violation of Federal Fair Credit Reporting Act

Dear Sir/Madam:

On *May 1, 1995*, I sent you a letter notifying you of your company's violation of the above-referenced statute and its possible effect on my credit. A copy of the letter is attached. To date the matter has not been corrected.

Please immediately correct the information or I shall be forced to take alternative measures available to me under the Act.

Sincerely,

Jake Dolan
Signature
Enclosure: copy of original letter

Follow-up Letter to Credit Agency

_____
Date

_____

Your Name

_____
Social Security Number

_____
Address

_____
City, State, Zip

_____

Credit Bureau

_____
Address

_____
City, State, Zip

Re: Account Number: _____
        Violation of Federal Fair Credit Reporting Act

Dear Sir/Madam:

On _____ , I sent you a letter notifying you of your company's violation of the above-referenced statute and its possible effect on my credit. A copy of the letter is attached.

Please immediately correct the information or I shall be forced to take alternative measures available to me under the Act.

Sincerely,

_____
Signature
Enclosure: copy of original letter

Letter to Creditor Requesting Removal of Old Information

May 1, 1995

Jake Dolan
682 Haines St.
Houston, TX 78237

DRI, Inc.
415 Deacon
Melrose, IL

Re: Account Number: _4712_
        Statute of Limitations

Dear Sir/Madam:

My credit report contains a continuing reference to the account listed above. All activity on the account is over seven years old.

According to the Fair Credit Reporting Act, information on an account more than seven years from its last activity must be deleted. The continued inclusion of this information is in clear violation of the referenced statute, and I respectfully request that it be immediately removed.

Please notify your credit reporting agency to remove this information.

Thank you for your attention to this matter.

Sincerely,

Jake Dolan
Signature
Social Security Number: _265-93-4217_
Date of Birth: _9/17/44_

Letter to Creditor Requesting Removal of Old Information

_____

Date

_____

Your Name

_____

Address

_____

City, State, Zip

_____

Creditor

_____

Address

_____

City, State, Zip

Re: Account Number: _____
            Statute of Limitations

Dear Sir/Madam:

My credit report contains a continuing reference to the account listed above. All activity on the account is over seven years old.

According to the Fair Credit Reporting Act, information on an account more than seven years from its last activity must be deleted. The continued inclusion of this information is in clear violation of the referenced statute, and I respectfully request that it be immediately removed.

Please notify your credit reporting agency to remove this information.

Thank you for your attention to this matter.

Sincerely,

_____

Signature
Social Security Number: _____
Date of Birth: _____

Credit Report Reverification Request

May 1, 1995

Jake Dolan
682 Haines St.
Houston, TX 78237

Easy Credit Bureau
102 Fast St.
Washington, DC 21234

Re: Credit Report Reverification

Gentlemen:

Recently, I received a copy of my credit report containing information that I request you verify for accuracy. I believe this information is harmful to my credit record and request that the following item be immediately investigated:

Name of Creditor: *DRI, Inc.*
Account Number: *4712*

In accordance with the Fair Credit Reporting Act, Title VI, Section 611, Subsection A-D, I am requesting within a reasonable time (30 days) either the removal of the information or the name of anyone with whom you verified the above information so that I may contact them if needed.

Upon completion of your investigation, please forward to me a copy of my updated credit report.

Thank you for your prompt attention to this matter.

Sincerely,

Jake Dolan
Signature
Social Security Number: *265-93-4217*
Date of Birth: *9/17/44*

Credit Report Reverification Request

_____
Date

_____
Your Name

_____
Address

_____
City, State, Zip

_____
Credit Bureau

_____
Address

_____
City, State, Zip

Re: Credit Report Reverification

Gentlemen:
Recently, I received a copy of my credit report containing information that I request you verify for accuracy. I believe this information is harmful to my credit record and request that the following be immediately investigated:

Name of Creditor: _____
Account Number: _____

In accordance with the Fair Credit Reporting Act, Title VI, Section 611, Subsection A-D, I am requesting within a reasonable time (30 days) either the removal of the information or the name of anyone with whom you verified the above information so that I may contact them if needed.

Upon completion of your investigation, please forward to me a copy of my updated credit report.

Thank you for your prompt attention to this matter.
Sincerely,

_____
Signature
Social Security Number: _____
Date of Birth: _____

Credit Report Request Following Rejection

May 1, 1995

Jake Dolan
682 Haines St.
Houston, TX 78237

Easy Credit Bureau
102 Fast St.
Washington, DC 21234

Re: Credit Application Rejection

Gentlemen:

I have been advised by the following creditor, *DRI, Inc., 415 Deacon, Melrose, IL.* , that my application for credit was rejected based in whole or in part on information in your file.

In order to verify the accuracy of the credit record, I am requesting that you forward to me a copy of my credit report in accordance with the provisions of the Fair Credit Reporting Act. This request is being made within thirty days of rejection, and thus I understand there will be no charge for the report.

Thank you for your prompt attention to this matter.

Sincerely,

Jake Dolan
Signature
Social Security Number: *265-93-4217*
Date of Birth: *9/17/44*

Credit Report Request Following Rejection

_____
Date

_____
Your Name

_____
Address

_____
City, State, Zip

_____
Credit Bureau

_____
Address

_____
City, State, Zip

Re: Credit Application Rejection

Gentlemen:
I have been advised by the following creditor:_____
_____
_____
_____
_____
_____
_____

that my application for credit was rejected based in whole or in part on information in your file.

In order to verify the accuracy of the credit record, I am requesting that you forward to me a copy of my credit report in accordance with the provisions of the Fair Credit Reporting Act. This request is being made within thirty days of rejection, and thus I understand there will be no charge for the report.

Thank you for your prompt attention to this matter.
Sincerely,

_____
Signature
Social Security No: _____
Date of Birth: _____

Commentary

Do you think it is possible that a credit bureau won't respond to your request? Well, unfortunately, it is. Consequently, we have a follow-up letter to let them know you weren't just kidding.

Credit File Follow-up after Thirty Days

June 1, 1995

Jake Dolan
682 Haines St.
Houston, TX 78237

Easy Credit Bureau
102 Fast St.
Washington, DC 21234

Re: Credit File Follow-up

Gentlemen:

On _May 1, 1995_ I forwarded to your office a certified letter requesting an investigation of my credit file. A copy of said letter is enclosed. To date, I have received no reply.

As you are aware, under the Fair Credit Reporting Act, I am entitled to an investigation of my file within a reasonable length of time. I respectfully request that you immediately forward to me a report of your investigation and a copy of my corrected credit report.

Thank you for your prompt attention to this matter.

Jake Dolan
Signature
Social Security Number: _265-93-4217_
Date of Birth: _9/17/44_

Credit File Follow-up after Thirty Days

_____
Date

_____
Your Name

_____
Address

_____
City, State, Zip

_____
Credit Bureau

_____
Address

_____
City, State, Zip

Re: Credit File Follow-up

Gentlemen:

On _____ I forwarded to your office a certified letter requesting an investigation of my credit file. A copy of said letter is enclosed. To date, I have received no reply.

As you are aware, under the Fair Credit Reporting Act, I am entitled to an investigation of my file within a reasonable length of time. I respectfully request that you immediately forward to me a report of your investigation and a copy of my corrected credit report.

Thank you for your prompt attention to this matter.

_____
Signature
Social Security Number: _____
Date of Birth: _____

Request Removal of Unauthorized Credit Inquiries

May 1, 1995

Jake Dolan
682 Haines Street
Houston, TX   78237

Easy Credit Bureau
102 Fast Street
Washington, DC   21234

Re: Removal of Unauthorized Credit Inquiries

Dear Sir/Madam:

The following inquiry appeared on my recent credit report and was never authorized by me. I request that the inquiry be immediately removed before it causes damage to my credit.

1. Name of Creditor: *DRI, Inc.*
    Date of Inquiry: *11/2/94*

Upon the removal of the unauthorized inquiry, please forward me an updated copy of my credit report.

Thank you for your prompt attention to this matter.

Sincerely,

Jake Dolan
Signature
Social Security Number: *265-93-4217*
Date of Birth: *9/17/44*

Request Removal of Unauthorized Credit Inquiries

_____
Date

_____
Your Name

_____
Address

_____
City, State, Zip

_____
Credit Bureau

_____
Address

_____
City, State, Zip

Re: Removal of Unauthorized Credit Inquiries

Dear Sir/Madam:

The following inquiry appeared on my recent credit report and was never authorized by me. I request that the inquiry be immediately removed before it causes damage to my credit.

1. Name of Creditor _____
    Date of Inquiry _____

Upon the removal of the unauthorized inquiries, please forward me an updated copy of my credit report.

Thank you for your prompt attention to this matter.

Sincerely,

_____
Signature
Social Security Number: _____
Date of Birth: _____

Complaint Letter to Federal Trade Commission

May 1, 1995

Jake Dolan
682 Haines Street
Houston, TX 78237

Federal Trade Commission
Pennsylvania Avenue and 6th Street, NW
Washington, DC 20580

Re: Complaint of Violation of Fair Debt Collection
         Practices Act

Gentlemen:

I am receiving continued harassment from _Brown's Collection Agency_ , which I believe is violating the Fair Debt Collection Practices Act by: _Calling my home after 11:00 P.M. on several occasions, most recently on April 26 and April 27._

I have requested _Brown's Collection Agency_ to stop its actions based on the statute, but it continues.

I respectfully request that you investigate this matter and take appropriate action to protect the public from such violation.

Sincerely,

Jake Dolan
Signature

cc: Brown's Collection Agency
         DRI, Inc.

Complaint Letter to Federal Trade Commission

_____
Date

_____
Your Name

_____
Address

_____
City, State, Zip

Federal Trade Commission
Pennsylvania Avenue and 6th Street, NW
Washington, DC 20580

Re: Complaint of Violation of Fair Debt Collection
         Practices Act

Gentlemen:
I am receiving continued harassment from _____ ,
                                    (Name of Collection Agency)
which I believe is violating the Fair Debt Collection Practices
Act by: _____
_____
_____
_____
_____
_____
_____

   I have requested _____ to stop its actions based on the
statute, but it continues.
   I respectfully request that you investigate this matter and
take appropriate action to protect the public from such
violation.
   Sincerely,

_____
Signature

cc: _____
          Collection Agency

          _____
          Original Creditor

Letter to Request Time Extension from Creditor

May 1, 1995

Jake Dolan
682 Haines Street
Houston, TX 78237

Stacy Jones
Tiger Supplies
6700 Dorral Street
Houston, TX 78024

Re: Account Number: *6721*
Account Name: *J .D. Hardware Store*

Dear Sir/Madam:

At the present time, I am unable to meet my present obligation under my agreement with your company.

I have carefully analyzed my current income and expenses and respectfully request an extension of time on my account. I will be able to forward to you a monthly payment of *$15.00* until my debt is paid in full.

If you have any questions regarding my proposal or if you need to discuss the matter further, I can be reached during the *day* at (*407*) *555-5456* . I appreciate your patience and any help you may be able to give me.

Sincerely,

Jake Dolan
Signature
J.D. Hardware Store

Letter to Request Time Extension from Creditor

_____

Date

_____

Your Name

_____

Address

_____

City, State, Zip

_____

Credit Manager

_____

Creditor

_____

Address

_____

City, State, Zip

Re: Account Number _____

         Account Name _____

Dear Sir/Madam:

At the present time, I am unable to meet my present obligation under my agreement with your company.

I have carefully analyzed my current income and expenses and respectfully request an extension of time on my account. I will be able to forward to you a monthly payment of $ _____ until my debt is paid in full.

If you have any questions regarding my proposal or if you need to discuss the matter further, I can be reached during the _____ (day or evening) at (___) _____ . I appreciate your patience and any help you may be able to give me.

Sincerely,

_____

Signature

_____

Name of Business (if applicable)

Chapter 6
Bill of Sale

Entrepreneurs buy and sell property and equipment all the time, and this chapter contains all the forms you will need to complete your transactions.

There is a big difference in price between new and used business equipment. However, when you are buying new equipment, there is usually a store you can go back to if you have a problem. With used equipment, it's not always that simple. If something is wrong with the equipment shortly after you buy it, sellers are likely to shrug their shoulders and tell you they're sorry, but it was working fine when they sold it to you. Without a bill of sale, and, more particularly, without a bill of sale with warranties, you are out of luck.

Bill of Sale—Quitclaim

FOR VALUE RECEIVED, the undersigned hereby sells and transfers to _Jeff Brown_ of _741 Pleasant Avenue_ ,city of _Dalton_ , state of _Georgia_ , the following personal property:
1. _10 metal desks and chairs_
2. _10 grey metal filing cabinets_

The seller is hereby selling only such right title and interest as he may have. The seller disclaims all warranties, and the property is conveyed to buyer "as is" and "where is."

Signed and sealed this _1st_ day of _June_ , 199 _7_ .

Joe Stiff
Seller

Bill of Sale—Quitclaim

FOR VALUE RECEIVED, the undersigned hereby sells and transfers to _____ of _____ , city of _____ , state of _____ , the following personal property: _____
_____
_____
_____
_____
_____
_____

The seller is hereby selling only such right title and interest as he may have. The seller disclaims all warranties, and the property is conveyed to buyer "as is" and "where is."

Signed and sealed this _____ day of _____ , 199 ___ .

_____
Seller

Bill of Sale

FOR VALUE RECEIVED, the undersigned hereby sells and transfers to _Jeff Brown_ of _741 Pleasant Avenue_ , city of _Dalton_ , state of _Georgia_ , the following personal property (describe as specifically as possible):

1. _10 metal desks and chairs_
2. _10 grey metal filing cabinets_

The Seller warrants that he is the sole owner of the property being conveyed and that he has full rights and authority to sell and transfer it. Seller warrants that he shall fully defend, protect, and indemnify the Buyer from any claims against the property.

The property is being sold free and clear of all liens and encumbrances.

The Seller specifically disclaims any implied warranty of condition or merchantability or fitness for a particular purpose, and the property is being sold "as is" and "where is."

Signed and sealed this _1st_ day of _June_ , 199 _7_ .

Joe Stiff
Seller

Bill of Sale

FOR VALUE RECEIVED, the undersigned hereby sells and transfers to _____ of _____ , city of _____ , state of _____ , the following personal property (Describe as specifically as possible): _____

_____

_____

_____

_____

_____

The Seller warrants that he or she is the sole owner of the property being conveyed and that he or she has full rights and authority to sell and transfer it. Seller warrants that he shall fully defend, protect, and indemnify the Buyer from any claims against the property.

The property is being sold free and clear of all liens and encumbrances.

The Seller specifically disclaims any implied warranty of condition or merchantability or fitness for a particular purpose, and the property is being sold "as is" and "where is."

Signed and sealed this _____ day of _____ , 199 ___ .

_____
Seller

Bill of Sale with Lien

FOR VALUE RECEIVED, the seller hereby sells and transfers to _Jeff Brown_ of _741 Pleasant Avenue_ , city of _Dalton_ , state of _Georgia_ , the following described property:

1. _10 metal desks and chairs_
2. _10 grey metal filing cabinets_

The seller warrants good title to the property subject to the following lien:

1. _$1,000 note to Aims Furniture Financing_

Buyer agrees to assume all obligations of the lien and indemnify seller from any claim arising from it.

Property is being sold "as is" and "where is" without any express or implied warranty as to condition, use, or working order.

Signed and sealed this _1st_ day of _June_ , 199 _7_ .

Joe Stiff
Seller

Bill of Sale with Lien

FOR VALUE RECEIVED, the seller hereby sells and transfers to
_____ of _____ , city of _____ , state of
_____ , the following described property: _____
_____
_____
_____
_____
_____
_____
_____

    The seller warrants good title to the property subject to the
following lien: _____
_____
_____
_____
_____
_____
_____

    Buyer agrees to assume all obligations of the lien and
indemnify seller from any claim arising from it.

    Property is being sold "as is" and "where is" without any
express or implied warranty as to condition, use, or working
order.

    Signed and sealed this _____ day of _____ , 199 ___ .

_____
Seller

Bill of Sale with Warranties

THE BILL OF SALE entered into this _1st_ day of _June_ , 199 _7_ , by and between _Joe Stiff_ (Seller) of _42 Boxer Court_ , city of _Dalton_ , state of _Georgia_ , and _Jeff Brown_ (Buyer) of _741 Pleasant Avenue_ , city of _Dalton_ , state of _Georgia_ .

For and in consideration of _One thousand and no/00_ dollars ($ _1,000_) paid by the Buyer, Seller hereby sells and transfers to the Buyer the following described property: _10 metal desks and 10 grey metal filing cabinets_

The Seller warrants that he is the owner of the property and has full authority to transfer it. The Seller also represents and warrants that the property is being sold free and clear of liens, encumbrances, and liabilities except: _None_

The Seller warrants that the property is in good working order as of the date of sale.

Signed on the day first above written.

                         Joe Stiff
                         Seller

Bill of Sale with Warranties

THE BILL OF SALE entered into this _____ day of
_____ , 199 ___ , by and between _____ (Seller) of
_____ , city of _____ , state of _____ , and
_____ (Buyer) of _____ , city of _____ , state of
_____ .

    For and in consideration of _____ dollars ($ _____)
paid by the Buyer, Seller hereby sells and transfers to the Buyer
the following described property: _____
_____
_____
_____
_____
_____
_____

    The Seller warrants that he is the owner of the property and
has full authority to transfer it. The Seller also represents and
warrants that the property is being sold free and clear of liens,
encumbrances, and liabilities except: _____
_____
_____
_____
_____
_____
_____

    The Seller warrants that the property is in good working order
as of the date of sale.
    Signed on the day first above written.

                                       _____

                                       Seller

Contract for Sale of Personal Property

THIS AGREEMENT, entered into this _1st_ day of _June_ , 199 _7_ , by and between _Jeff Baron_ (_Baron_) of _741 Pleasant Avenue_ , city of _Dalton_ , state of _Georgia_ , and _Joe Stiff_ (_Stiff_) of _42 Boxer Court_ , city of _Dalton_ , state of _Georgia_ .

FOR AND IN CONSIDERATION of the mutual promises and benefits to be derived by the parties, they do hereby agree to the following terms and conditions:

1. Description of property to be purchased: _10 metal filing cabinets and 10 matching chairs, each original 1950 pieces from the executive offices of the White House, and 10 grey metal filing cabinets, also from the White House._

2. Purchase price $ _10,000_
   Terms: ☒ Cash
   ☐ Other (describe) _____

3. Transfer of property shall take place at _9:00_ A.M. at _741 Pleasant Avenue_ , city of _Dalton_ , state of _Georgia_ .

4. The Seller represents he has legal title to the property and has full right and authority to convey. Seller also represents that the property is free and clear of all encumbrances. Seller will on the date of sale provide buyer with a notarized bill of sale.

5. Seller is selling property "as is," disclaiming any warranty of merchantability, fitness, or working order.

6. This document represents the full understanding between the parties and can only be altered by a written agreement signed by both parties.

7. In any dispute that may arise as a result of this agreement, the governing law shall be that of the state of _Georgia_ , and the venue shall be _Dalton County_ .

8. The prevailing party to any disagreement regarding this contract shall be awarded reasonable attorneys' fees and costs.

9. This contract shall bind the successors and assigns.

_6/1/97_	_Jeff Baron_
Date	Buyer
_6/1/97_	_Joe Stiff_
Date	Seller

Contract for Sale of Personal Property

THIS AGREEMENT, entered into this _____ day of _____ ,
199 ___ , by and between _____ (_____) of _____ ,
city of _____ , state of _____ , and _____
(_____) of _____ , city of _____ , state of
_____ .

FOR AND IN CONSIDERATION of the mutual promises and benefits
to be derived by the parties, they do hereby agree to the
following terms and conditions:

1. Description of property to be purchased: _____
   _____
   _____
   _____
   _____
   _____
   _____

2. Purchase price $ _____
   Terms: ❏ Cash
            ❏ Other (describe) _____

3. Transfer of property shall take place at _____
   A.M./P.M. at _____ , city of _____ , state of
   _____ .

4. The Seller represents he has legal title to the property
   and has full right and authority to convey. Seller also
   represents that the property is free and clear of all
   encumbrances. Seller will on the date of sale provide
   buyer with a notarized bill of sale.

5. Seller is selling property "as is," disclaiming any
   warranty of merchantability, fitness, or working order.

6. This document represents the full understanding between
   the parties and can only be altered by a written agreement
   signed by both parties.

7. In any dispute that may arise as a result of this
   agreement, the governing law shall be that of the state of
   _____ , and the venue shall be _____ .

8. The prevailing party to any disagreement regarding this
   contract shall be awarded reasonable attorneys' fees and
   costs.

9. This contract shall bind the successors and assigns.

_____   _____
Date   Buyer

_____   _____
Date   Seller

Chapter 7
Partnerships and Joint Ventures

Business partnerships can be both the best of times and the worst of times. When they go bad, they can be worse than the most heated divorce imaginable. When they are good, they make business worthwhile. In my career, I have been cursed and blessed with both extremes and a great deal in between. One thing I have learned is that except on rare occasions, it is in everyone's best interest to put your agreement in writing. It doesn't have to be fancy, but you need to get your thoughts down on paper. If you can do this yourself, great. However, if you have any hesitancy, see an attorney.

Joint ventures are partnerships, but for a very defined purpose. I have included for your review a short-form and a long-form agreement.

The long-form joint venture agreement covers almost every conceivable aspect of a partnership. In fact, you may consider using a modification of the agreement for a general partnership. The major difference would simply be the business contemplated by the partners.

When you use a long agreement like the one included in this chapter, you can expect that the other parties will want their attorneys to review it, and the process will probably not be a short one. In the actual transaction for which I first designed this form, millions of dollars were at stake, and the joint venture ultimately had difficulty. In that case, having a well-planned, thorough contract saved tens of thousands of dollars.

Partnership Agreement

THIS AGREEMENT, entered into this <u>14th</u> day of <u>September</u>, 199 <u>7</u>, by and between <u>Lindsay Simmons</u> (<u>Simmons</u>) of <u>521 Crystal Lane</u>, city of <u>Oklahoma City</u>, state of <u>Oklahoma</u>, and <u>Jennifer Jones</u> (<u>Jones</u>) of <u>64 Summer Street</u>, city of <u>Oklahoma City</u>, state of <u>Oklahoma</u>.

FOR AND IN CONSIDERATION of the mutual promises and benefits to be derived by the parties, they do hereby agree to the following terms and conditions.

1. The parties will form a partnership effective <u>October 1</u>, 199 <u>7</u>, to be known as <u>L & G Enterprises</u>.
2. The general purpose of the partnership shall be <u>to sell a line of health care products</u>.
3. Profits and losses will be split <u>50/50</u>.
4. The parties will contribute the following to the partnership: <u>$2,000 each for working capital</u>.
5. The parties further agree: <u>to purchase for $1,000 a Wonder Life Health Care System</u>.
6. The parties' signatures below indicate acceptance to the terms of this agreement.

<u>Kathleen Shuman</u>
Witness

<u>Sarah Barrett</u>
Witness

<u>Greg Taylor</u>
Witness

<u>Lindsay Simmons</u>
Signature

<u>Jennifer Jones</u>
Signature

Partnership Agreement

THIS AGREEMENT, entered into this _____ day of _____ ,
199 ___ , by and between _____ (_____) of _____
, city of _____ , state of _____ , and _____ (
_____) of _____ , city of _____ , state of
_____ .

FOR AND IN CONSIDERATION of the mutual promises and benefits
to be derived by the parties, they do hereby agree to the
following terms and conditions.

1. The parties will form a partnership effective _____ ,
   199 ___ , to be known as _____ .

2. The general purpose of the partnership shall be _____
   _____
   _____
   _____
   _____
   _____
   _____
   _____ .

3. Profits and losses will be split _____ .

4. The parties will contribute the following to the
   partnership: _____
   _____
   _____
   _____
   _____
   _____ .

5. The parties further agree: _____
   _____
   _____
   _____
   _____
   _____ .

6. The parties' signatures below indicate acceptance to the
   terms of this agreement.

_____   _____
Witness   Signature

_____
Witness

_____   _____
Witness   Signature

Partnership Amendment

THIS AMENDMENT, entered into this _3rd_ day of _December_ , 199 _7_ , by and between _Lindsay Simmons_ (_Simmons_) of _521 Crystal Lane_ , city of _Oklahoma City_ , state of _Oklahoma_ , and _Jennifer Jones_ (_Jones_) of _64 Summer Street_ , city of _Oklahoma City_ , state of _Oklahoma_ .

WHEREAS, the parties have entered into a Partnership Agreement on _9/14/97_ , a copy of which is attached, and

WHEREAS the parties wish to modify the Agreement,

NOW THEREFORE, in consideration of the mutual promises and benefits to be derived by the parties, they do hereby agree to the following terms and conditions (state modifications): _Add Heather Valley as an additional partner upon the investment of $2,000. All profits to be shared equally._

All other terms and conditions of the original Partnership Agreement shall remain in full force and effect.

Kathleen Shuman
Witness

Lindsay Simmons
Signature

Sarah Barrett
Witness

Greg Taylor
Witness

Jennifer Jones
Signature

Chris Johnson
Witness

Partnership Amendment

THIS AMENDMENT, entered into this _____ day of _____ , 199 ___ , by and between _____ (_____) of _____ , city of _____ , state of _____ , and _____ (_____) of _____ , city of _____ , state of _____ .

WHEREAS, the parties have entered into a Partnership Agreement on _____ , a copy of which is attached, and

WHEREAS the parties wish to modify the Agreement,

NOW THEREFORE, in consideration of the mutual promises and benefits to be derived by the parties, they do hereby agree to the following terms and conditions (state modifications): _____

_____

_____

_____

_____

_____

_____

All other terms and conditions of the original Partnership Agreement shall remain in full force and effect.

_____ _____
Witness   Signature

_____
Witness

_____ _____
Witness   Signature

_____
Witness

Partnership Agreement Clauses

Term

How long do you want the partnership to last? If you know or have an idea, great. Put it down. If you don't know, the partnership will last until someone dissolves it by saying he or she doesn't want to be a part of the partnership or until one of the parties dies.

Examples:

The Partnership shall continue in existence until it is dissolved by all of the Partners or until a Partner withdraws, dies, or otherwise leaves the Partnership.

The Partnership shall continue until _January 1, 2001_ or until a Partner withdraws or otherwise leaves the Partnership.

Contribution

Any time you start talking about money, you open the door to confusion—real or otherwise. These clauses will help everyone organize his or her thoughts.

Examples:

The initial capital of the Partnership shall be $ _2,000_ . Each Partner shall contribute an equal share in cash no later than _June 1_ , 199 _7_ , and shall own an equal share of the business.

A way to show unequal contributions:

Each Partner shall contribute the following amount to the Partnership on or before _June 1_ , 199 _7_ .

Name	Amount
Lindsay Simmons	_$2,000_
Jennifer Jones	_$1,000_
Heather Valley	_$ 500_

If ownership of the partnership is to be different from the cash contribution, you can add the next clause immediately thereafter.

Notwithstanding cash contributions, ownership in the Partnership shall be:

Name	Ownership
Lindsay Simmons	_1/3_
Jennifer Jones	_1/3_
Heather Valley	_1/3_

If the initial cash contribution is unequal because one partner is contributing work, you can add this type of clause immediately after the cash contribution breakdown.

> In addition to the cash contribution, _Lindsay Simmons_ shall contribute the following amount of work to the Partnership (describe):
>
> _Provide all accounting for the partnership without charge._

Note: Since the work contributed would be in exchange for a share equal to a certain dollar value, the partner will pay income tax on the value of the interest received.

Occasionally a partner will contribute property (real or personal) for his or her partnership interest. This can be handled as follows:

> In lieu of cash, _Jennifer Jones_ shall contribute the following property valued at $ _2,000_ :
>
> _office desk, chairs, copier, fax, phone_

What happens if a partner doesn't make his or her contribution? It doesn't happen often, but when it does, this clause is very helpful.

> If a Partner fails to make his contribution to the Partnership as required, the Partnership shall not terminate, but shall continue as a Partnership of only those Partners who have made their contributions. In this event, the share forfeited shall be reallocated to the remaining Partners in proportion to their respective shares in the Partnership.

Management

If you must have a clause on management, you probably already have a problem. Nevertheless, it is a good idea to let everyone know how the show will be run and who will run it.

Example:

In the management, control, and direction of the business, the Partners shall have the following percentages of voting power:

Name	Percentages
Lindsay Simmons	_25_ %
Jennifer Jones	_25_ %
Heather Valley	_50_ %

All decisions require a _75_ % vote.

Once you get the voting interest down on paper, you may find that one person has control over the partnership. This may or may not be a good idea. If it isn't, you can adjust the percentage of voting power.

Amendments

I believe that a partnership document should allow for change, because change will occur. You need to decide whether it should require a majority or a unanimous vote to make the change. Remember, using a majority vote may allow one person to dominate every aspect of the partnership. That isn't a good idea.

Example:

This Agreement may be amended only by written consent of all parties.

Naturally, unanimous consent becomes more difficult the larger your partnership. So the more partners you have, the greater flexibility you can allow for amendments.

Sale or Transfer of a Partner's Interest

Things change. A partner may want to get out of a partnership, or his or her circumstances may require that he or she do so. Most people don't like to think about the end of things, including their own demise, and so this consideration is often put off to last.

There are a variety of ways to decide about the sale of a partnership interest. If it's just because you want to split up, and you both would like the business, you will have lots of emotion and conflict. In these cases, I like the old saying, "You name the price, and I will say buy or sell." It isn't complicated, and it is extremely fair. The easy way to formalize this is to set the decision for an arbitration hearing with the arbitrators instructed to apply this formula.

Examples:

> In the event the Partners are unable to decide on a buyout arrangement, the Partners agree to submit the matter to binding arbitration. At arbitration, the arbitrator shall reach a decision under the following formula: One partner shall state a price and the other party shall decide whether he will buy or sell the Partnership interest at that price. If the Partners are unable to decide which partner names the price, then the arbitrator shall determine by a coin toss.

Another problem that occurs in dissolving partnerships is that one partner decides to sell or convey his or her interest to someone that the remaining partners don't wish to be in partnership with. This can happen for a variety of reasons, an example of which is a divorce proceeding where the spouse is awarded the partnership interest. They may not have anything against the spouse personally, but being partners with him or her is something else. The solution is to give existing partners the right of first refusal for a partner's interest.

> If a Partner receives a written offer to purchase his interest in the Partnership that he is willing to accept, he shall first give written notice to the Partnership of the amount, terms of the offer, and identity of the buyer. The remaining Partners shall have the option within ten (10) business days after receipt of notice to purchase the Partner's interest on the same terms and conditions presented in the offer.

The right of first refusal is not a panacea because it hampers the sale of partnership interests. Some people won't consider negotiating for an interest encumbered by a right of first refusal because they may spend a lot of time and effort, only to have someone else benefit by their negotiations. Nevertheless, it is a frequently used solution to dissolution.

Partnership Agreement Clauses

Term

How long do you want the partnership to last? If you know or have an idea, great. Put it down. If you don't know, the partnership will last until someone dissolves it by saying he or she doesn't want to be a part of the partnership or until one of the parties dies.

Examples:

The Partnership shall continue in existence until it is dissolved by all of the Partners or until a Partner withdraws, dies, or otherwise leaves the Partnership.

The Partnership shall continue until _____ or until a Partner withdraws or otherwise leaves the Partnership.

Contribution

Any time you start talking about money, you open the door to confusion—real or otherwise. These clauses will help everyone organize his or her thoughts.

Examples:

The initial capital of the Partnership shall be $ _____ . Each Partner shall contribute an equal share in cash no later than _____ , 199 ___ , and shall own an equal share of the business.

A way to show unequal contributions:

Each Partner shall contribute the following amount to the Partnership on or before _____ , 199 ___ .

Name	Amount
_____	_____
_____	_____
_____	_____

If ownership of the partnership is to be different from the cash contribution, you can add the next clause immediately thereafter.

Notwithstanding cash contributions, ownership in the Partnership shall be:

Name   Ownership

_____   _____

_____   _____

_____   _____

If the initial cash contribution is unequal because one partner is contributing work, you can add this type of clause immediately after the cash contribution breakdown.

In addition to the cash contribution, _____ shall contribute the following amount of work to the Partnership (describe):

_____

_____

Note: Since the work contributed would be in exchange for a share equal to a certain dollar value, the partner will pay income tax on the value of the interest received.

Occasionally a Partner will contribute property (real or personal) for his or her Partnership interest. This can be handled as follows:

In lieu of cash, _____ shall contribute the following property valued at $ _____ :

What happens if a partner doesn't make his or her contribution? It doesn't happen often, but when it does, this clause is very helpful.

If a Partner fails to make his contribution to the Partnership as required, the Partnership shall not terminate, but shall continue as a Partnership of only those Partners who have made their contributions. In this event, the share forfeited shall be reallocated to the remaining Partners in proportion to their respective shares in the Partnership.

Management

If you have to have a clause on management, you probably already have a problem. Nevertheless, it is a good idea to let everyone know how the show will be run and who will run it.

Example:

In the management, control, and direction of the business, the Partners shall have the following percentages of voting power:

Name	Percentages
_____	_____ %
_____	_____ %
_____	_____ %

All decisions require a _____ % vote.

Once you get the voting interest down on paper, you may find that one person has control over the partnership. This may or may not be a good idea. If it isn't, you can adjust the percentage of voting power.

Amendments

I believe that a partnership document should allow for change, because change will occur. You need to decide whether it should require a majority or a unanimous vote to make the change. Remember, using a majority vote may allow one person to dominate every aspect of the partnership. That isn't a good idea.

Example:

This Agreement may be amended only by written consent of all parties.

Naturally, unanimous consent becomes more difficult the larger your partnership. So the more partners you have, the greater flexibility you can allow for amendments.

Sale or Transfer of a Partner's Interest

Things change. A partner may want to get out of a partnership, or his or her circumstances may require that he or she do so. Most people don't like to think about the end of things, including their own demise, and so this consideration is often put off to last.

There are a variety of ways to decide about the sale of a partnership interest. If it's just because you want to split up, and you both would like the business, you will have lots of emotion and conflict. In these cases, I like the old saying, "You name the price, and I will say buy or sell." It isn't complicated, and it is extremely fair. The easy way to formalize this is to set the decision for an arbitration hearing with the arbitrators instructed to apply this formula.

Examples:

> In the event the Partners are unable to decide on a buyout arrangement, the Partners agree to submit the matter to binding arbitration. At arbitration, the arbitrator shall reach a decision under the following formula: One partner shall state a price and the other party shall decide whether he will buy or sell the Partnership interest at that price. If the Partners are unable to decide which partner names the price, then the arbitrator shall determine by a coin toss.

Another problem that occurs in dissolving partnerships is that one partner decides to sell or convey his or her interest to someone that the remaining partners don't wish to be in partnership with. This can happen for a variety of reasons, not the least of which is divorce. Partners may find that a partnership interest went to the spouse of the partner. They may not have anything against the spouse personally, but being partners with him or her is something else. The solution is to give partners the right of first refusal for a partner's interest.

> If a Partner receives a written offer to purchase his interest in the Partnership that he is willing to accept, he shall first give written notice to the Partnership of the amount, terms of the offer, and identity of the buyer. The remaining Partners shall have the option within ten (10) business days after receipt of notice to purchase the Partner's interest on the same terms and conditions presented in the offer.

The right of first refusal is not a panacea because it hampers the sale of partnership interests. Some people won't consider negotiating for an interest encumbered by a right of first refusal because they may spend a lot of time and effort, only to have someone else benefit by their negotiations. Nevertheless, it is a frequently used solution to dissolution.

Joint Venture (Short Form)

THIS JOINT VENTURE AGREEMENT is made and entered into this
_4th_ day of _June_ , 199 _7_ , by and between _Lindsay Simmons_
(_Simmons_) of _521 Crystal Lane_ , city of _Oklahoma City_ ,
state of _Oklahoma_ , and _Jennifer Jones_ (_Jones_) of _64
Summer Street_ , city of _Oklahoma City_ , state of _Oklahoma_ ,
hereinafter collectively referred to as the "Venturers."

WITNESSETH:

WHEREAS, _Simmons_ has substantial experience in _computers_ ;
and

WHEREAS, _Jones_ has substantial experience in
telecommunications ; and

WHEREAS, the parties desire to put in writing their oral
understanding of responsibilities and enumeration relating to
this Venture;

NOW, THEREFORE, in consideration of the mutual covenants
hereinafter contained, the Venturers agree as follows:

1. **Prior Agreements.** It is the intention of the parties that
    this Agreement replace all written and/or oral agreements,
    understandings, and business ventures, previously, or
    otherwise, existing between the parties with respect to
    the subject matter hereof.
2. **Contributions.** _Simmons_ shall contribute _$5,000 plus 20
    hours per week_ , and _Jones_ shall contribute _$5,000
    plus 20 hours per work week_ .
3. **Interests and Distributions.** _Simmons_ shall receive a
    _50%_ interest in the Venture, and _Jones_ shall receive a
    _50%_ interest in the Venture. All profits and losses of
    the Venture shall be distributed according to their
    respective interests.
4. **Miscellaneous Provisions.**
    a. This Agreement supersedes any and all prior agreements
        of the parties, whether oral or written.
    b. The parties agree to execute any and all documents
        necessary to carry out the terms and intent of this
        Agreement.
    c. Section headings contained in this Agreement are
        included for convenience only and form no part of the
        Agreement between the parties.

d. If any provision of this Agreement is or becomes invalid, illegal, or unenforceable in any jurisdiction, such provision shall be deemed amended to conform to applicable laws so as to be valid and enforceable or, if it cannot be so amended without materially altering the intention of the parties, it shall be stricken and the remainder of this Agreement shall remain in full force and effect.

e. Unless specifically disallowed by law, should litigation arise hereunder, service of process therefor may be obtained through certified mail, return receipt requested, the parties hereto waiving any and all rights they may have to object to the method by which service was perfected.

f. No waiver of any right under this Agreement shall be deemed effective unless contained in a writing signed by the party charged with such waiver, and no waiver of any right arising from any breach or failure to perform shall be deemed to be a waiver of any future such right or of any other right arising under this Agreement.

g. This instrument contains the entire Agreement of the Venturers with respect to the subject matter hereof, and the terms and conditions thereof may not be further modified except by a writing signed by all the Venturers.

h. This Agreement shall be construed and enforced in accordance with the laws of the state of _Oklahoma_ . The parties hereby waive trial by jury and agree to submit to the personal jurisdiction and venue of a court of subject matter jurisdiction located in _Sussex_ County , _Oklahoma_ . In the event that litigation results from or arises out of this Agreement or the performance thereof, the prevailing party shall be entitled to an award of reasonable attorneys' fees and costs.

i. This Agreement shall be binding upon and shall inure to the benefit of the parties hereto, their respective heirs, legal representatives, executors, administrators, successors, and assigns, as the case may be.

IN WITNESS WHEREOF, the Venturers have executed or caused this instrument to be executed this _4th_ day of _June_ , 199 _7_ .

Signed, sealed, and delivered in the presence of:

Kathleen Shuman   _Lindsay Simmons_
Witness   Signature

Sarah Barrett
Witness

Greg Taylor   _Jennifer Jones_
Witness   Signature

Chris Johnson
Witness

Joint Venture (Short Form)

THIS JOINT VENTURE AGREEMENT is made and entered into this day of _____ , 199___ , by and between _____ (_____) of _____ , city of _____ , state of _____ , and _____ (_____) of _____ , city of _____ , state of _____ , hereinafter collectively referred to as the "Venturers."

WITNESSETH:

WHEREAS, _____ has substantial experience in _____ ; and

WHEREAS, _____ has substantial experience in _____ ; and

WHEREAS, the parties desire to put in writing their oral understanding of responsibilities and enumeration relating to this Venture;

NOW, THEREFORE, in consideration of the mutual covenants hereinafter contained, the Venturers agree as follows:

1. **Prior Agreements.** It is the intention of the parties that this Agreement replace all written and/or oral agreements, understandings, and business ventures, previously, or otherwise, existing between the parties with respect to the subject matter hereof.

2. **Contributions.** _____ shall contribute _____ _____ , and _____ shall contribute _____ .

3. **Interests and Distributions.** _____ shall receive a _____ interest in the Venture, and _____ shall receive a _____ interest in the Venture. All profits and losses of the Venture shall be distributed according to their respective interests.

4. **Miscellaneous Provisions.**

   a. This Agreement supersedes any and all prior agreements of the parties, whether oral or written.

   b. The parties agree to execute any and all documents necessary to carry out the terms and intent of this Agreement.

   c. Section headings contained in this Agreement are included for convenience only and form no part of the Agreement between the parties.

   d. If any provision of this Agreement is or becomes invalid, illegal, or unenforceable in any jurisdiction, such provision shall be deemed amended to conform to applicable laws so as to be valid and enforceable or, if it cannot be so amended without materially altering the intention of the parties, it shall be stricken and the remainder of this Agreement shall remain in full force and effect.

e. Unless specifically disallowed by law, should litigation arise hereunder, service of process therefor may be obtained through certified mail, return receipt requested; the parties hereto waiving any and all rights they may have to object to the method by which service was perfected.

f. No waiver of any right under this Agreement shall be deemed effective unless contained in a writing signed by the party charged with such waiver, and no waiver of any right arising from any breach or failure to perform shall be deemed to be a waiver of any future such right or of any other right arising under this Agreement.

g. This instrument contains the entire Agreement of the Venturers with respect to the subject matter hereof, and the terms and conditions thereof may not be further modified except by a writing signed by all the Venturers.

h. This Agreement shall be construed and enforced in accordance with the laws of the state of _____ . The parties hereby waive trial by jury and agree to submit to the personal jurisdiction and venue of a court of subject matter jurisdiction located in _____ County, _____ . In the event that litigation results from or arises out of this Agreement or the performance thereof, the prevailing party shall be entitled to an award of reasonable attorneys' fees and costs.

i. This Agreement shall be binding upon and shall inure to the benefit of the parties hereto, their respective heirs, legal representatives, executors, administrators, successors, and assigns, as the case may be.

IN WITNESS WHEREOF, the Venturers have executed or caused this instrument to be executed this _____ day of _____ , 199 ___ .

Signed, sealed, and delivered in the presence of:

_____   _____
Witness   Signature

_____
Witness

_____   _____
Witness   Signature

_____
Witness

Joint Venture Agreement

THIS AGREEMENT entered into this the _1st_ day of _June_ , 199 _7_ , by and between _Lindsay Simmons_ (_Simmons_), of _531 Crystal Lane_ , city of _Oklahoma City_ , state of _Oklahoma_ , and _Jennifer Jones_ (_Jones_) of _64 Summer Street_ , city of _Oklahoma City_ , state of _Oklahoma_ ;

WITNESSETH:

WHEREAS, (_Simmons_) is in the business of: _computer consulting and software development_ , and

WHEREAS, (_Jones_) is in the business of: _telephone consulting and systems design_ , and

WHEREAS, both parties desire to work together for the purpose of: _developing a new computer telephone interface_

NOW THEREFORE, for good and valuable consideration, receipt of which is hereby acknowledged, and the mutual promises and benefits to be derived by the parties, they do hereby agree to the following terms and conditions:

Article I
Formation

Section 1.1 **Formation and Name.**

    1.1.1 **Formation.** The Joint Venturers hereby confirm that they have formed a Joint Venture for the purposes and scope set forth in this Agreement.

    1.1.2 **Name.** The name of the Joint Venture is and shall continue to be _Comtel_ . The business and affairs of the Joint Venture shall be conducted solely under that name and under no other unless modified in writing by addendum to this agreement.

Section 1.2 **Purposes and Scope of the Joint Venture.**

    The purpose of the Joint Venture is to: _develop a new computer telephone interface to be marketed to home office businesses_

Section 1.3 **Principal Place of Business.**

    The principal place of business of the Joint Venture shall be initially located at _521 Crystal Lane, Oklahoma City, Oklahoma_

Section 1.4 **Term.**

The term of the Joint Venture shall commence on the first above written day, and shall continue, unless sooner terminated in accordance with other provisions of this Agreement, until _June 4_ , 199 _9_ .

Section 1.5 **No Partition.**

No Joint Venturer shall have the right and each Joint Venturer hereby agrees not to withdraw from the Joint Venture nor to dissolve, terminate, partition, or liquidate, or to petition a court for the dissolution, termination, partition, or liquidation of the Joint Venture or its assets, except as provided in this Agreement, and no Joint Venturer at any time shall have the right to petition or to take any action to subject the operation of the Project or any part thereof or the Joint Venture assets or any part thereof to the authority of any court of bankruptcy, insolvency, receivership, or similar proceeding.

Article II
Capital Contributions, Reserves, Voting, Financing, and Distributions

Section 2.1 **Joint Venture Percentage Interest.**

The Joint Venturers shall have the following undivided percentage interests in the Joint Venture (individually a "Percentage Interest" and joint "Percentage Interests"):

Simmons	_50_ %
Jones	_50_ %
	_100_ %

Section 2.2 **Adjustments and Interest.**

Unless otherwise approved by the Joint Venturers, no adjustment to the Percentage Interest of any Joint Venturer shall be made except as otherwise provided herein or as a result of a transfer of a Joint Venturer's Joint Venture interest or a portion thereof. It is the specific intent of the parties to equally split all fees and profits generated from the joint venture.

Section 2.3 **Capital Accounts.**

2.3.1 **General.** As used herein, the term "Capital Account" shall refer to the capital account of each Joint Venturer reflecting the value of each Joint Venturer's relative interest in the capital of the Joint Venture as calculated pursuant to this Agreement. A Capital Account, as defined herein, shall be maintained for each Joint Venturer and shall be subject to adjustment as provided in subsection 2.3.3.

2.3.2 **Initial Capital Contribution and Initial Capital**. Upon the execution of this Agreement, the parties shall mutually decide an amount for initial capitalization of the venture. The determined amount will be fulfilled by contributions proportionate to ownership. Thereafter, as additional capital is needed for the operation of the venture, it will be contributed in the same ratio.

2.3.3 **Adjustments to Capital Accounts**. The Capital Account of each Joint Venturer shall from time to time be:

(a) increased by:

(i) any additional capital contributions of such Joint Venturer.

(b) decreased by:

(i) all distributions to or for the account of such Joint Venturer, whether of capital or income (other than payments received by a Joint Venturer in payment of a loan permitted by the provisions hereof or a Contribution Loan);

(ii) such Joint Venturer's allocable share of Net Capital Loss and Net Ordinary Loss of the Joint Venture during such fiscal year.

Section 2.4 **Additional Capital Contributions.**

2.4.1 **General**. If additional capital for the operation of the venture is needed, then the parties shall make such additional capital contributions in the same percentage as their percentage interests.

2.4.2 **Notice by Manager**. Notice of any additional capital contributions required to be made pursuant to this Section 2.4 shall be given by the Manager as hereinafter defined to each Joint Venturer in the manner provided in this Agreement. Such notice shall name the Joint Venturers voting for additional capital contributions and shall specify in reasonable detail the amount of and purpose of any such additional capital contributions. Each Joint Venturer shall, within _forty-five_ (_45_) days of the receipt of such notice from the Manager, contribute to the Joint Venture the additional capital contribution required of such Joint Venturer as set forth in such notice.

2.4.3 **Contribution Loans**. In the event any Joint Venturer ("Noncontributing Joint Venturer") fails to make a required additional capital contribution pursuant to subsection 2.4.2 within the time specified, the other Joint Venturers (the "Contributing Joint Venturers") shall have the right to contribute an amount equal to such Noncontributing Joint Venturer's additional capital contribution. Any amounts so advanced to the Joint Venture by the Contributing Joint Venturers pursuant to this subsection 2.4.3 shall be treated as a loan by such Contributing Joint Venturers to the Noncontributing Joint Venturer ("Contribution Loan"), followed by the Noncontributing Joint Venturer making his or its required additional capital contribution to the Joint Venture of the proceeds of such Contribution Loan.

2.4.4 **Interest Repayment through Distributions**. In the event the Contributing Joint Venturers elect to make a Contribution Loan, then the Contribution Loan shall bear interest at a rate equal to the maximum allowed by law. In addition to other remedies, including, without limitation, those set forth in subsection 2.4.5, the Contribution Loan to the Noncontributing Joint Venturer shall be repaid out of any subsequent distributions from the Joint Venture made pursuant to this Agreement to which the Noncontributing Joint Venturer for whose account the Contribution Loan was made would otherwise be entitled, which amounts shall be applied first to interest accrued on the Contribution Loan and then to the principal due under the Contribution Loan, until the Contribution Loan is paid in full. In no event shall the principal or interest on any such Contribution Loan be an obligation of or paid by the Joint Venture. Contribution Loans shall be repaid on a first-in, first-out basis.

2.4.5 **Remedies**. In the event any Contribution Loan has not been repaid in full by the Noncontributing Joint Venturer within _thirty_ (_30_) days of the date the Contribution Loan is made, then at any time thereafter the Contributing Joint Venturers may proceed under subparagraphs (a) or (b) below:

(a) Upon _thirty_ (_30_) days' prior written notice, such Contributing Joint Venturer may elect to convert the Contribution Loan to an interest in the Joint Venture, whereupon, as of the effective date of such election, the Percentage Interest of the Contributing Joint Venturer and the Noncontributing Joint Venturer with respect to which the Contribution Loan relates shall be recalculated as provided below and the capital account of such Contributing Joint Venturer shall be increased by an amount equal to the principal plus accrued but unpaid interest on such Contribution Loan and the capital account of the Noncontributing Joint Venturer with respect to which the Contribution Loan relates shall be reduced accordingly. Upon determination of such value, the Noncontributing Joint Venturer shall be deemed to have transferred to the Contributing Joint Venturer that portion of the Noncontributing Joint Venturer's Percentage Interest of a value, calculated as provided above, as is equal to the Contributing Joint Venturer's Contribution Loan plus accrued but unpaid interest.

(b) Until a Contributing Joint Venturer has elected to proceed under subparagraph (a) above, such Contributing Joint Venturer's Contribution Loan shall remain in place and shall bear interest and be repaid as provided in subsection 2.4.4 above; provided, however, that this provision shall not operate to prohibit the Contributing Joint Venturer from declaring the Noncontributing Joint Venturer to be in default in the payment of any such Contribution Loan by reason of such nonpayment or from exercising any other rights or remedies of the Contributing Joint Venturer provided herein or at law.

Section 2.5 **Distributions to Joint Venturers of Cash Flow.**

  2.5.1 **Definition of Net Cash Flow.** In each fiscal year of the Joint Venture, the Manager shall determine the Joint Venture's "Net Cash Flow." Net Cash Flow shall be distributed between the parties according to their ownership interest subject to the adjustments described in Section 2.5.2 hereafter.

  2.5.2 **Definition of Distributable Cash Flow.** "Distributable Cash Flow" shall consist of the Net Cash Flow reduced by all reasonable amounts of reserved cash as shall be determined by a majority in interest of the Joint Venturers to be necessary or advisable for: (i) the repayment of Joint Venture indebtedness due or coming due in a future time period; (ii) the improvement, development, management, operation (including, but not limited to, insurance and property taxes and assessments), maintenance, replacement, or preservation of the Project; (iii) increases in working capital and other contingencies.

Section 2.6 **Allocations of Profits and Losses to Joint Venturers.**

  All profits and losses shall be allocated according to ownership interest.

Section 2.7 **Withdrawals of Capital.**

  Except as otherwise provided herein, no portion of the capital of the Joint Venture may be withdrawn at any time without the approval of all the parties. However, upon termination of the Joint Venture, the Joint Venture's capital shall be distributed pursuant to Section 6.3.4 hereof.

Section 2.8 **Voting.**

  Except as otherwise provided, all actions of the venture shall be mutually agreed upon by the parties.

Section 2.9 **Time Limit for Approval**

  Where an issue arises needing a vote, such vote shall be given within five (5) calendar days of a written request by the other party for a vote. Should a response not be returned within the stated period, then the vote will be considered in the affirmative.

Article III
Management

Section 3.1 **Joint Venture Manager.**

  Simmons is hereby appointed Manager or "Venture Manager" of the Joint Venture and shall be responsible for the internal operation of the venture. Any direct cost incurred shall be paid out of Joint Venture funds.

Section 3.2 **Other Business Activities.**

Nothing herein is to be construed as giving any party an interest in other business of the parties except those construed specifically by this Agreement or incorporated by an amendment hereto.

The parties mutually acknowledge that each is involved in additional businesses and are not restricted to participating with each other except as stated in the first right of refusal for additional projects.

Article IV
Accounting

Section 4.1 **Books, Records, and Fiscal Year.**

4.1.1 General. The Joint Venture's books and records of account shall be maintained in accordance with generally accepted accounting principles consistently applied on the cash basis and shall be adequate to provide any Joint Venturer with all financial information as may be needed by any Joint Venturer or any Affiliate of any Joint Venturer for purposes of satisfying the financial reporting obligations of any Joint Venturer or his or its respective affiliate or affiliates. The fiscal year of the Joint Venture shall end on December 31 of each year. The books and records shall be maintained at the Joint Venturer's principal place of business and shall be available to any Joint Venturer or its representative during normal business hours. Any such Joint Venturer may at any time request that the Joint Venture's independent accountants audit the books and records. The cost of such audit shall be borne by the requesting Joint Venturer unless said audit shall disclose a substantial discrepancy, in which case it shall be borne by the Joint Venture.

Section 4.2 **Budget.**

The Joint Venture Manager of the business shall prepare and submit to the Joint Venturers for their approval a budget (the "Budget") setting forth the estimated receipts and expenditures of the Joint Venture for the operation, management, and marketing of the business. No later than sixty (60) days prior to the end of each fiscal year of the Joint Venture, the Joint Venture manager shall prepare and submit a proposed Budget for the operation of the business of the Joint Venture in the next fiscal year for approval by the Joint Venturers. Upon adoption of an annual Budget, the Joint Venture manager shall be authorized, without the need for further approval by the Joint Venturers (except as otherwise provided), to make the expenditures and incur the obligations provided for in the Budget.

Section 4.3 **Statements of Financial Condition.**

The Joint Venture Manager shall prepare statements of financial condition of the Joint Venture as of the last day of each month of each fiscal year, and such statements shall be submitted promptly to the Joint Venturers. The Joint Venture's accountants shall prepare financial statements showing, among other things, income and Net Cash Flow of the Joint Venture for each fiscal year, copies of which shall be furnished to each of the Joint Venturers within thirty (30) days after they are prepared.

Section 4.4 **Other Accounting Decisions.**

All accounting decisions and tax elections for the Joint Venture (other than those specifically provided for in other Sections of this Agreement) shall be made from time to time as required and approved by the Joint Venturers.

Article V
Sale, Transfer, or Mortgage

Section 5.1 **General.**

Except as expressly permitted herein, no Joint Venturer shall sell, assign, transfer, mortgage, charge, or otherwise encumber, or permit any of the foregoing, whether voluntarily or by operation of law (herein sometimes collectively called a "transfer"), any part or all of his or its Joint Venture interest without the prior written approval of the other Joint Venturers, and any attempt to do so shall be void.

5.1.1 **Permitted Transfers**

(a) Any Joint Venturer may transfer or assign his or its interest in the Joint Venture to any corporation or general partnership that is controlled by such Joint Venturer, or to any limited partnership in which the Joint Venturer would be the general partner, and such transfers or assignments shall not be subject to this subsection, but the transferee thereof shall be subject to all the terms and conditions of this Agreement, including without limitation this subsection, and as a condition precedent to any such transfer, such transferee shall enter into a written agreement agreeing to be bound by the terms hereof.

(b) Except as provided in subsection 5.1.1.(a) above, no Joint Venturer may assign his or its interest in this Joint Venture without first obtaining the written approval and waiver of right of first refusal from the other Joint Venturers.

Section 5.2 **Right of First Refusal.**

5.2.1 Except for permitted transfers, each party to this Agreement shall give the others thirty (30) days to meet any offer to purchase his interest in the Joint Venture on the same terms and conditions being offered.

If, within the thirty (30) day period a modification of acceptance by the offering party is not received, he is free to sell his interest for the offered amount, but not on terms more favorable.

Any purchasing party must agree in writing to execute this Agreement and be bound as though he were an original party.

5.2.2 **Limitations on Exercise**. Notwithstanding anything to the contrary contained in this Section 5.2, an Offeree who has committed an Event of Default that is still continuing and that has not been cured shall not be entitled to exercise its or his right to purchase any portion of the Offeror's interest in the Joint Venture.

5.2.3 **Death of a Joint Venturer**. The death of a Joint Venturer shall not dissolve the Joint Venture as to the other Joint Venturers, nor shall such a death cause any interruption in the conduct of the business of the Joint Venture. Upon the death of a Joint Venturer, the remaining Joint Venturers shall have the right, privilege, and option of purchasing, from the personal representative of the estate of the deceased Joint Venturer, all, but not less than all, of the interest in the Joint Venture owned by the deceased Joint Venturer at the time of his or her death, at the price and upon the terms and conditions hereinafter set forth. Should the other Joint Venturers desire to exercise such option, they shall give notice in writing to the personal representative of the estate of the deceased Joint Venturer within sixty (60) days after the date of death of the deceased Joint Venturer. The estate of the deceased Joint Venturer shall be obligated to sell its interest in the Joint Venture should any of the surviving Joint Venturers desire to exercise the option as set forth above. In the event that none of the surviving Joint Venturers desire to purchase the interest in the Joint Venture of the deceased Joint Venturer, the interest of such deceased Joint Venturer shall be transferred by testamentary instrument or by operation of law to any other person or persons or to any public charitable organization so designated by the deceased Joint Venturer.

The purchase price of a deceased Joint Venturer's interest in the Joint Venture shall be an amount equal to the fair market value of such interest as determined in Article VII hereof. An amount equal to _fifty_ percent (_50_ %) of the total purchase price of the deceased Joint Venturer's interest in the Joint Venture shall be paid at closing, and the balance of the purchase price shall be paid in three (3) equal consecutive annual installments of principal and interest, with the first of said remaining installments being due and payable on the anniversary of the Closing. The deferred portion of the purchase price shall be evidenced by the purchasing Joint Venturer's negotiable promissory note(s), payable with interest at the rate of _ten_ percent (_10_ %) per annum from Closing until paid in full. Such note or notes shall provide for the acceleration of the due date of the remaining balance due in the event of default of the payment of any installment due on any such note, or interest due thereon, and shall also give the maker thereof the option of prepayment, in whole or in part, at any time, without penalty. If any of such notes are executed by a corporation as maker, then the shareholders of such corporation shall guarantee the payment thereof.

In the event a corporation is a Joint Venturer in the Joint Venture, the restrictions on the transfer of a shareholder's stock in such corporation upon his or her death shall be governed by a separate stock transfer agreement to be entered into between such corporate Joint Venturer and its shareholders, which agreement shall generally provide for restrictions as set forth above upon the death of an individual Joint Venturer, except that the remaining shareholders in the corporate Joint Venturer shall first have the option to purchase the deceased shareholder's stock in the corporation before the stock is offered for sale to the other Joint Venturers in the Joint Venture.

Section 5.3 **Closings.**

5.3.1 **Termination of Obligations.** As of the effective date of any transfer not prohibited hereunder by a Joint Venturer of its entire interest in the Joint Venture, such Joint Venturer's rights and obligations hereunder shall terminate except as to items accrued as of such date and except as to any indemnity obligations of such Joint Venturer attributable to acts or events occurring prior to such date. Thereupon, except as limited by the preceding sentence, this Agreement shall terminate as to the transferring Joint Venturer but shall remain in effect as to the other Joint Venturers. In the event of a transfer of its or his entire Joint Venture interest by a Joint Venturer to another Joint Venturer, the Joint Venturer to whom such interest is transferred shall indemnify, defend, and hold harmless the Joint Venturer so transferring its or his Joint Venture interest from and against any and all claims, demands, liabilities, expenses, actions, lawsuits, and other proceedings, judgments, awards, and costs (including reasonable attorneys' fees) incurred in or arising directly or indirectly, in whole or in part, out of operation of the business of the Joint Venture, excluding only those matters listed above, if any, accruing prior to the date of such transfer.

Section 5.4 **Withdrawals.**

Each of the Joint Venturers does hereby covenant and agree that it will not withdraw or retire from the Joint Venture, except as a result of a permitted transfer of its entire interest in the Joint Venture pursuant to the terms of this Agreement, and that it will carry out its duties and responsibilities hereunder until the Joint Venture is terminated, liquidated, and dissolved.

Article VI
Default and Dissolution

Section 6.1 **Events of Default.**

6.1.1 **Definitions and Cure Periods.** The occurrence of any of the following events shall constitute an event of default ("Event of Default") hereunder on the part of the Joint Venturer with respect to whom such event occurs ("Defaulter") if within thirty (30) days following written notice of such default from the Joint Venture Manager the Defaulter fails to pay such monies, or in the case of nonmonetary defaults, fails to commence substantial efforts to cure such default or thereafter fails within a reasonable time to prosecute to completion with diligence and continuity the curing of such default; provided, however, that the occurrence of any Act of Insolvency (as hereafter defined in subsection 6.1.2) shall constitute an Event of Default immediately upon such occurrence without any requirement of notice or passage of time except as specifically set forth in any such subparagraph:

(a) the failure by a Joint Venturer to make any additional capital contribution to the Joint Venture as required;

(b) the violation by a Joint Venturer of any of the restrictions set forth in Article V of this Agreement upon the right of a Joint Venturer to transfer its Joint Venture interest;

(c) the failure of a Joint Venturer to repay a Contribution Loan as required;

(d) the failure of a Joint Venturer's personal representative or heirs to assume in writing and agree to be bound by all of the deceased Joint Venturer's obligations;

(e) the occurrence of an Act of Insolvency by any Joint Venturer (as defined in subsection 6.1.2); and

(f) default in performance of or failure to comply with any other agreements, obligations, or undertakings of a Joint Venturer herein contained.

The death of a Joint Venturer shall not comprise an Event of Default, nor shall it result in the dissolution of the Joint Venture.

6.1.2 **Act of Insolvency.** The occurrence of any of the following events shall constitute an "Act of Insolvency," as said term is used in this Agreement:

(a) institution by a Joint Venturer of proceedings of any nature under any laws of the United States or of any state, whether now existing or subsequently enacted or amended, for the relief of debtors wherein such Joint Venturer is seeking relief as debtor;

(b) a general assignment by a Joint Venturer for the benefit of creditors;

(c) the institution by a Joint Venturer of a proceeding under any section or chapter of the Federal Bankruptcy Act as now existing or hereafter amended or becoming effective;

(d) the institution against a Joint Venturer of a proceeding under any section or chapter of the Federal Bankruptcy Act as now existing or hereafter amended or becoming effective, which proceeding is not dismissed, stayed, or discharged within a period sixty (60) days after the filing thereof, or if stayed, which stay is thereafter lifted without contemporaneous discharge or dismissal of such proceeding.

Section 6.2 **Causes of Dissolution.**

The Joint Venture shall be dissolved only if a Dissolving Event shall occur. A "Dissolving Event" shall occur when:

(a) an Event of Default has occurred as provided in Section 6.1 and the nondefaulting Joint Venturers elect to dissolve the Joint Venture as provided in Section 6.3 hereof;

(b) one or more of the Joint Venturers elect to dissolve or terminate the Joint Venture pursuant to any provision of this Agreement permitting such election to be made; or

(c) the Joint Venture, by its terms as set forth in this Agreement, is terminated.

Section 6.3 **Election of Nondefaulting Joint Venturer.**

6.3.1 **Purchase of Defaulter's Interest.** Upon the occurrence of an Event of Default by any Joint Venturer ("Defaulter"), the other Joint Venturers ("Nondefaulters") shall have the right to acquire all, but not less than all, of the Joint Venture interest of the Defaulter for cash, except as provided in subsection 6.3.2 hereof, at a price determined pursuant to the appraisal procedure set forth in Article VII, subject to adjustment as otherwise herein set forth (and except for the provisions set forth in subsection 2.4.5, which shall govern in such circumstances). In furtherance of such right, a Nondefaulter (the "Electing Nondefaulter") may notify the Defaulter at any time following an Event of Default of its election to institute the appraisal procedure set forth in Article VII. Upon receipt of notice of determination of the fair market value of the Defaulter's Joint Venture interest, the Electing Nondefaulter may notify the Defaulter of its election to purchase the interest of the Defaulter.

6.3.2 **Purchase in Event of Act of Insolvency.** If the Event of Default is also an Act of Insolvency, a Joint Venturer who elects to purchase the Joint Venture interest of the Defaulter shall have the right to purchase such Joint Venturer's interest by down payment of _twenty_ percent (_20_ %) of the purchase price, as determined by the appraisal procedure pursuant to Article VII, of such Joint Venture interest at Closing, with the balance of the purchase price to be payable in equal monthly installments over a period of _five_ (_5_) years, and with the unpaid balance of such purchase price bearing interest equal to the prime rate in effect at that time at _First Bank_ , city of _Oklahoma City_ , state of _Oklahoma_ , or its successors in interest as of the date of Closing, with the right of prepayment of any amount at any time without penalty.

6.3.3 **Defaulter's Right to Cure.** The right of a Defaulter to cure an Event of Default shall expire upon a Joint Venturer giving to the Defaulter a notice of election to purchase the Defaulter's interest in the Joint Venture.

6.3.4 **Distribution upon Dissolution.** The assets of the Joint Venture shall be applied or distributed in liquidation upon the happening of a Dissolving Event in the following order of priority:

(a) in payment of debts and obligations of the Joint Venture owed to third parties, which shall include any Joint Venturer as the holder of any secured loan;

(b) in payment of debts and obligations of the Joint Venture to any Joint Venturer;

(c) to the Joint Venturers in the same manner and in the same priorities and percentages as Net Proceeds are allocated and distributed to the Joint Venturers as set forth herein.

Notwithstanding the foregoing, in the event that there are any outstanding Contribution Loans at the time of any distribution pursuant to this subsection 6.3.4, then the Joint Venturer to whom such Contribution Loan is owed shall be entitled to payment of the Contribution Loan on a priority basis out of the distributions to which the Joint Venturer for whose benefit the Contribution Loans were made is entitled, to be applied to the Contribution Loans in order of priority based on the chronological order in which they were made, the earliest to be paid first in full, and to each Contribution Loan in payment first of interest and then of principal.

Article VII
Appraisal

Section 7.1 **General.**

Whenever this Agreement provides for the valuation of an interest in the Joint Venture to be purchased or sold, the value of such interest in the Joint Venture shall be determined in the following manner. The parties shall first attempt to agree upon the "net fair market value" of the Joint Venture and of the interests in the Joint Venture to be purchased or sold. Net fair market value of the Joint Venture shall be determined using accepted appraisal methods utilized in the appraisal industry, including the capitalization of income approach and the comparable sale approach. The "net fair market value" of a Joint Venture interest shall mean the value of the interest to be sold or purchased, based on the net fair market value of the Joint Venture.

Section 7.2 **Appraisal Procedure.**

In the event the Joint Venturers are unable to mutually agree upon the net fair market value of the Joint Venture and of the Joint Venture interests to be sold or purchased within thirty (30) days of the date the appraisal procedure of this Article VII is instituted, the Joint Venturers shall then attempt to agree upon the appointment of three disinterested appraisers, who shall be members of the American Institute of Appraisers. If the Joint Venturers are unable to agree upon the selection of three appraisers within thirty (30) days of the date the appraisal procedure is instituted, then a petition may be made by any Joint Venturer to the presiding judge of the Circuit Court for the county of _Sussex_ , state of _Oklahoma_ , for such selection. Each Joint Venturer shall have the right to submit the names of three (3) appraisers so qualified, and the judge shall select the three (3) appraisers from the names so submitted. Each appraiser so selected shall furnish the Joint Venturers and the certified public accountants for the Joint Venture with a written appraisal within ninety (90) days of his selection, setting forth his determination of the net fair market value of all real estate and other tangible assets owned by the Joint Venture as of the date of institution of this appraisal procedure. Such appraisal shall assume that the use of the Property, Improvements, and other tangible Joint Venture assets shall be the use for which the Property, Improvements, and other tangible Joint Venture assets are then being utilized, and the appraisal shall not include any value for goodwill. The average of the two closest evaluations of such appraisers shall be treated as the net fair market value of the Property, Improvements and other tangible assets of the Joint Venture. Upon receipt of the appraisals of the net fair market value of such assets, the independent certified public accountants of the Joint Venture shall make the final determination as to the net fair market value of the Joint Venture and of the Joint Venture interest to be sold or purchased, and in making their determination shall decide what effect, if any, should be given to the terms and provisions of this Agreement. The accountants shall notify the Joint Venturers in writing of their determination within sixty (60) days of the date of receipt of the appraisals prepared by the appraisers. The determination of the accountants shall be treated as the net fair market value of the Joint Venture and of the Joint Venture interest to be sold or purchased determined pursuant to this Article VII, and the determination shall be final and binding on the Joint Venturers. The cost of the appraisal shall be an expense of the Joint Venture.

Article VIII
Insurance

Section 8.1 **General.**

The Joint Venture shall carry and maintain in force the following insurance, the premium for which shall be a cost and expense in connection with the operation of the Joint Venture.

Section 8.2 **Workers' Compensation.**

Workers' Compensation Insurance covering all employees of the Joint Venture employed in, on, or about the property of the Joint Venture to provide statutory benefits as required by the laws of the state of _Oklahoma_ .

Section 8.3 **Comprehensive General Liability.**

Comprehensive General Liability Insurance on an occurrence basis for the benefit of the Joint Venturers and the Joint Venture as named insureds against claims for personal injury liability, including, without limitation, bodily injury, death, or property damage liability with limits of not less than _Three Million and No/100_ Dollars ($ _3,000,000.00_) in the event of personal injury to one (1) person and not less than _Five Million and No/100_ Dollars ($ _5,000,000.00_) in the event of injury to any number of persons in any one (1) occurrence, with a limit of not less than _Five Hundred Thousand and No/100_ Dollars ($ _500,000.00_) for property damage; such insurance shall also include coverage against liability for bodily injury or property damage arising out of the use by or on behalf of the Joint Venturers of any owned, nonowned, or hired automotive equipment for limits not less than those specified above.

Section 8.4 **Umbrella.**

Comprehensive umbrella coverage for the benefit of the Joint Venturers and the Joint Venture with limits of not less than _Three Million and No/100_ Dollars ($ _3,000,000.00_).

Section 8.5 **Extended Coverage.**

The Joint Venturers shall keep the Improvements insured against loss or damage by fire and the risks embraced within the term "Extended Coverage" in such amount or amounts as a majority in interest of the Joint Venturers may require and insured against such other hazards and risks as may be reasonably required by the Joint Venturers, in such amount or amounts as may be reasonably required by said Joint Venturers, with such insurance company or companies as the Joint Venturers or their respective successors or assigns may approve, and the Manager shall retain the policies of such insurance and of any additional insurance that shall be taken out upon such buildings.

Section 8.6 **Other Insurance.**

Such other insurance as may be approved by the Joint Venturers.

Section 8.7 **Named Insured.**

All such aforesaid policies shall be issued in the name of the Joint Venturers and the Joint Venture, as named insureds.

Article IX
General Provisions

Section 9.1 **Complete Agreement; Amendment; Notice.**

9.1.1 **Entire Agreement.** This Agreement embodies the entire understanding of the parties, and any changes must be made in writing and signed by all parties.

9.1.2 **Amendment.** This instrument may be amended or modified only by an instrument of equal formality signed by all of the respective parties hereto.

9.1.3 **Notice.** All notices under this Agreement shall be in writing and shall be delivered by personal service, or by certified or registered mail, postage prepaid, return receipt requested, to the Joint Venturers (and where required, to the person required to be copied with the notice) at the addresses herein or at such other address as the addressee may designate in writing, and to the Joint Venture at its principal place of business as set forth in Section 1.3 hereof, and shall be effective upon receipt (or refusal to accept).

The addresses for notices to the Joint Venturers are as follows:

Lindsay Simmons
521 Central Lane
Oklahoma City, Oklahoma 73149
Jennifer Jones
64 Summer Street
Oklahoma City, Oklahoma 73160

Section 9.2 **Attorneys' Fees.**

Should any litigation be commenced between the parties hereto or their representatives, or should any party institute any proceeding in a bankruptcy or similar court which has jurisdiction over any other party hereto or any or all of his or its property or assets concerning any provision of this Agreement or the rights and duties of any person or entity in relation thereto, the party or parties prevailing in such litigation shall be entitled, in addition to such other relief as may be granted, to a reasonable sum as and for his or its or their attorneys' fees and court costs in such litigation or in a separate action brought for that purpose.

Section 9.3 **Validity.**

In the event that any provision of this Agreement shall be held to be invalid or unenforceable, the same shall not affect in any respect whatsoever the validity or enforceability of the remainder of this Agreement.

Section 9.4 **Survival of Rights.**

Except as provided herein to the contrary, this Agreement shall be binding upon and inure to the benefit of the parties signatory hereto, their respective heirs, executors, legal representatives, and permitted successors and assigns.

Section 9.5 **Governing Law.**

This Agreement has been entered into in the state of _Oklahoma_ , and all questions with respect to this Agreement and the rights and liabilities of the parties hereto shall be governed by the laws of _Oklahoma_ , and the venue of any action brought hereunder shall be in _Sussex_ County, state of _Oklahoma_ .

Section 9.6 **Waiver.**

No consent or waiver, express or implied, by a Joint Venturer to or of any breach or default by another Joint Venturer in the performance by such other Joint Venturer of its obligations hereunder shall be deemed or construed to be a consent or waiver to or of any other breach or default in the performance by such other Joint Venturer hereunder. Failure on the part of a Joint Venturer to complain of any act or failure to act of another Joint Venturer or to declare another Joint Venturer in default, irrespective of how long such failure continues, shall not constitute a waiver by such Joint Venturer of its rights hereunder. The giving of consent by a Joint Venturer in any one instance shall not limit or waive the necessity to obtain such Joint Venturer's consent in any future instance.

Section 9.7 **Remedies in Equity.**

The rights and remedies of any of the Joint Venturers hereunder shall not be mutually exclusive, i.e., the exercise of one or more of the provisions hereof shall not preclude the exercise of any other provisions hereof. Each of the Joint Venturers confirm that damages at law may be an inadequate remedy for a breach or threatened breach of this Agreement and agree that, in the event of a breach or threatened breach of any provision hereof, the respective rights and obligations hereunder shall be enforceable by specific performance, injunction, or other equitable remedy, but nothing herein contained is intended to, nor shall it, limit or affect any rights at law or by statute or otherwise of any party aggrieved as against the other for a breach or threatened breach of any provision hereof, it being the intention by this Section to make clear the agreement of the

Joint Venturers that the respective rights and obligations of the Joint Venturers hereunder shall be enforceable in equity as well as at law or otherwise.

Section 9.8 **Indemnification.**

Each Joint Venturer ("Indemnifying Venturer") hereby agrees to indemnify and hold the other Joint Venturers and the Joint Venture harmless from and against any and all claims, demands, actions, and rights of action (including attorneys' fees and costs) that shall or may arise by virtue of anything done or omitted to be done by the Indemnifying Venturer (through or by its agents, employees, or other representatives) outside the scope of, or in breach of the terms of, this Agreement; provided, however, that the other Joint Venturers shall be notified promptly of the existence of any such claim, demand, action, or cause of action and shall be given reasonable opportunity to participate in the defense thereof. In the event that one Joint Venturer shall be held severally liable for the debts of the joint venture he shall be awarded contribution from the other Venturers so that each Joint Venturer shall only be obligated to pay that portion of such liability as shall be proportionate to such Joint Venturer's interest in the Joint Venture.

Section 9.9 **Counterparts.**

This Agreement may be executed in any number of counterparts, each of which shall be deemed to be an original and all of which shall constitute one and the same Agreement.

Section 9.10 **Further Assurances.**

Each party hereto agrees to do all acts and things and to make, execute, and deliver such written instruments as shall from time to time be reasonably required to carry out the terms and provisions of this Agreement.

IN WITNESS WHEREOF, the parties have executed this Agreement as of the day and year first above set forth.

Kathleen Shuman   _Lindsay Simmons_
Witness   Signature

Sarah Barrett
Witness

Greg Taylor   _Jennifer Jones_
Witness   Signature

Chris Johnson
Witness

Joint Venture Agreement

THIS AGREEMENT entered into this the _____ day of
_____ , 199 ___ , by and between _____ (_____)
of _____ , city of _____ , state of _____ , and
_____ (_____) of _____ , city of _____ ,
state of _____ ;

WITNESSETH:

WHEREAS, (_____) is in the business of: _____
_____ , and

WHEREAS, (_____) is in the business of:
_____ , and

WHEREAS, both parties desire to work together for the purpose
of: _____
_____
_____
_____
_____
_____
_____

NOW THEREFORE, for good and valuable consideration, receipt of
which is hereby acknowledged, and the mutual promises and
benefits to be derived by the parties, they do hereby agree to
the following terms and conditions:

Article I
Formation

Section 1.1 **Formation and Name.**

1.1.1 **Formation.** The Joint Venturers hereby confirm that they
have formed a Joint Venture for the purposes and scope set forth
in this Agreement.

1.1.2 **Name.** The name of the Joint Venture is and shall
continue to be _____ . The business and affairs of the Joint
Venture shall be conducted solely under that name and under no
other unless modified in writing by addendum to this agreement.

Section 1.2 **Purposes and Scope of the Joint Venture.**

The purpose of the Joint Venture is to: _____
_____
_____

Section 1.3 **Principal Place of Business.**

The principal place of business of the Joint Venture shall be
initially located at _____
_____
_____

Section 1.4 **Term.**

The term of the Joint Venture shall commence on the first above written day, and shall continue, unless sooner terminated in accordance with other provisions of this Agreement, until _____ , 199 ___ .

Section 1.5 **No Partition.**

No Joint Venturer shall have the right and each Joint Venturer hereby agrees not to withdraw from the Joint Venture nor to dissolve, terminate, partition, or liquidate, or to petition a court for the dissolution, termination, partition, or liquidation of the Joint Venture or its assets, except as provided in this Agreement, and no Joint Venturer at any time shall have the right to petition or to take any action to subject the operation of the Project or any part thereof or the Joint Venture assets or any part thereof to the authority of any court of bankruptcy, insolvency, receivership, or similar proceeding.

Article II
Capital Contributions, Reserves, Voting, Financing, and Distributions

Section 2.1 **Joint Venture Percentage Interest.**

The Joint Venturers shall have the following undivided percentage interests in the Joint Venture (individually a "Percentage Interest" and joint "Percentage Interests"):

_____   _____ %

_____   _____ %

                      _____ %

Section 2.2 **Adjustments and Interest.**

Unless otherwise approved by the Joint Venturers, no adjustment to the Percentage Interest of any Joint Venturer shall be made except as otherwise provided herein or as a result of a transfer of a Joint Venturer's Joint Venture interest or a portion thereof. It is the specific intent of the parties to equally split all fees and profits generated from the joint venture.

Section 2.3 **Capital Accounts.**

2.3.1 **General.** As used herein, the term "Capital Account" shall refer to the capital account of each Joint Venturer reflecting the value of each Joint Venturer's relative interest in the capital of the Joint Venture as calculated pursuant to this Agreement. A Capital Account, as defined herein, shall be maintained for each Joint Venturer and shall be subject to adjustment as provided in subsection 2.3.3.

2.3.2 **Initial Capital Contribution and Initial Capital**. Upon the execution of this Agreement, the parties shall mutually decide an amount for initial capitalization of the venture. The determined amount will be fulfilled by contributions proportionate to ownership. Thereafter, as additional capital is needed for the operation of the venture, it will be contributed in the same ratio.

2.3.3 **Adjustments to Capital Accounts**. The Capital Account of each Joint Venturer shall from time to time be:

(a) increased by:

    (i) any additional capital contributions of such Joint Venturer.

(b) decreased by:

    (i) all distributions to or for the account of such Joint Venturer, whether of capital or income (other than payments received by a Joint Venturer in payment of a loan permitted by the provisions hereof or a Contribution Loan);

    (ii) such Joint Venturer's allocable share of Net Capital Loss and Net Ordinary Loss of the Joint Venture during such fiscal year.

Section 2.4 **Additional Capital Contributions.**

2.4.1 **General**. If additional capital for the operation of the venture is needed, then the parties shall make such additional capital contributions in the same percentage as their percentage interests.

2.4.2 **Notice by Manager**. Notice of any additional capital contributions required to be made pursuant to this Section 2.4 shall be given by the Manager as hereinafter defined to each Joint Venturer in the manner provided in this Agreement. Such notice shall name the Joint Venturers voting for additional capital contributions and shall specify in reasonable detail the amount of and purpose of any such additional capital contributions. Each Joint Venturer shall, within _____ (_____) days of the receipt of such notice from the Manager, contribute to the Joint Venture the additional capital contribution required of such Joint Venturer as set forth in such notice.

2.4.3 **Contribution Loans**. In the event any Joint Venturer ("Noncontributing Joint Venturer") fails to make a required additional capital contribution pursuant to subsection 2.4.2 within the time specified, the other Joint Venturers (the "Contributing Joint Venturers") shall have the right to contribute an amount equal to such Noncontributing Joint Venturer's additional capital contribution. Any amounts so advanced to the Joint Venture by the Contributing Joint Venturers pursuant to this subsection 2.4.3 shall be treated as a loan by such Contributing Joint Venturers to the Noncontributing Joint Venturer ("Contribution Loan"), followed by the Noncontributing Joint Venturer making his or its required additional capital contribution to the Joint Venture of the proceeds of such Contribution Loan.

2.4.4 **Interest Repayment through Distributions**. In the event the Contributing Joint Venturers elect to make a Contribution Loan, then the Contribution Loan shall bear interest at a rate equal to the maximum allowed by law. In addition to other remedies, including, without limitation, those set forth in subsection 2.4.5, the Contribution Loan to the Noncontributing Joint Venturer shall be repaid out of any subsequent distributions from the Joint Venture made pursuant to this Agreement to which the Noncontributing Joint Venturer for whose account the Contribution Loan was made would otherwise be entitled, which amounts shall be applied first to interest accrued on the Contribution Loan and then to the principal due under the Contribution Loan, until the Contribution Loan is paid in full. In no event shall the principal or interest on any such Contribution Loan be an obligation of or paid by the Joint Venture. Contribution Loans shall be repaid on a first-in, first-out basis.

2.4.5 **Remedies**. In the event any Contribution Loan has not been repaid in full by the Noncontributing Joint Venturer within _____ (_____) days of the date the Contribution Loan is made, then at any time thereafter the Contributing Joint Venturers may proceed under subparagraphs (a) or (b) below:

(a) Upon _____ (_____) days' prior written notice, such Contributing Joint Venturer may elect to convert the Contribution Loan to an interest in the Joint Venture, whereupon, as of the effective date of such election, the Percentage Interest of the Contributing Joint Venturer and the Noncontributing Joint Venturer with respect to which the Contribution Loan relates shall be recalculated as provided below and the capital account of such Contributing Joint Venturer shall be increased by an amount equal to the principal plus accrued but unpaid interest on such Contribution Loan and the capital account of the Noncontributing Joint Venturer with respect to which the Contribution Loan relates shall be reduced accordingly. Upon determination of such value, the Noncontributing Joint Venturer shall be deemed to have transferred to the Contributing Joint Venturer that portion of the Noncontributing Joint Venturer's Percentage Interest of a value, calculated as provided above, as is equal to the Contributing Joint Venturer's Contribution Loan plus accrued but unpaid interest.

(b) Until a Contributing Joint Venturer has elected to proceed under subparagraph (a) above, such Contributing Joint Venturer's Contribution Loan shall remain in place and shall bear interest and be repaid as provided in subsection 2.4.4 above; provided, however, that this provision shall not operate to prohibit the Contributing Joint Venturer from declaring the Noncontributing Joint Venturer to be in default in the payment of any such Contribution Loan by reason of such nonpayment or from exercising any other rights or remedies of the Contributing Joint Venturer provided herein or at law.

Section 2.5 **Distributions to Joint Venturers of Cash Flow.**

2.5.1 **Definition of Net Cash Flow.** In each fiscal year of the Joint Venture, the Manager shall determine the Joint Venture's "Net Cash Flow." Net Cash Flow shall be distributed between the parties according to their ownership interest subject to the adjustments described in Section 2.5.2 hereafter.

2.5.2 **Definition of Distributable Cash Flow.** "Distributable Cash Flow" shall consist of the Net Cash Flow reduced by all reasonable amounts of reserved cash as shall be determined by a majority in interest of the Joint Venturers to be necessary or advisable for: (i) the repayment of Joint Venture indebtedness due or coming due in a future time period; (ii) the improvement, development, management, operation (including, but not limited to, insurance and property taxes and assessments), maintenance, replacement, or preservation of the Project; (iii) increases in working capital and other contingencies.

Section 2.6 **Allocations of Profits and Losses to Joint Venturers.**

All profits and losses shall be allocated according to ownership interest.

Section 2.7 **Withdrawals of Capital.**

Except as otherwise provided herein, no portion of the capital of the Joint Venture may be withdrawn at any time without the approval of all the parties. However, upon termination of the Joint Venture, the Joint Venture's capital shall be distributed pursuant to Section 6.3.4 hereof.

Section 2.8 **Voting.**

Except as otherwise provided, all actions of the venture shall be mutually agreed upon by the parties.

Section 2.9 **Time Limit for Approval**

Where an issue arises needing a vote, such vote shall be given within five (5) calendar days of a written request by the other party for a vote. Should a response not be returned within the stated period, then the vote will be considered in the affirmative.

Article III
Management

Section 3.1 **Joint Venture Manager.**

_____ is hereby appointed Manager or "Venture Manager" of the Joint Venture and shall be responsible for the internal operation of the venture. Any direct cost incurred shall be paid out of Joint Venture funds.

Section 3.2 **Other Business Activities.**

Nothing herein is to be construed as giving any party an interest in other business of the parties except those construed specifically by this Agreement or incorporated by an amendment hereto.

The parties mutually acknowledge that each is involved in additional businesses and are not restricted to participating with each other except as stated in the first right of refusal for additional projects.

Article IV
Accounting

Section 4.1 **Books, Records, and Fiscal Year.**

4.1.1 **General.** The Joint Venture's books and records of account shall be maintained in accordance with generally accepted accounting principles consistently applied on the cash basis and shall be adequate to provide any Joint Venturer with all financial information as may be needed by any Joint Venturer or any Affiliate of any Joint Venturer for purposes of satisfying the financial reporting obligations of any Joint Venturer or his or its respective affiliate or affiliates. The fiscal year of the Joint Venture shall end on December 31 of each year. The books and records shall be maintained at the Joint Venturer's principal place of business and shall be available to any Joint Venturer or its representative during normal business hours. Any such Joint Venturer may at any time request that the Joint Venture's independent accountants audit the books and records. The cost of such audit shall be borne by the requesting Joint Venturer unless said audit shall disclose a substantial discrepancy, in which case it shall be borne by the Joint Venture.

Section 4.2 **Budget.**

The Joint Venture Manager of the business shall prepare and submit to the Joint Venturers for their approval a budget (the "Budget") setting forth the estimated receipts and expenditures of the Joint Venture for the operation, management, and marketing of the business. No later than sixty (60) days prior to the end of each fiscal year of the Joint Venture, the Joint Venture manager shall prepare and submit a proposed Budget for the operation of the business of the Joint Venture in the next fiscal year for approval by the Joint Venturers. Upon adoption of an annual Budget, the Joint Venture manager shall be authorized, without the need for further approval by the Joint Venturers (except as otherwise provided), to make the expenditures and incur the obligations provided for in the Budget.

Section 4.3 **Statements of Financial Condition.**

The Joint Venture Manager shall prepare statements of financial condition of the Joint Venture as of the last day of each month of each fiscal year, and such statements shall be submitted promptly to the Joint Venturers. The Joint Venture's accountants shall prepare financial statements showing, among other things, income and Net Cash Flow of the Joint Venture for each fiscal year, copies of which shall be furnished to each of the Joint Venturers within thirty (30) days after they are prepared.

Section 4.4 **Other Accounting Decisions.**

All accounting decisions and tax elections for the Joint Venture (other than those specifically provided for in other Sections of this Agreement) shall be made from time to time as required and approved by the Joint Venturers.

Article V
Sale, Transfer, or Mortgage

Section 5.1 **General.**

Except as expressly permitted herein, no Joint Venturer shall sell, assign, transfer, mortgage, charge, or otherwise encumber, or permit any of the foregoing, whether voluntarily or by operation of law (herein sometimes collectively called a "transfer"), any part or all of his or its Joint Venture interest without the prior written approval of the other Joint Venturers, and any attempt to do so shall be void.

5.1.1 **Permitted Transfers**

(a) Any Joint Venturer may transfer or assign his or its interest in the Joint Venture to any corporation or general partnership that is controlled by such Joint Venturer, or to any limited partnership in which the Joint Venturer would be the general partner, and such transfers or assignments shall not be subject to this subsection, but the transferee thereof shall be subject to all the terms and conditions of this Agreement, including without limitation this subsection, and as a condition precedent to any such transfer, such transferee shall enter into a written agreement agreeing to be bound by the terms hereof.

(b) Except as provided in subsection 5.1.1.(a) above, no Joint Venturer may assign his or its interest in this Joint Venture without first obtaining the written approval and waiver of right of first refusal from the other Joint Venturers.

Section 5.2 **Right of First Refusal.**

5.2.1 Except for permitted transfers, each party to this Agreement shall give the others thirty (30) days to meet any offer to purchase his interest in the Joint Venture on the same terms and conditions being offered.

If, within the thirty (30) day period a modification of acceptance by the offering party is not received, he is free to sell his interest for the offered amount, but not on terms more favorable.

Any purchasing party must agree in writing to execute this Agreement and be bound as though he were an original party.

5.2.2 **Limitations on Exercise.** Notwithstanding anything to the contrary contained in this Section 5.2, an Offeree who has committed an Event of Default that is still continuing and that has not been cured shall not be entitled to exercise its or his right to purchase any portion of the Offeror's interest in the Joint Venture.

5.2.3 **Death of a Joint Venturer.** The death of a Joint Venturer shall not dissolve the Joint Venture as to the other Joint Venturers, nor shall such a death cause any interruption in the conduct of the business of the Joint Venture. Upon the death of a Joint Venturer, the remaining Joint Venturers shall have the right, privilege, and option of purchasing, from the personal representative of the estate of the deceased Joint Venturer, all, but not less than all, of the interest in the Joint Venture owned by the deceased Joint Venturer at the time of his or her death, at the price and upon the terms and conditions hereinafter set forth. Should the other Joint Venturers desire to exercise such option, they shall give notice in writing to the personal representative of the estate of the deceased Joint Venturer within sixty (60) days after the date of death of the deceased Joint Venturer. The estate of the deceased Joint Venturer shall be obligated to sell its interest in the Joint Venture should any of the surviving Joint Venturers desire to exercise the option as set forth above. In the event that none of the surviving Joint Venturers desire to purchase the interest in the Joint Venture of the deceased Joint Venturer, the interest of such deceased Joint Venturer shall be transferred by testamentary instrument or by operation of law to any other person or persons or to any public charitable organization so designated by the deceased Joint Venturer.

The purchase price of a deceased Joint Venturer's interest in the Joint Venture shall be an amount equal to the fair market value of such interest as determined in Article VII hereof. An amount equal to _____ percent (_____ %) of the total purchase price of the deceased Joint Venturer's interest in the Joint Venture shall be paid at closing, and the balance of the purchase price shall be paid in three (3) equal consecutive annual installments of principal and interest, with the first of said remaining installments being due and payable on the anniversary of the Closing. The deferred portion of the purchase price shall be evidenced by the purchasing Joint Venturer's negotiable promissory note(s), payable with interest at the rate of _____ percent (_____ %) per annum from Closing until paid in full. Such note or notes shall provide for the acceleration of the due date of the remaining balance due in the event of default of the payment of any installment due on any such note, or interest due thereon, and shall also give the maker thereof the option of prepayment, in whole or in part, at any time, without penalty. If any of such notes are executed by a corporation as maker, then the shareholders of such corporation shall guarantee the payment thereof.

In the event a corporation is a Joint Venturer in the Joint Venture, the restrictions on the transfer of a shareholder's stock in such corporation upon his or her death shall be governed by a separate stock transfer agreement to be entered into between such corporate Joint Venturer and its shareholders, which agreement shall generally provide for restrictions as set forth above upon the death of an individual Joint Venturer, except that the remaining shareholders in the corporate Joint Venturer shall first have the option to purchase the deceased shareholder's stock in the corporation before the stock is offered for sale to the other Joint Venturers in the Joint Venture.

Section 5.3 **Closings.**

5.3.1 Termination of Obligations. As of the effective date of any transfer not prohibited hereunder by a Joint Venturer of its entire interest in the Joint Venture, such Joint Venturer's rights and obligations hereunder shall terminate except as to items accrued as of such date and except as to any indemnity obligations of such Joint Venturer attributable to acts or events occurring prior to such date. Thereupon, except as limited by the preceding sentence, this Agreement shall terminate as to the transferring Joint Venturer but shall remain in effect as to the other Joint Venturers. In the event of a transfer of its or his entire Joint Venture interest by a Joint Venturer to another Joint Venturer, the Joint Venturer to whom such interest is transferred shall indemnify, defend, and hold harmless the Joint Venturer so transferring its or his Joint Venture interest from and against any and all claims, demands, liabilities, expenses, actions, lawsuits, and other proceedings, judgments, awards, and costs (including reasonable attorneys' fees) incurred in or arising directly or indirectly, in whole or in part, out of operation of the business of the Joint Venture, excluding only those matters listed above, if any, accruing prior to the date of such transfer.

Section 5.4 **Withdrawals.**

Each of the Joint Venturers does hereby covenant and agree that it will not withdraw or retire from the Joint Venture, except as a result of a permitted transfer of its entire interest in the Joint Venture pursuant to the terms of this Agreement, and that it will carry out its duties and responsibilities hereunder until the Joint Venture is terminated, liquidated, and dissolved.

Article VI
Default and Dissolution

Section 6.1 **Events of Default.**

   6.1.1 **Definitions and Cure Periods.** The occurrence of any of the following events shall constitute an event of default ("Event of Default") hereunder on the part of the Joint Venturer with respect to whom such event occurs ("Defaulter") if within thirty (30) days following written notice of such default from the Joint Venture Manager the Defaulter fails to pay such monies, or in the case of nonmonetary defaults, fails to commence substantial efforts to cure such default or thereafter fails within a reasonable time to prosecute to completion with diligence and continuity the curing of such default; provided, however, that the occurrence of any Act of Insolvency (as hereafter defined in subsection 6.1.2) shall constitute an Event of Default immediately upon such occurrence without any requirement of notice or passage of time except as specifically set forth in any such subparagraph:

   (a) the failure by a Joint Venturer to make any additional capital contribution to the Joint Venture as required;

   (b) the violation by a Joint Venturer of any of the restrictions set forth in Article V of this Agreement upon the right of a Joint Venturer to transfer its Joint Venture interest;

   (c) the failure of a Joint Venturer to repay a Contribution Loan as required;

   (d) the failure of a Joint Venturer's personal representative or heirs to assume in writing and agree to be bound by all of the deceased Joint Venturer's obligations;

   (e) the occurrence of an Act of Insolvency by any Joint Venturer (as defined in subsection 6.1.2); and

   (f) default in performance of or failure to comply with any other agreements, obligations, or undertakings of a Joint Venturer herein contained.

   The death of a Joint Venturer shall not comprise an Event of Default, nor shall it result in the dissolution of the Joint Venture.

   6.1.2 **Act of Insolvency.** The occurrence of any of the following events shall constitute an "Act of Insolvency," as said term is used in this Agreement:

   (a) institution by a Joint Venturer of proceedings of any nature under any laws of the United States or of any state, whether now existing or subsequently enacted or amended, for the relief of debtors wherein such Joint Venturer is seeking relief as debtor;

   (b) a general assignment by a Joint Venturer for the benefit of creditors;

   (c) the institution by a Joint Venturer of a proceeding under any section or chapter of the Federal Bankruptcy Act as now existing or hereafter amended or becoming effective;

(d) the institution against a Joint Venturer of a proceeding under any section or chapter of the Federal Bankruptcy Act as now existing or hereafter amended or becoming effective, which proceeding is not dismissed, stayed, or discharged within a period sixty (60) days after the filing thereof, or if stayed, which stay is thereafter lifted without contemporaneous discharge or dismissal of such proceeding.

Section 6.2 **Causes of Dissolution.**

The Joint Venture shall be dissolved only if a Dissolving Event shall occur. A "Dissolving Event" shall occur when:

(a) an Event of Default has occurred as provided in Section 6.1 and the nondefaulting Joint Venturers elect to dissolve the Joint Venture as provided in Section 6.3 hereof;

(b) one or more of the Joint Venturers elect to dissolve or terminate the Joint Venture pursuant to any provision of this Agreement permitting such election to be made; or

(c) the Joint Venture, by its terms as set forth in this Agreement, is terminated.

Section 6.3 **Election of Nondefaulting Joint Venturer.**

6.3.1 **Purchase of Defaulter's Interest.** Upon the occurrence of an Event of Default by any Joint Venturer ("Defaulter"), the other Joint Venturers ("Nondefaulters") shall have the right to acquire all, but not less than all, of the Joint Venture interest of the Defaulter for cash, except as provided in subsection 6.3.2 hereof, at a price determined pursuant to the appraisal procedure set forth in Article VII, subject to adjustment as otherwise herein set forth (and except for the provisions set forth in subsection 2.4.5, which shall govern in such circumstances). In furtherance of such right, a Nondefaulter (the "Electing Nondefaulter") may notify the Defaulter at any time following an Event of Default of its election to institute the appraisal procedure set forth in Article VII. Upon receipt of notice of determination of the fair market value of the Defaulter's Joint Venture interest, the Electing Nondefaulter may notify the Defaulter of its election to purchase the interest of the Defaulter.

6.3.2 **Purchase in Event of Act of Insolvency.** If the Event of Default is also an Act of Insolvency, a Joint Venturer who elects to purchase the Joint Venture interest of the Defaulter shall have the right to purchase such Joint Venturer's interest by down payment of _____ percent (_____ %) of the purchase price, as determined by the appraisal procedure pursuant to Article VII, of such Joint Venture interest at Closing, with the balance of the purchase price to be payable in equal monthly installments over a period of _____ (_____) years, and with the unpaid balance of such purchase price bearing interest equal to the prime rate in effect at that time at _____ , city of _____ , state of _____ , or its successors in interest as of the date of Closing, with the right of prepayment of any amount at any time without penalty.

    6.3.3 **Defaulter's Right to Cure**. The right of a Defaulter to cure an Event of Default shall expire upon a Joint Venturer giving to the Defaulter a notice of election to purchase the Defaulter's interest in the Joint Venture.

    6.3.4 **Distribution upon Dissolution**. The assets of the Joint Venture shall be applied or distributed in liquidation upon the happening of a Dissolving Event in the following order of priority:

    (a) in payment of debts and obligations of the Joint Venture owed to third parties, which shall include any Joint Venturer as the holder of any secured loan;

    (b) in payment of debts and obligations of the Joint Venture to any Joint Venturer;

    (c) to the Joint Venturers in the same manner and in the same priorities and percentages as Net Proceeds are allocated and distributed to the Joint Venturers as set forth herein.

Notwithstanding the foregoing, in the event that there are any outstanding Contribution Loans at the time of any distribution pursuant to this subsection 6.3.4, then the Joint Venturer to whom such Contribution Loan is owed shall be entitled to payment of the Contribution Loan on a priority basis out of the distributions to which the Joint Venturer for whose benefit the Contribution Loans were made is entitled, to be applied to the Contribution Loans in order of priority based on the chronological order in which they were made, the earliest to be paid first in full, and to each Contribution Loan in payment first of interest and then of principal.

Article VII
Appraisal

Section 7.1 **General.**

    Whenever this Agreement provides for the valuation of an interest in the Joint Venture to be purchased or sold, the value of such interest in the Joint Venture shall be determined in the following manner. The parties shall first attempt to agree upon the "net fair market value" of the Joint Venture and of the interests in the Joint Venture to be purchased or sold. Net fair market value of the Joint Venture shall be determined using accepted appraisal methods utilized in the appraisal industry, including the capitalization of income approach and the comparable sale approach. The "net fair market value" of a Joint Venture interest shall mean the value of the interest to be sold or purchased, based on the net fair market value of the Joint Venture.

Section 7.2 **Appraisal Procedure.**

In the event the Joint Venturers are unable to mutually agree upon the net fair market value of the Joint Venture and of the Joint Venture interests to be sold or purchased within thirty (30) days of the date the appraisal procedure of this Article VII is instituted, the Joint Venturers shall then attempt to agree upon the appointment of three disinterested appraisers, who shall be members of the American Institute of Appraisers. If the Joint Venturers are unable to agree upon the selection of three appraisers within thirty (30) days of the date the appraisal procedure is instituted, then a petition may be made by any Joint Venturer to the presiding judge of the Circuit Court for the county of _____ , state of _____ , for such selection. Each Joint Venturer shall have the right to submit the names of three (3) appraisers so qualified, and the judge shall select the three (3) appraisers from the names so submitted. Each appraiser so selected shall furnish the Joint Venturers and the certified public accountants for the Joint Venture with a written appraisal within ninety (90) days of his selection, setting forth his determination of the net fair market value of all real estate and other tangible assets owned by the Joint Venture as of the date of institution of this appraisal procedure. Such appraisal shall assume that the use of the Property, Improvements, and other tangible Joint Venture assets shall be the use for which the Property, Improvements, and other tangible Joint Venture assets are then being utilized, and the appraisal shall not include any value for goodwill. The average of the two closest evaluations of such appraisers shall be treated as the net fair market value of the Property, Improvements and other tangible assets of the Joint Venture. Upon receipt of the appraisals of the net fair market value of such assets, the independent certified public accountants of the Joint Venture shall make the final determination as to the net fair market value of the Joint Venture and of the Joint Venture interest to be sold or purchased, and in making their determination shall decide what effect, if any, should be given to the terms and provisions of this Agreement. The accountants shall notify the Joint Venturers in writing of their determination within sixty (60) days of the date of receipt of the appraisals prepared by the appraisers. The determination of the accountants shall be treated as the net fair market value of the Joint Venture and of the Joint Venture interest to be sold or purchased determined pursuant to this Article VII, and the determination shall be final and binding on the Joint Venturers. The cost of the appraisal shall be an expense of the Joint Venture.

Article VIII
Insurance

Section 8.1 **General.**

The Joint Venture shall carry and maintain in force the following insurance, the premium for which shall be a cost and expense in connection with the operation of the Joint Venture.

Section 8.2 **Workers' Compensation.**

Workers' Compensation Insurance covering all employees of the Joint Venture employed in, on, or about the property of the Joint Venture to provide statutory benefits as required by the laws of the state of _____ .

Section 8.3 **Comprehensive General Liability.**

Comprehensive General Liability Insurance on an occurrence basis for the benefit of the Joint Venturers and the Joint Venture as named insureds against claims for personal injury liability, including, without limitation, bodily injury, death, or property damage liability with limits of not less than _____ Dollars ($ _____) in the event of personal injury to one (1) person and not less than _____ Dollars ($ _____) in the event of injury to any number of persons in any one (1) occurrence, with a limit of not less than _____ Dollars ($ _____) for property damage; such insurance shall also include coverage against liability for bodily injury or property damage arising out of the use by or on behalf of the Joint Venturers of any owned, nonowned, or hired automotive equipment for limits not less than those specified above.

Section 8.4 **Umbrella.**

Comprehensive umbrella coverage for the benefit of the Joint Venturers and the Joint Venture with limits of not less than _____ Dollars ($ _____).

Section 8.5 **Extended Coverage.**

The Joint Venturers shall keep the Improvements insured against loss or damage by fire and the risks embraced within the term "Extended Coverage" in such amount or amounts as a majority in interest of the Joint Venturers may require and insured against such other hazards and risks as may be reasonably required by the Joint Venturers, in such amount or amounts as may be reasonably required by said Joint Venturers, with such insurance company or companies as the Joint Venturers or their respective successors or assigns may approve, and the Manager shall retain the policies of such insurance and of any additional insurance that shall be taken out upon such buildings.

Section 8.6 **Other Insurance.**
Such other insurance as may be approved by the Joint Venturers.

Section 8.7 **Named Insured.**
All such aforesaid policies shall be issued in the name of the Joint Venturers and the Joint Venture, as named insureds.

Article IX
General Provisions

Section 9.1 **Complete Agreement; Amendment; Notice.**
9.1.1 **Entire Agreement.** This Agreement embodies the entire understanding of the parties, and any changes must be made in writing and signed by all parties.
9.1.2 **Amendment.** This instrument may be amended or modified only by an instrument of equal formality signed by all of the respective parties hereto.
9.1.3 **Notice.** All notices under this Agreement shall be in writing and shall be delivered by personal service, or by certified or registered mail, postage prepaid, return receipt requested, to the Joint Venturers (and where required, to the person required to be copied with the notice) at the addresses herein or at such other address as the addressee may designate in writing, and to the Joint Venture at its principal place of business as set forth in Section 1.3 hereof, and shall be effective upon receipt (or refusal to accept).

The addresses for notices to the Joint Venturers are as follows:

_____
_____
_____
_____
_____
_____

Section 9.2 **Attorneys' Fees.**
Should any litigation be commenced between the parties hereto or their representatives, or should any party institute any proceeding in a bankruptcy or similar court which has jurisdiction over any other party hereto or any or all of his or its property or assets concerning any provision of this Agreement or the rights and duties of any person or entity in relation thereto, the party or parties prevailing in such litigation shall be entitled, in addition to such other relief as may be granted, to a reasonable sum as and for his or its or their attorneys' fees and court costs in such litigation or in a separate action brought for that purpose.

Section 9.3 **Validity.**

In the event that any provision of this Agreement shall be held to be invalid or unenforceable, the same shall not affect in any respect whatsoever the validity or enforceability of the remainder of this Agreement.

Section 9.4 **Survival of Rights.**

Except as provided herein to the contrary, this Agreement shall be binding upon and inure to the benefit of the parties signatory hereto, their respective heirs, executors, legal representatives, and permitted successors and assigns.

Section 9.5 **Governing Law.**

This Agreement has been entered into in the state of _____ , and all questions with respect to this Agreement and the rights and liabilities of the parties hereto shall be governed by the laws of _____ , and the venue of any action brought hereunder shall be in _____ County, state of _____ .

Section 9.6 **Waiver.**

No consent or waiver, express or implied, by a Joint Venturer to or of any breach or default by another Joint Venturer in the performance by such other Joint Venturer of its obligations hereunder shall be deemed or construed to be a consent or waiver to or of any other breach or default in the performance by such other Joint Venturer hereunder. Failure on the part of a Joint Venturer to complain of any act or failure to act of another Joint Venturer or to declare another Joint Venturer in default, irrespective of how long such failure continues, shall not constitute a waiver by such Joint Venturer of its rights hereunder. The giving of consent by a Joint Venturer in any one instance shall not limit or waive the necessity to obtain such Joint Venturer's consent in any future instance.

Section 9.7 **Remedies in Equity.**

The rights and remedies of any of the Joint Venturers hereunder shall not be mutually exclusive, i.e., the exercise of one or more of the provisions hereof shall not preclude the exercise of any other provisions hereof. Each of the Joint Venturers confirm that damages at law may be an inadequate remedy for a breach or threatened breach of this Agreement and agree that, in the event of a breach or threatened breach of any provision hereof, the respective rights and obligations hereunder shall be enforceable by specific performance, injunction, or other equitable remedy, but nothing herein contained is intended to, nor shall it, limit or affect any rights at law or by statute or otherwise of any party aggrieved as against the other for a breach or threatened breach of any provision hereof, it being the intention by this Section to make clear the agreement of the

Joint Venturers that the respective rights and obligations of the Joint Venturers hereunder shall be enforceable in equity as well as at law or otherwise.

Section 9.8 **Indemnification.**

Each Joint Venturer ("Indemnifying Venturer") hereby agrees to indemnify and hold the other Joint Venturers and the Joint Venture harmless from and against any and all claims, demands, actions, and rights of action (including attorneys' fees and costs) that shall or may arise by virtue of anything done or omitted to be done by the Indemnifying Venturer (through or by its agents, employees, or other representatives) outside the scope of, or in breach of the terms of, this Agreement; provided, however, that the other Joint Venturers shall be notified promptly of the existence of any such claim, demand, action, or cause of action and shall be given reasonable opportunity to participate in the defense thereof. In the event that one Joint Venturer shall be held severally liable for the debts of the joint venture he shall be awarded contribution from the other Venturers so that each Joint Venturer shall only be obligated to pay that portion of such liability as shall be proportionate to such Joint Venturer's interest in the Joint Venture.

Section 9.9 **Counterparts.**

This Agreement may be executed in any number of counterparts, each of which shall be deemed to be an original and all of which shall constitute one and the same Agreement.

Section 9.10 **Further Assurances.**

Each party hereto agrees to do all acts and things and to make, execute, and deliver such written instruments as shall from time to time be reasonably required to carry out the terms and provisions of this Agreement.

IN WITNESS WHEREOF, the parties have executed this Agreement as of the day and year first above set forth.

Witness

Witness

Witness

Witness

Signature

By _____
Authorized Representative

Signature

By _____
Authorized Representative

Chapter 8
Corporations

This chapter represents a corporation start-up kit. It contains all the forms and information you need to form your corporation and begin business.

In today's business climate, I feel strongly that there are very few businesses that should not incorporate. The potential liability of a business today is tremendous. An entrepreneur can be faced with litigation from customers, competitors, lenders, employees, and the government. This problem is compounded by the fact that few businesses can even afford to fight a lawsuit. What you as an entrepreneur want to be assured of is that any action against your business does not move over into your personal life and family assets. The corporation is the major vehicle to accomplish that protection.

Recently, a number of states have begun to adopt statutes authorizing a limited liability companies. The beauty of this corporate form is that you have all of the advantages of a regular corporation, all of the advantages of an S corporation and none of their disadvantages. A complete explanation of limited liability companies is beyond the scope of this book. If you would like more information I would recommend you contact your local library or seek the opinion of an attorney.

Agreement to Form Corporation

THIS AGREEMENT, made this _12th_ day of _September_ , 199 _5_ , by and between the following:

Name	Address
Steve Ponder	_62 Winter Dr., Annandale, VA 22003_
Ed Jones	_1421 Park Cr., Annandale, VA 22003_
Cathy Kline	_21 E. Marks Pl., Annandale, VA 22003_

WHEREAS the above named individuals desire to form a corporation for the purpose of _Consulting in the computer and telecommunications field and to do any lawful business in the state._

WHEREAS the parties wish to put their understanding in written form.

NOW THEREFORE, in consideration of the mutual promises and benefits to be derived by the parties, they do hereby agree to the following:

1. The parties shall organize a corporation under the laws of the state of _Virginia_ , to be called _Comtel, Inc._ .
2. The capital stock of the corporation shall consist of _1,000_ shares of common stock.
3. Each of the undersigned agrees to take the number of shares indicated by his or her name and to pay the amount listed.

Name	Number of Shares	Amount of Subscription
Steve Ponder	_100_	_$1.00 per share_
Ed Jones	_100_	_$1.00 per share_
Cathy Kline	_100_	_$1.00 per share_

4. _Steve Ponder_ is authorized to file all appropriate documents for incorporation and to schedule a shareholders' meeting as soon as practical thereafter to elect a board of directors.

Signed and sealed on the date first above written.

Steve Ponder
Signature
Ed Jones
Signature
Cathy Kline
Signature

Agreement to Form Corporation

THIS AGREEMENT, made this _____ day of _____ , 199 ___ ,
by and between the following:

Name   Address

_____   _____
_____   _____
_____   _____

WHEREAS the above named individuals desire to form a
corporation for the purpose of _____
_____
_____

WHEREAS the parties wish to put their understanding in written
form.

NOW THEREFORE, in consideration of the mutual promises and
benefits to be derived by the parties, they do hereby agree to
the following:

1. The parties shall organize a corporation under the laws of
   the state of _____ , to be called _____ .
2. The capital stock of the corporation shall consist of
   _____ shares of common stock.
3. Each of the undersigned agrees to take the number of
   shares indicated by his or her name and to pay the amount
   listed.

Name	Number of Shares	Amount of Subscription
_____	_____	_____
_____	_____	_____

4. _____ is authorized to file all appropriate documents
   for incorporation and to schedule a shareholders' meeting
   as soon as practical thereafter to elect a board of
   directors.

Signed and sealed on the date first above written.

_____
Signature

_____
Signature

_____
Signature

Stock Subscription Agreement

FOR VALUE RECEIVED, the undersigned parties hereby agree to subscribe to the capital stock of a corporation to be formed in the state of _Virginia_ for the purpose of _consulting_ and to be named _Comtel, Inc._ . The corporation will have an initial capital of $ _1,000_ , with _1,000_ shares of Common Stock with a par value of $ _1.00_ per share. We agree to subscribe to the number of shares designated as follows and to pay cash or property as stipulated:

Name	Number of Shares	Cash or Property
Steve Ponder	_100_	_$100_
Ed Jones	_100_	_$100_
Cathy Kline	_100_	_$100_

The payment for said shares shall be made within _5_ days of the commencement of existence of the corporation.

This agreement shall be considered among the parties and shall additionally be enforceable by the corporation when formed.

IN WITNESS WHEREOF, the parties hereto have affixed their hands and seals on this the _30th_ day of _September_ , 19 _95_ .

Steve Ponder	(Seal)
Ed Jones	(Seal)
Cathy Kline	(Seal)

Stock Subscription Agreement

FOR VALUE RECEIVED, the undersigned parties hereby agree to subscribe to the capital stock of a corporation to be formed in the state of _____ for the purpose of _____ and to be named _____ . The corporation will have an initial capital of $ _____ , with _____ shares of Common Stock with a par value of $ _____ per share. We agree to subscribe to the number of shares designated as follows and to pay cash or property as stipulated:

Name	Number of Shares	Cash or Property
_____	_____	_____
_____	_____	_____
_____	_____	_____

The payment for said shares shall be made within days of the commencement of existence of the corporation.

This agreement shall be considered among the parties and shall additionally be enforceable by the corporation when formed.

IN WITNESS WHEREOF, the parties hereto have affixed their hands and seals on this the _____ day of _____ , 19 ___ .

_____ (Seal)
Signature

_____ (Seal)
Signature

_____ (Seal)
Signature

_____ (Seal)
Signature

Assignment of Subscription Obligation

FOR VALUE RECEIVED, the undersigned hereby assigns to _Rebekah Johnson_ of _632 Forest Lane_ , city of _Annandale_ , state of _Virginia_ , all of his/her right, title, and interest as a subscriber to _Comtel, Inc._ , a corporation under the laws of the state of _Virginia_ , for _100_ shares.

Dated _October 1_ , 199 _5_

> Ed Jones
> Assignor

Agreement to Assignment by Assignee

The undersigned assignee, in consideration of the above assignment of the shares, hereby agrees to assume all the obligations, liabilities, and duties of the assignor attendant to said subscription.

Dated _October 1_ , 199 _5_

> _Rebekah Johnson_
> Assignee

Acceptance of Assignment by Corporation

The undersigned corporation hereby agrees to the above assignment and agreement to assignment of subscription rights.

Dated _October 1_ , 199 _5_

> _Comtel, Inc._
> Name of Corporation
> By _Steve Ponder_
> President (or other authorized officer)

Assignment of Subscription Obligation

FOR VALUE RECEIVED, the undersigned hereby assigns to _____ of _____ , city of _____ , state of _____ , all of his/her right, title, and interest as a subscriber to _____ , a corporation under the laws of the state of _____ , for _____ shares.

Dated _____ , 199 ___

_____
Assignor

Agreement to Assignment by Assignee

The undersigned assignee, in consideration of the above assignment of the shares, hereby agrees to assume all the obligations, liabilities, and duties of the assignor attendant to said subscription.

Dated _____ , 199 ___

_____
Assignor

Acceptance of Assignment by Corporation

The undersigned corporation hereby agrees to the above assignment and agreement to assignment of subscription rights.

Dated _____ , 199 ___

_____
Name of Corporation
By _____
President (or other
   authorized officer)

Stock Transfer

FOR VALUE RECEIVED, the undersigned hereby sells and transfers to _Rebekah Johnson_ of _623 Forest Lane_ , city of _Annandale_ , state of _Virginia_ , the following:

_100_ shares of stock of _Comtel, Inc._ .

The undersigned irrevocably appoints and authorizes the appropriate office of the named company as attorney-in-fact to transfer shares on the corporate records.

Ed Jones
Signature

I, _Bob Cleveland_ , an authorized representative of _First City_ bank, do acknowledge and guarantee the signature of _Ed Jones_ .

Bob Cleveland
Signature Guaranteed

Stock Transfer

FOR VALUE RECEIVED, the undersigned hereby sells and transfers to _____ of _____ , city of _____ , state of _____ , the following:

_____ shares of stock of _____ .

The undersigned irrevocably appoints and authorizes the appropriate office of the named company as attorney-in-fact to transfer shares on the corporate records.

_____
Signature

I, _____ , an authorized representative of _____ bank, do acknowledge and guarantee the signature of _____ .

_____
Signature Guarantee

Reservation of Corporate Name

To the Department of State
of the State of _Virginia_ :

October 1, 1995
Date

The undersigned hereby applies for reservation of the following corporate name for a period of _one hundred twenty_ days: _Comtel, Inc._ .

By _Steve Ponder_
Authorized Representative

Notice of Transfer of Reserved Corporate Name of

Comtel, Inc.

To the Department of State
of the state of _Florida_ :

November 5, 1995
Date

You are hereby notified that the undersigned has transferred to _American Communications, Inc._ , whose address is _241 Telegraph Rd., Orlando, FL_ , the corporate name of _Comtel, Inc._ , which was reserved in your office for the exclusive use of the undersigned on _October 1_ , 199 _5_ .

By _Steve Ponder_
Authorized Representative

Reservation of Corporate Name

To the Department of State   _____
of the state of _____ :   Date

    The undersigned hereby applies for reservation of the following
corporate name for a period of _____ *days*: _____ .

                        By _____
                        Authorized Representative

Notice of Transfer of Reserved Corporate Name of

                _____
                Name of Corporation

To the Department of State   _____
of the state of _____ :   Date

    You are hereby notified that the undersigned has transferred to
_____ , whose address is _____ , the corporate
name of _____ , which was reserved in your office for the
exclusive use of the undersigned on _____ , 199 ___ .

                        By _____
                        Authorized Representative

Articles of Incorporation

THE UNDERSIGNED, acting as incorporator(s) of a corporation, adopt the following articles of incorporation for such corporation:

1. The name of the corporation is _Comtel, Inc._ .
2. The period of its duration is perpetual.
3. The purpose is to engage in any activities or business permitted under the laws of the United States and the state of _Virginia_ .
4. The corporation shall have authority to issue _1,000_ shares, all of one class, $ _1.00_ par value.
5. The address of the corporate office is _1821 Central Ave., Annandale, Virginia 22003_ .
6. The name and address of its registered agent is _Steve Ponder, 62 Winter Drive, Annandale, Virginia 22003_ .
7. The number of directors constituting its initial Board of Directors is _3_ , whose name(s) and address(es) is (are):

Name	Address
Steve Ponder	62 Winter Dr., Annandale, VA 22003
Ed Jones	1421 Park Cr., Annandale, VA 22003
Cathy Kline	21 E. Marks Pl., Annandale, VA 22003

8. The name(s) and address(es) of the incorporator(s) is (are):

Name	Address
Steve Ponder	62 Winter Dr., Annandale, VA 22003
Ed Jones	1421 Park Cr., Annandale, VA 22003
Cathy Kline	21 E. Marks Pl., Annandale, VA 22003

Steve Ponder

Ed Jones

Cathy Kline
Signature(s) of Incorporator(s)

State of _Virginia_
County of _Arlington_

Before me, the undersigned authority, personally appeared _Steve Ponder, Ed Jones, and Cathy Kline_ , who are to me well known to be the persons described in and who subscribed the above articles of incorporation, and did freely and voluntarily acknowledge before me according to law that they made and subscribed the same for the uses and purposes therein mentioned and set forth.

IN WITNESS WHEREOF, I have hereunto set my hand and my official seal, at _1821 Central Avenue, Annandale_ in said county and state this _1st_ , day of _October_ , 199 _5_ .

Jonathan Edwards
Notary Public, state of _Virginia_
Jonathan Edwards
Printed Notary Name

My Commission Expires: _January 1996_

Articles of Incorporation

THE UNDERSIGNED, acting as incorporator(s) of a corporation, adopt the following articles of incorporation for such corporation:

1. The name of the corporation is _____ .
2. The period of its duration is perpetual.
3. The purpose is to engage in any activities or business permitted under the laws of the United States and the state of _____ .
4. The corporation shall have authority to issue _____ shares, all of one class, $ _____ par value.
5. The address of the corporate office is _____ .
6. The name and address of its registered agent is _____ _____ .
7. The number of directors constituting its initial Board of Directors is _____ , whose name(s) and address(es) is (are):

Name	Address
_____	_____
_____	_____
_____	_____

8. The name(s) and address(es) of the incorporator(s) is (are):

Name	Address
_____	_____
_____	_____
_____	_____

_____

_____

_____

Signature(s) of Incorporator(s)

State of _____
County of _____

Before me, the undersigned authority, personally appeared
_____ , who are to me well known to be the persons
described in and who subscribed the above articles of
incorporation, and did freely and voluntarily acknowledge before
me according to law that they made and subscribed the same for
the uses and purposes therein mentioned and set forth.

IN WITNESS WHEREOF, I have hereunto set my hand and my
official seal, at _____ in said county and state
this _____ , day of _____ , 199 ___ .

_____
Notary Public, state of _____

_____
Printed Notary Name

My Commission Expires: _____

Articles of Incorporation of

Comtel, Inc.

THE UNDERSIGNED, acting as (an) incorporator(s) of a corporation, adopt(s) the following Articles of Incorporation for such corporation:

1. The name of the corporation is *Comtel, Inc.* .
2. The period of duration of the corporation is perpetual.
3. The purpose or purposes for which the corporation is organized are to engage in *consulting in the computer and telecommunications industry* and to do everything necessary, proper, advisable, or convenient for the accomplishment of said purposes, and to do all other things incidental to them or connected with them that are not forbidden by the state of *Virginia* . In addition to the stated purpose, the corporation is authorized to conduct all lawful business activity in the state and outside.
4. Authorized Shares.
   Number. The aggregate number of shares that the corporation shall have the authority to issue is *1,000* shares of Capital Stock with a par value of $ *1.00* per share.
   Initial issue. *300* shares of the Capital Stock of the corporation shall be issued for cash at a par value of *$1.00* per share.
   Dividends. The holders of the outstanding capital stock shall be entitled to receive, when and as declared by the Board of Directors, dividends payable either in cash, in property, or in shares of the capital stock of the corporation.
   No classes of stock. The shares of the corporation are not to be divided into classes.
5. The street address of the initial registered office of the corporation is *1821 Central Avenue, Annandale, Virginia* , and the name of the initial registered agent at such address is *Steve Ponder* .

6. The initial Board of Directors shall consist of _3_ members, who need not be residents of this state or shareholders of the corporation.

7. The names and addresses of the persons who shall serve as directors until the first annual meeting of shareholders, or until their successors have been elected and qualified, are as follows:

Name	Number & Street, City, State, Zip Code
Steve Ponder	*62 Winter Dr., Annandale, VA 22003*
Ed Jones	*1421 Park Cr., Annandale, VA 22003*
Cathy Kline	*21 E. Marks Pl., Annandale, VA 22003*

8. The name(s) and address(es) of the initial incorporator(s) is (are) as follows:

Name	Number & Street, City, State, Zip Code
Steve Ponder	*62 Winter Dr., Annandale, VA 22003*
Ed Jones	*1421 Park Cr., Annandale, VA 22003*
Cathy Kline	*21 E. Marks Pl., Annandale, VA 22003*

9. An affirmative vote of (three-fourths) (all) of the shares of the corporation shall be required for any shareholder action.

10. The shareholders shall have the power to adopt, amend, alter, change, or repeal the articles of incorporation when proposed and approved at a stockholders meeting with not less than a (majority) (two-thirds) (three-fourths) (unanimous) vote of the common stock.

11. The holders of the common stock of this corporation shall have preemptive rights to purchase, at prices, terms, and conditions that shall be fixed by the Board of Directors, such shares of stock of this corporation as may be issued for money (money, or any property or services) from time to time, in addition to that stock authorized (authorized and issued) by the corporation. The preemptive right of any holder is determined by the ratio of the authorized (authorized and issued) shares of common stock held by the holder to all shares of common stock currently authorized (authorized and issued).

12. The shareholders of this corporation shall be allowed to vote their shares cumulatively so as to give one candidate as many votes as the number of directors to be elected multiplied by the number of their shares, to distribute them among as many candidates as they may wish. Notice must be given by any shareholder to the President or a Vice President of said corporation not less than 24 hours prior to the time set for the holding of a shareholders' meeting for the election of the directors that said

shareholder intends to cumulate his vote at said election.

IN WITNESS WHEREOF, THE UNDERSIGNED has (have) made and subscribed these articles of incorporation on the _1st_ day of _October_ , 199 _5_ .

Steve Ponder

Ed Jones

Cathy Kline
Incorporators(s)

State of _Virginia_
County of _Arlington_

Before me, the undersigned authority, personally appeared _Steve Ponder, Ed Jones, and Cathy Kline_ , who are to me well known to be the persons described in and who subscribed the above articles of incorporation, and they did freely and voluntarily acknowledge before me according to law that they made and subscribed the same for the uses and purposes therein mentioned and set forth.

IN WITNESS WHEREOF, I have hereunto set my hand and my official seal in said county and state this _1st_ day of _October_ , 199 _5_ .

Debi Cade
Notary Public, state of _Virginia_
Debi Cade
Printed Notary Name

My Commission Expires: _October 31, 1997_

Articles of Incorporation of

_____

Name of Corporation

THE UNDERSIGNED, acting as (an) incorporator(s) of a corporation, adopt(s) the following Articles of Incorporation for such corporation:

1. The name of the corporation is _____ .
2. The period of duration of the corporation is perpetual.
3. The purpose or purposes for which the corporation is organized are to engage in _____ and to do everything necessary, proper, advisable, or convenient for the accomplishment of said purposes, and to do all other things incidental to them or connected with them that are not forbidden by the state of _____ . In addition to the stated purpose, the corporation is authorized to conduct all lawful business activity in the state and outside.
4. Authorized Shares.

   Number. The aggregate number of shares that the corporation shall have the authority to issue is _____ shares of Capital Stock with a par value of $ _____ per share.

   Initial issue. _____ shares of the Capital Stock of the corporation shall be issued for cash at a par value of $1.00 per share.

   Dividends. The holders of the outstanding capital stock shall be entitled to receive, when and as declared by the Board of Directors, dividends payable either in cash, in property, or in shares of the capital stock of the corporation.

   No classes of stock. The shares of the corporation are not to be divided into classes.
5. The street address of the initial registered office of the corporation is _____ , and the name of the initial registered agent at such address is _____ .
6. The initial Board of Directors shall consist of _____ members, who need not be residents of this state or shareholders of the corporation.

7. The names and addresses of the persons who shall serve as directors until the first annual meeting of shareholders, or until their successors have been elected and qualified, are as follows:

Name   Number & Street, City, State, Zip Code

_____   _____

_____   _____

_____   _____

8. The name(s) and address(es) of the initial incorporator(s) is (are) as follows:

Name   Number & Street, City, State, Zip Code

_____   _____

_____   _____

_____   _____

9. An affirmative vote of (three-fourths) (all) of the shares of the corporation shall be required for any shareholder action.

10. The shareholders shall have the power to adopt, amend, alter, change, or repeal the articles of incorporation when proposed and approved at a stockholders meeting with not less than a (majority) (two-thirds) (three-fourths) (unanimous) vote of the common stock.

11. The holders of the common stock of this corporation shall have preemptive rights to purchase, at prices, terms, and conditions that shall be fixed by the Board of Directors, such shares of stock of this corporation as may be issued for money (money, or any property or services) from time to time, in addition to that stock authorized (authorized and issued) by the corporation. The preemptive right of any holder is determined by the ratio of the authorized (authorized and issued) shares of common stock held by the holder to all shares of common stock currently authorized (authorized and issued).

12. The shareholders of this corporation shall be allowed to vote their shares cumulatively so as to give one candidate as many votes as the number of directors to be elected multiplied by the number of their shares, to distribute them among as many candidates as they may wish. Notice must be given by any shareholder to the President or a Vice President of said corporation not less than 24 hours prior to the time set for the holding of a shareholders' meeting for the election of the directors that said shareholder intends to cumulate his vote at said election.

IN WITNESS WHEREOF, THE UNDERSIGNED has (have) made and subscribed these articles of incorporation on the _____ day of _____ , 199 ___ .

_____

_____

_____
Incorporators(s)

State of *Virginia*
County of *Arlington*

Before me, the undersigned authority, personally appeared _____ , who are to me well known to be the persons described in and who subscribed the above articles of incorporation, and they did freely and voluntarily acknowledge before me according to law that they made and subscribed the same for the uses and purposes therein mentioned and set forth.

IN WITNESS WHEREOF, I have hereunto set my hand and my official seal in said county and state this _____ day of _____ , 199 ___ .

_____
Notary Public, state of _____

_____
Printed Notary Name

My Commission Expires: _____

Amendment to the Articles of Incorporation of

Comtel, Inc.

THE UNDERSIGNED corporation adopts the following Amendments to its Articles of Incorporation:

1. The name of the corporation is _Comtel, Inc._ .

2. The following amendments to the Articles of Incorporation were adopted by the shareholders of the corporation on _December 20_ , 199 _5_ :

    A. _The number of directors shall be increased from three to five._

3. The number of shares of the corporation outstanding at the time of adoption was _300_ , and the number of shares entitled to vote thereon was _300_ .

4. The number of shares of each class entitled to vote thereon as a class voted for and against such amendment, respectfully, was:

Class	Number of Shares Voted	
	For	Against
Common	_300_	_0_

Dated _December 20_ , 199 _5_

                     Comtel, Inc.
                     Name of Corporation

                     By _Steve Ponder_
                     President

                     and _Ed Jones_
                     Secretary

State of _Virginia_
County of _Arlington_

Before me, the undersigned authority, personally appeared _Steve Ponder_ , who is to me well known to be the person described in and who subscribed the above articles of amendment to the articles of incorporation, and he did freely and voluntarily acknowledge before me according to law that he made and subscribed the same for the use and purposes therein mentioned and set forth.

IN WITNESS WHEREOF, I have hereunto set my hand and my official seal in said county and state this _20th_ day of _December_ , 199 _5_ .

> _Kay Robinson_
> Notary Public, state of _Virginia_
> Kay Robinson
> Notary Printed Name

My Commission Expires: _October 31, 1997_

Amendment to the Articles of Incorporation of

_____
Name of Corporation

THE UNDERSIGNED corporation adopts the following Amendments to its Articles of Incorporation:

1. The name of the corporation is _____ .

2. The following amendments to the Articles of Incorporation were adopted by the shareholders of the corporation on _____ , 199 ___ :

    _____
    _____
    _____
    _____
    _____
    _____

3. The number of shares of the corporation outstanding at the time of adoption was _____ , and the number of shares entitled to vote thereon was _____ .

4. The number of shares of each class entitled to vote thereon as a class voted for and against such amendment, respectfully, was:

Class	Number of Shares Voted	
	For	Against
_____	_____	_____
_____	_____	_____

Dated _____ , 199 ___

_____
Name of Corporation

By _____
President (or vice-president)

and _____
Secretary (or assistant secretary)

State of _Virginia_
County of _Arlington_

Before me, the undersigned authority, personally appeared _____ (either of above officers), who is to me well known to be the person described in and who subscribed the above articles of amendment to the articles of incorporation, and he did freely and voluntarily acknowledge before me according to law that he made and subscribed the same for the use and purposes therein mentioned and set forth.

IN WITNESS WHEREOF, I have hereunto set my hand and my official seal in at _____ in said county and state this _____ day of _____ , 199 ___ .

_____
Notary Public, state of _____

_____
Notary Printed Name

My Commission Expires: _____

Bylaws of

Comtel, Inc.

Article I. Shareholders

Section 1. The shareholders shall hold at least one annual meeting per year, which shall be held at the corporate office or a place so designated by the corporation. Additional meetings may be held upon proper notice according to state statute.

Article II. Directors

Section 1. The number of directors shall be _3_ .

Section 2. A regular meeting of the Board of Directors shall be held without notice immediately following the annual meeting of shareholders and at the same place. The Board of Directors may provide for the holding without notice of additional regular meetings.

Section 3. Special meetings of the Board of Directors may be called by the president or any _1_ director(s) on a 24-hour notice given personally or by telephone or telegraph or on four days' notice by mail. Special meetings shall be held at a place fixed by the Board of Directors.

Article III. Officers

Section 1. The officers of the corporation shall be a president, a vice president, a secretary, and a treasurer, who shall be elected annually. Their term of office shall be at the discretion of Board of Directors.

Section 2. The president shall be the principal executive officer of the corporation to execute the decisions of the Board of Directors. He shall supervise and control the business and affairs of the corporation and preside at meetings of the shareholders and directors.

Section 3. The vice president, secretary, and treasurer shall act under the direction of the president. The vice president shall perform the duties of the president when the president is absent or unable to act. The secretary shall prepare and keep minutes of the meetings of the shareholders and the directors and shall have general charge of stock records of the corporation. The treasurer shall have custody of the funds and keep financial records.

Article IV. Miscellaneous

Section 1. The Board of Directors may authorize any officer or agent to enter into any contract or to execute any instrument for the corporation. Such authority may be general or be confined to specific instances.

Section 2. Certificates representing shares of the corporation shall be in such form as the Board of Directors shall determine. Transfers of shares shall be made only on the stock transfer books of the corporation.

Article V. Amendments

Section 1. These bylaws may be altered, amended, or repealed and new bylaws may be adopted by a majority of the Board of Directors or the shareholders.

Article VI. Miscellaneous

Section 1. The location of the principal office shall be *1821 Central Avenue, Annandale, Virginia* .

Section 2. The address of the resident agent shall be *1821 Central Avenue, Annandale, Virginia* .

Section 3. The seal of the corporation shall be as follows:

(Seal of the Corporation)

Section 4. The fiscal year of the corporation shall be from *January 1* to *December 31* .

Adopted this *1st* day of *October* , 199 *6* .

Steve Ponder
Director

Ed Jones
Director

Cathy Kline
Director

Bylaws of

_____

Name of Corporation

Article I. Shareholders

Section 1. The shareholders shall hold at least one annual meeting per year, which shall be held at the corporate office or a place so designated by the corporation. Additional meetings may be held upon proper notice according to state statute.

Article II. Directors

Section 1. The number of directors shall be _____ .

Section 2. A regular meeting of the Board of Directors shall be held without notice immediately following the annual meeting of shareholders and at the same place. The Board of Directors may provide for the holding without notice of additional regular meetings.

Section 3. Special meetings of the Board of Directors may be called by the president or any _____ directors on a 24-hour notice given personally or by telephone or telegraph or on four days' notice by mail. Special meetings shall be held at a place fixed by the Board of Directors.

Article III. Officers

Section 1. The officers of the corporation shall be a president, a vice president, a secretary, and a treasurer, who shall be elected annually. Their term of office shall be at the discretion of Board of Directors.

Section 2. The president shall be the principal executive officer of the corporation to execute the decisions of the Board of Directors. He shall supervise and control the business and affairs of the corporation and preside at meetings of the shareholders and directors.

Section 3. The vice president, secretary, and treasurer shall act under the direction of the president. The vice president shall perform the duties of the president when the president is absent or unable to act. The secretary shall prepare and keep minutes of the meetings of the shareholders and the directors and shall have general charge of stock records of the corporation. The treasurer shall have custody of the funds and keep financial records.

Article IV. Miscellaneous

Section 1. The Board of Directors may authorize any officer or agent to enter into any contract or to execute any instrument for the corporation. Such authority may be general or confined to specific instances.

Section 2. Certificates representing shares of the corporation shall be in such form as the Board of Directors shall determine. Transfers of shares shall be made only on the stock transfer books of the corporation.

Article V. Amendments

Section 1. These bylaws may be altered, amended, or repealed and new bylaws may be adopted by the Board of Directors or by the shareholders.

Article VI. Miscellaneous

Section 1. The location of the principal office shall be _____

_____

_____ .

Section 2. The address of the resident agent shall be _____

_____

_____ .

Section 3. The seal of the corporation shall be as follows: __

_____

_____ .

(Seal of the Corporation)

Section 4. The fiscal year of the corporation shall be from _____ to _____ .

Adopted this _____ day of _____ , 199 ___ .

                              _____
                              Director

                              _____
                              Director

                              _____
                              Director

Bylaws of

Comtel, Inc.

Article I. Offices

The principal office of the corporation shall be located in the city of *Annandale* , county of *Arlington* , state of *Virginia* . The corporation may have such other offices, either within or without the state of *Virginia* , as the Board of Directors may designate or as the business of the corporation may require from time to time.

The registered office of the corporation shall be *1821 Central Avenue* , city of *Annandale* , state of *Virginia* .

Article II. Shareholders

Section 1. Annual Meeting. The shareholders of the corporation shall hold a meeting at least annually each year for the purpose of electing directors and for the transaction of such other business as may come before the meeting.

Section 2. Special Meetings. Special meetings of the shareholders may be called by the president or by the Board of Directors, and shall be called by the president at the request of the holders of not less than *a majority* of all outstanding shares of the corporation entitled to vote at the meeting.

Section 3. Place of Meeting. The Board of Directors may designate any place, either within or without the state of *Virginia* , as the place of meeting called by the Board of Directors.

Section 4. Notice of Meeting. Written notice stating the place, day, and hour of the meeting and, in case of a special meeting, the purpose or purposes for which the meeting is called shall be delivered not less than ten nor more than sixty days before the date of the meeting, either personally or by first class mail, by or at the direction of the president, or the secretary, or the officer or other persons calling the meeting, to each shareholder of record entitled to vote at such meeting. If mailed, such notice shall be deemed to be delivered when deposited in the United States mail, addressed to the shareholder at his address as it appears on the stock transfer books of the corporation, with postage thereon prepaid.

Section 5. Closing of Transfer Books or Fixing of Record Date. For the purpose of determining shareholders entitled to notice of or to vote at any meeting of shareholders or entitled to receive payment of any dividend, or in order to make a determination of shareholders for any other proper purpose, the board of directors of the corporation may provide that the stock transfer books shall be closed for a stated period but not to exceed, in any case, sixty days. If the stock transfer books shall be closed for the purpose of determining shareholders entitled to notice of or to vote at a meeting of shareholders, such books shall be closed for at least ten days immediately preceding such meeting. In lieu of closing the stock transfer books, the board of directors may fix in advance a date as the record date for any such determination of shareholders, such date in any case to be not more than sixty days and, in case of a meeting of shareholders, not less than ten days prior to the date on which the particular action requiring such determination of shareholders is to be taken.

Section 6. Voting Record. The officer or agent having charge of the stock transfer books for shares of the corporation shall make, at least ten days before each meeting of shareholders, a complete list of the shareholders entitled to vote at such meeting of shareholders. Such list shall be kept on file at the registered office of the corporation. The list shall be available for inspection of any shareholder during the meeting.

Section 7. Quorum. A majority of the outstanding shares of the corporation entitled to vote, represented in person or by proxy, shall constitute a quorum at a meeting of shareholders. If less than a majority of the outstanding shares are represented at a meeting, a majority of the shares so represented may adjourn the meeting without further notice.

Section 8. Proxies. At all meetings of shareholders, a shareholder may vote in person or by proxy. Such proxy shall be filed with the secretary of the corporation before or at the time of the meeting.

Section 9. Informal Action by Shareholders. Any action required or permitted to be taken at a meeting of the shareholders may be taken without a meeting if a consent in writing, setting forth the action so taken, shall be signed by the holders of outstanding stock having not less than the minimum number of votes that would be necessary to authorize or take such action at a meeting at which all shares entitled to vote thereon were present and voted.

Section 10. Cumulative Voting. At each election for directors every shareholder entitled to vote at such election shall have the right to vote, in person or by proxy, the number of shares owned by him for as many persons as there are directors to be elected and for whose election he has a right to vote, or to cumulate his votes by giving one candidate as many votes as the number of such directors multiplied by the number of shares shall equal, or by distributing such votes on the same principle among any number of such candidates.

Article III. Board of Directors

Section 1. General Powers. The business and affairs of the corporation shall be managed by its Board of Directors.

Section 2. Number, Tenure, and Qualifications. The number of directors of the corporation shall be __3__ . Each director shall hold office until the next annual meeting of shareholders and until his successor shall have been elected and qualified.

Section 3. Regular Meetings. An annual meeting of the Board of Directors shall be held without notice immediately after the annual meeting of shareholders. Additional meetings may be held at the option of the directors with two days written notice. Any director may waive notice, and attendance at the meeting shall constitute waiver unless an objection is made.

Section 4. Quorum. A majority of the number of directors shall constitute a quorum for the transaction of business at any meeting of the Board of Directors.

Section 5. Action without a Meeting. Any action required or permitted to be taken by the Board of Directors at a meeting may be taken without a meeting if a consent in writing, setting forth the action so taken, shall be signed by all of the directors.

Section 6. Vacancies. A vacancy occurring in the Board of Directors may be filled by the affirmative vote of a majority of the remaining directors. A director elected to fill a vacancy shall be elected for the unexpired term of his predecessor in office.

Section 7. Compensation. By resolution of the Board of Directors, each director may be paid his expenses, if any, of attendance at each meeting of the Board of Directors, and may be paid a stated salary as director or a fixed sum for attendance at each meeting of the Board of Directors or both. No such payment shall preclude any director from serving the corporation in any other capacity and receiving compensation therefor. Directors may set their own compensation for service as officers as well as for service as directors.

Article IV. Officers

Section 1. The officers of the corporation shall be a president, one or more vice presidents, a secretary, and a treasurer, each of whom shall be elected by the Board of Directors. Such other officers and assistant officers as may be deemed necessary may be elected or appointed by the Board of Directors. Any two or more offices may be held by the same person.

Section 2. Election and Term of Office. The officers of the corporation to be elected by the Board of Directors shall be elected annually by the Board of Directors. Each officer shall hold office until his successor shall have been duly elected and shall have qualified or until his death or until he shall resign or shall have been removed from office.

Section 3. Removal. Any officer or agent may be removed by the Board of Directors whenever in its judgment the best interest of the corporation will be served thereby.

Section 4. Vacancies. A vacancy in any office because of death, resignation, removal, disqualification, or otherwise, may be filled by the Board of Directors for the unexpired portion of the term.

Section 5. President. The president shall be the principal executive officer of the corporation and, subject to the control of the Board of Directors, shall in general supervise and control all of the business and affairs of the corporation. He shall, when present, preside at all meetings of the shareholders and of the Board of Directors. He may sign, with the secretary or any other proper officer of the corporation, certificates for shares of the corporation and deeds, mortgages, bonds, contracts, or other instruments that the Board of Directors has authorized to be executed.

Section 6. The Vice Presidents. In the absence of the president or in the event of his death, inability, or refusal to act, the vice president designated the "senior vice president" shall perform the duties of the president, and when so acting, shall have all the powers of and be subject to all the restrictions upon the president. Any vice president may sign, with the secretary or an assisting secretary, certificates for shares of the corporation, and shall perform such other duties as from time to time may be assigned to him by the president or by the Board of Directors.

Section 7. The Secretary. The secretary shall: (a) keep the minutes of the proceedings of the shareholders and of the Board of Directors in one or more books provided for that purpose; (b) see that all notices are duly given in accordance with the provisions of these Bylaws or as required by law; (c) be custodian of the corporate records and of the seal of the corporation and see that the seal of the corporation is affixed to all documents the execution of which on behalf of the corporation under its seal is duly authorized; (d) keep a register of the post office address of each shareholder, which shall be furnished to the secretary by such shareholder; (e) sign with the president, or a vice president, certificates for shares of the corporation, the issuance of which shall have been authorized by resolution of the Board of Directors; (f) have general charge of the stock transfer books of the corporation; and (g) in general perform all duties as from time to time may be assigned to him by the president or by the Board of Directors.

Section 8. The Treasurer. The treasurer shall: (a) have charge and custody of and be responsible for all funds and securities of the corporation; (b) receive and give receipts for moneys due and payable to the corporation from any source whatsoever, and deposit all such moneys in the name of the corporation in such banks, trust companies, or other depositaries as shall be selected in accordance with the provisions of Article V of these Bylaws; and (c) in general perform all duties as from time to time may be assigned to him by the president or by the Board of Directors.

Article V. Contracts, Loans, Checks, and Deposits

Section 1. Contracts. The Board of Directors may authorize any officer or agent to enter into any contract on behalf of the corporation. The authority may be general or confined to specific instances.

Section 2. Loans. All loans taken on behalf of the corporation must be authorized by a specific resolution of the Board of Directors.

Section 3. Checks, Drafts, etc. All checks, drafts, or other orders for the payment of money, notes, or other evidences of indebtedness issued in the name of the corporation shall be signed by such officer or agent of the corporation as shall from time to time be determined by resolution of the Board of Directors.

Section 4. Deposits. All funds of the corporation not otherwise employed shall be deposited to the credit of the corporation in such banks, money markets, or other depositaries as the Board of Directors may select.

Article VI. Certificates for Shares and Their Transfer

Section 1. Certificates for Shares. Certificates representing shares of the corporation shall be in such form as shall be determined by the Board of Directors. Such certificates shall be signed by the president and by the secretary and sealed with the corporate seal. The name and address of the person to whom the shares represented thereby are issued, with the number of shares and date of issue, shall be entered on the stock transfer books of the corporation. All certificates surrendered to the corporation for transfer shall be canceled and no new certificate shall be issued until the former certificate for a like number of shares shall have been surrendered and canceled, except that in case of a lost, destroyed, or mutilated certificate, a new one may be issued therefor upon such terms and indemnity to the corporation as the Board of Directors may prescribe.

Section 2. Transfer of Shares. Transfer of shares of the corporation shall be made only on the stock transfer books of the corporation by the holder of record thereof or by his legal representative, who shall furnish proper evidence of authority to transfer such shares. The person in whose name shares appear on the books of the corporation shall be deemed by the corporation to be the owner thereof for all purposes.

Article VII. Fiscal Year

The fiscal year of the corporation shall begin on the first day of January and end on the thirty-first day of December each year.

Article VIII. Dividends

The Board of Directors may, from time to time, declare and the corporation may pay dividends on its outstanding shares in the manner and upon the terms and conditions provided by law and the Articles of Incorporation.

Article IX. Corporate Seal

The Board of Directors shall provide a corporate seal, which shall be circular in form and shall have inscribed thereon the name of its corporation and the state of its incorporation and the words "Corporate Seal."

Article X. Waiver of Notice

Whenever any notice is required to be given to any shareholder or director of the corporation under the provisions of these Bylaws or under the provisions of the Articles of Incorporation or under the provisions of the state, a waiver thereof in writing signed by the person or persons entitled to such notice, whether before or after the time stated therein, shall be deemed equivalent to the giving of such notice.

Article XI. Amendments

These Bylaws may be altered, amended, or repealed and new Bylaws may be adopted by the Board of Directors or by the shareholders at any regular or special meeting.

Adopted the _1st_ day of _October_ , 199 _5_ .

> _Steve Ponder_
> Director
>
> _Ed Johnson_
> Director
>
> _Cathy Kline_
> Director

Bylaws of

Article I. Offices

The principal office of the corporation shall be located in the city of _____ , county of _____ , state of _____ . The corporation may have such other offices, either within or without the state of _____ , as the Board of Directors may designate or as the business of the corporation may require from time to time.

The registered office of the corporation shall be _____ , city of _____ , state of _____ .

Article II. Shareholders

Section 1. Annual Meeting. The shareholders of the corporation shall hold a meeting at least annually each year for the purpose of electing directors and for the transaction of such other business as may come before the meeting.

Section 2. Special Meetings. Special meetings of the shareholders may be called by the president or by the Board of Directors, and shall be called by the president at the request of the holders of not less than _____ of all outstanding shares of the corporation entitled to vote at the meeting.

Section 3. Place of Meeting. The Board of Directors may designate any place, either within or without the state of _____ , as the place of meeting called by the Board of Directors.

Section 4. Notice of Meeting. Written notice stating the place, day, and hour of the meeting and, in case of a special meeting, the purpose or purposes for which the meeting is called shall be delivered not less than ten nor more than sixty days before the date of the meeting, either personally or by first class mail, by or at the direction of the president, or the secretary, or the officer or other persons calling the meeting, to each shareholder of record entitled to vote at such meeting. If mailed, such notice shall be deemed to be delivered when deposited in the United States mail, addressed to the shareholder at his address as it appears on the stock transfer books of the corporation, with postage thereon prepaid.

Section 5. Closing of Transfer Books or Fixing of Record Date. For the purpose of determining shareholders entitled to notice of or to vote at any meeting of shareholders or entitled to receive payment of any dividend, or in order to make a determination of shareholders for any other proper purpose, the board of directors of the corporation may provide that the stock transfer books shall be closed for a stated period but not to exceed, in any case, sixty days. If the stock transfer books shall be closed for the purpose of determining shareholders entitled to notice of or to vote at a meeting of shareholders, such books shall be closed for at least ten days immediately preceding such meeting. In lieu of closing the stock transfer books, the board of directors may fix in advance a date as the record date for any such determination of shareholders, such date in any case to be not more than sixty days and, in case of a meeting of shareholders, not less than ten days prior to the date on which the particular action requiring such determination of shareholders is to be taken.

Section 6. Voting Record. The officer or agent having charge of the stock transfer books for shares of the corporation shall make, at least ten days before each meeting of shareholders, a complete list of the shareholders entitled to vote at such meeting of shareholders. Such list shall be kept on file at the registered office of the corporation. The list shall be available for inspection of any shareholder during the meeting.

Section 7. Quorum. A majority of the outstanding shares of the corporation entitled to vote, represented in person or by proxy, shall constitute a quorum at a meeting of shareholders. If less than a majority of the outstanding shares are represented at a meeting, a majority of the shares so represented may adjourn the meeting without further notice.

Section 8. Proxies. At all meetings of shareholders, a shareholder may vote in person or by proxy. Such proxy shall be filed with the secretary of the corporation before or at the time of the meeting.

Section 9. Informal Action by Shareholders. Any action required or permitted to be taken at a meeting of the shareholders may be taken without a meeting if a consent in writing, setting forth the action so taken, shall be signed by the holders of outstanding stock having not less than the minimum number of votes that would be necessary to authorize or take such action at a meeting at which all shares entitled to vote thereon were present and voted.

Section 10. Cumulative Voting. At each election for directors every shareholder entitled to vote at such election shall have the right to vote, in person or by proxy, the number of shares owned by him for as many persons as there are directors to be elected and for whose election he has a right to vote, or to cumulate his votes by giving one candidate as many votes as the number of such directors multiplied by the number of shares shall equal, or by distributing such votes on the same principle among any number of such candidates.

Article III. Board of Directors

Section 1. General Powers. The business and affairs of the corporation shall be managed by its Board of Directors.

Section 2. Number, Tenure, and Qualifications. The number of directors of the corporation shall be _____ . Each director shall hold office until the next annual meeting of shareholders and until his successor shall have been elected and qualified.

Section 3. Regular Meetings. An annual meeting of the Board of Directors shall be held without notice immediately after the annual meeting of shareholders. Additional meetings may be held at the option of the directors with two days written notice. Any director may waive notice, and attendance at the meeting shall constitute waiver unless an objection is made.

Section 4. Quorum. A majority of the number of directors shall constitute a quorum for the transaction of business at any meeting of the Board of Directors.

Section 5. Action without a Meeting. Any action required or permitted to be taken by the Board of Directors at a meeting may be taken without a meeting if a consent in writing, setting forth the action so taken, shall be signed by all of the directors.

Section 6. Vacancies. A vacancy occurring in the Board of Directors may be filled by the affirmative vote of a majority of the remaining directors. A director elected to fill a vacancy shall be elected for the unexpired term of his predecessor in office.

Section 7. Compensation. By resolution of the Board of Directors, each director may be paid his expenses, if any, of attendance at each meeting of the Board of Directors, and may be paid a stated salary as director or a fixed sum for attendance at each meeting of the Board of Directors or both. No such payment shall preclude any director from serving the corporation in any other capacity and receiving compensation therefor. Directors may set their own compensation for service as officers as well as for service as directors.

Article IV. Officers

Section 1. The officers of the corporation shall be a president, one or more vice presidents, a secretary, and a treasurer, each of whom shall be elected by the Board of Directors. Such other officers and assistant officers as may be deemed necessary may be elected or appointed by the Board of Directors. Any two or more offices may be held by the same person.

Section 2. Election and Term of Office. The officers of the corporation to be elected by the Board of Directors shall be elected annually by the Board of Directors. Each officer shall hold office until his successor shall have been duly elected and shall have qualified or until his death or until he shall resign or shall have been removed from office.

Section 3. Removal. Any officer or agent may be removed by the Board of Directors whenever in its judgment the best interest of the corporation will be served thereby.

Section 4. Vacancies. A vacancy in any office because of death, resignation, removal, disqualification, or otherwise, may be filled by the Board of Directors for the unexpired portion of the term.

Section 5. President. The president shall be the principal executive officer of the corporation and, subject to the control of the Board of Directors, shall in general supervise and control all of the business and affairs of the corporation. He shall, when present, preside at all meetings of the shareholders and of the Board of Directors. He may sign, with the secretary or any other proper officer of the corporation, certificates for shares of the corporation and deeds, mortgages, bonds, contracts, or other instruments that the Board of Directors has authorized to be executed.

Section 6. The Vice Presidents. In the absence of the president or in the event of his death, inability, or refusal to act, the vice president designated the "senior vice president" shall perform the duties of the president, and when so acting, shall have all the powers of and be subject to all the restrictions upon the president. Any vice president may sign, with the secretary or an assisting secretary, certificates for shares of the corporation, and shall perform such other duties as from time to time may be assigned to him by the president or by the Board of Directors.

Section 7. The Secretary. The secretary shall: (a) keep the minutes of the proceedings of the shareholders and of the Board of Directors in one or more books provided for that purpose; (b) see that all notices are duly given in accordance with the provisions of these Bylaws or as required by law; (c) be custodian of the corporate records and of the seal of the corporation and see that the seal of the corporation is affixed to all documents the execution of which on behalf of the corporation under its seal is duly authorized; (d) keep a register of the post office address of each shareholder, which shall be furnished to the secretary by such shareholder; (e) sign with the president, or a vice president, certificates for shares of the corporation, the issuance of which shall have been authorized by resolution of the Board of Directors; (f) have general charge of the stock transfer books of the corporation; and (g) in general perform all duties as from time to time may be assigned to him by the president or by the Board of Directors.

Section 8. The Treasurer. The treasurer shall: (a) have charge and custody of and be responsible for all funds and securities of the corporation; (b) receive and give receipts for moneys due and payable to the corporation from any source whatsoever, and deposit all such moneys in the name of the corporation in such banks, trust companies, or other depositaries as shall be selected in accordance with the provisions of Article V of these Bylaws; and (c) in general perform all duties as from time to time may be assigned to him by the president or by the Board of Directors.

Article V. Contracts, Loans, Checks, and Deposits

Section 1. Contracts. The Board of Directors may authorize any officer or agent to enter into any contract on behalf of the corporation. The authority may be general or confined to specific instances.

Section 2. Loans. All loans taken on behalf of the corporation must be authorized by a specific resolution of the Board of Directors.

Section 3. Checks, Drafts, etc. All checks, drafts, or other orders for the payment of money, notes, or other evidences of indebtedness issued in the name of the corporation shall be signed by such officer or agent of the corporation as shall from time to time be determined by resolution of the Board of Directors.

Section 4. Deposits. All funds of the corporation not otherwise employed shall be deposited to the credit of the corporation in such banks, money markets, or other depositaries as the Board of Directors may select.

Article VI. Certificates for Shares and Their Transfer

Section 1. Certificates for Shares. Certificates representing shares of the corporation shall be in such form as shall be determined by the Board of Directors. Such certificates shall be signed by the president and by the secretary and sealed with the corporate seal. The name and address of the person to whom the shares represented thereby are issued, with the number of shares and date of issue, shall be entered on the stock transfer books of the corporation. All certificates surrendered to the corporation for transfer shall be canceled and no new certificate shall be issued until the former certificate for a like number of shares shall have been surrendered and canceled, except that in case of a lost, destroyed, or mutilated certificate, a new one may be issued therefor upon such terms and indemnity to the corporation as the Board of Directors may prescribe.

Section 2. Transfer of Shares. Transfer of shares of the corporation shall be made only on the stock transfer books of the corporation by the holder of record thereof or by his legal representative, who shall furnish proper evidence of authority to transfer such shares. The person in whose name shares appear on the books of the corporation shall be deemed by the corporation to be the owner thereof for all purposes.

Article VII. Fiscal Year

The fiscal year of the corporation shall begin on the first day of January and end on the thirty-first day of December each year.

Article VIII. Dividends

The Board of Directors may, from time to time, declare and the corporation may pay dividends on its outstanding shares in the manner and upon the terms and conditions provided by law and the Articles of Incorporation.

Article IX. Corporate Seal

The Board of Directors shall provide a corporate seal, which shall be circular in form and shall have inscribed thereon the name of its corporation and the state of its incorporation and the words "Corporate Seal."

Article X. Waiver of Notice

Whenever any notice is required to be given to any shareholder or director of the corporation under the provisions of these Bylaws or under the provisions of the Articles of Incorporation or under the provisions of the state, a waiver thereof in writing signed by the person or persons entitled to such notice, whether before or after the time stated therein, shall be deemed equivalent to the giving of such notice.

Article XI. Amendments

These Bylaws may be altered, amended, or repealed and new Bylaws may be adopted by the Board of Directors or by the shareholders at any regular or special meeting.

Adopted the _____ day of _____ , 199 ___ .

_____
Director

_____
Director

_____
Director

Minutes of the First Meeting of the Incorporators

Comtel, Inc.

The first meeting of the incorporators was held at _9_ o'clock A.M. on the _5th_ day of _October_ , 199 _5_ at _1821 Central Avenue_ , city of _Annandale_ , state of _Virginia_ .

The following incorporators were present in person at the meeting:

Name	Address	Number of Shares
Steve Ponder	*62 Winter Dr., Annandale, VA 22003*	*100*
Ed Jones	*1421 Park Cr., Annandale, VA 22003*	*100*
Cathy Kline	*21 E. Marks Pl., Annandale, VA 22003*	*100*

The above persons constitute all of the incorporators of the corporation.

Steve Ponder was elected as Chairman, and _Ed Jones_ as Secretary of the meeting.

The Secretary presented a written Waiver of Notice of the First Meeting of Incorporators, signed by all the incorporators. The Secretary was directed to include said waiver in the minute book.

The Secretary next presented and read a copy of the Articles of Incorporation of the corporation, which was filed with the state on _October 1_ , 199 _5_ . The Secretary was directed to include a copy of the Articles of Incorporation in the minute book as the first document appearing therein.

The Secretary next presented and read the proposed bylaws for the corporation.

The bylaws were unanimously approved, with the directors granted the power to adopt new and amend existing bylaws without the approval of the shareholders, unless inconsistent with provisions of the corporate laws of the state of _Virginia_ , and the Secretary was directed to include a copy of the bylaws in the minute book.

The corporate seal was presented to the incorporators and approved, and the Secretary was directed to place an imprint of the corporate seal at the bottom of these minutes.

The proposed stock certificate form was presented to the incorporators and approved, and the Secretary was directed to include a copy of the stock certificate in the minute book.

The following were nominated for directors of the corporation:

Name	Address
Steve Ponder	*62 Winter Dr., Annandale, VA 22003*
Ed Jones	*1421 Park Cr., Annandale, VA 22003*
Cathy Kline	*21 E. Marks Pl., Annandale, VA 22003*

to serve from the date of election until their respective successors shall be elected and qualified. No further nominations were made. The incorporators then unanimously elected the nominees as directors.

The incorporators next unanimously voted to authorize the Board of Directors to issue the shares of capital stock as authorized by the Articles of Incorporation in such amounts and for such consideration in cash, property, or services as from time to time the Board of Directors may determine and as may be allowed by law.

Upon motion duly made, seconded, and unanimously approved, the meeting was adjourned.

Ed Jones
Secretary of the Meeting

Approval of minutes

Ed Ponder

Ed Jones

Cathy Kline
Signatures of all present

Minutes of the First Meeting of the Incorporators

_____

Name of Corporation

The first meeting of the incorporators was held at _____ o'clock
A.M. on the _____ day of _____ , 199 ___ at
_____ , city of _____ , state of _____ .
The following incorporators were present in person at the
meeting:

Name	Address	Number of Shares
_____	_____	_____
_____	_____	_____
_____	_____	_____

The above persons constitute all of the incorporators of the
corporation.

_____ was elected as Chairman, and _____ as
Secretary of the meeting.

The Secretary presented a written Waiver of Notice of the
First Meeting of Incorporators, signed by all the incorporators.
The Secretary was directed to include said waiver in the minute
book.

The Secretary next presented and read a copy of the Articles
of Incorporation of the corporation, which was filed with the
state on _____ , 199 ___ . The Secretary was directed to
include a copy of the Articles of Incorporation in the minute
book as the first document appearing therein.

The Secretary next presented and read the proposed bylaws for
the corporation.

The bylaws were unanimously approved, with the directors
granted the power to adopt new and amend existing bylaws without
the approval of the shareholders, unless inconsistent with
provisions of the corporate laws of the state of _____ , and
the Secretary was directed to include a copy of the bylaws in the
minute book.

The corporate seal was presented to the incorporators and
approved, and the Secretary was directed to place an imprint of
the corporate seal at the bottom of these minutes.

The proposed stock certificate form was presented to the
incorporators and approved, and the Secretary was directed to
include a copy of the stock certificate in the minute book.

The following were nominated for directors of the corporation:

Name   Address

_____   _____

_____   _____

_____   _____

to serve from the date of election until their respective
successors shall be elected and qualified. No further nominations
were made. The incorporators then unanimously elected the
nominees as directors.

The incorporators next unanimously voted to authorize the
Board of Directors to issue the shares of capital stock as
authorized by the Articles of Incorporation in such amounts and
for such consideration in cash, property, or services as from
time to time the Board of Directors may determine and as may be
allowed by law.

Upon motion duly made, seconded, and unanimously approved, the
meeting was adjourned.

                              _____
                              Secretary of the Meeting

Approval of minutes

_____

_____

_____
Signatures of all present

Waiver of Notice of the First Meeting of Incorporators

Comtel, Inc.

THE UNDERSIGNED, being all of the incorporators of _Comtel, Inc._ , waive notice of the first meeting of the incorporators of the said corporation, and do hereby consent that the time and place for holding said meeting shall be _9_ o'clock A.M. on the _5th_ day of _October_ , 199 _5_ , at _1821 Central Avenue_ in the city of _Annandale_ , state of _Virginia_ , and do hereby further consent to the transaction of such business as may lawfully come before said meeting, including the election of directors and the adoption of bylaws.

    Dated _October 5_ , 199 _5_

                    Steve Ponder
                    Incorporator

                    Ed Jones
                    Incorporator

                    Cathy Kline
                    Incorporator

Waiver of Notice of the First Meeting of Incorporators

_____

Name of Corporation

    THE UNDERSIGNED, being all of the incorporators of _____ ,
waive notice of the first meeting of the incorporators of the
said corporation, and do hereby consent that the time and place
for holding said meeting shall be _____ o'clock (A.M.) (P.M.)
on the _____ day of _____ , 199 ___ , at _____ in
the city of _____ , state of _____ , and do hereby
further consent to the transaction of such business as may
lawfully come before said meeting, including the election of
directors and the adoption of bylaws.

    Dated _____ , 199 ___

_____

Incorporator

_____

Incorporator

_____

Incorporator

Waiver of Notice of the Organizational Meeting of Directors

Comtel, Inc.

THE UNDERSIGNED, being all of the directors of the corporation, severally waive notice of the organizational meeting of the directors of the said corporation, and do hereby consent that the time and place for holding said meeting shall be _9_ o'clock A.M., on the _15th_ day of _October_ , 199 _5_ , at _1821 Central Ave._ in the city of _Annandale_ , state of _Virginia_ , and do hereby further consent to the transaction of such business as may lawfully come before said meeting.

October 15, 1995   *Steve Ponder, Director*

Ed Jones, Director

Cathy Kline, Director
Signatures

Waiver of Notice of the Organizational Meeting of Directors

_____
Name of Corporation

    THE UNDERSIGNED, being all of the directors of the corporation, severally waive notice of the organizational meeting of the directors of the said corporation, and do hereby consent that the time and place for holding said meeting shall be _____ o'clock (A.M.) (P.M.), on the _____ day of _____ , 199 ___ , at _____ in the city of _____ , state of _____ , and do hereby further consent to the transaction of such business as may lawfully come before said meeting.

    Dated _____ , 199 ___

_____

_____

_____
Signatures

Minutes of the Organizational Meeting of the Board of Directors

Comtel, Inc.

The organizational meeting of the Board of Directors of _Comtel, Inc._ was held at _9_ o'clock A.M. on the _15th_ day of _October_, 199 _5_, at _1821 Central Avenue_ in the city of _Annandale_, state of _Virginia_.

The following directors were present in person at the meeting:

Name	Address	Number of Shares
Steve Ponder	_62 Winter Dr., Annandale, VA 22003_	_100_
Ed Jones	_1421 Park Cr., Annandale, VA 22003_	_100_
Cathy Kline	_21 E. Marks Pl., Annandale, VA 22003_	_100_

The above members constitute all of the directors of the corporation.

By majority vote, _Steve Ponder_ was elected Chairman of the Board, and _Ed Jones_ was elected Secretary of the meeting.

The Secretary presented the written Waiver of Notice of the First Meeting of the Board of Directors signed by all of the directors.

The Secretary next presented and read to the meeting the Minutes of the First Meeting of the Incorporators, which were then, upon motion duly made, seconded and unanimously approved and ratified.

The Secretary next presented and read to the meeting the bylaws, which were then, upon motion duly made, seconded, and unanimously approved and ratified.

The Chairman then accepted as nominations for the appointment of officers the following persons, said officers to serve until their respective successors should be appointed and qualify.

President	_Steve Ponder_
Vice President	_Cathy Kline_
Secretary	_Ed Jones_
Treasurer	_Ed Jones_

No other nominations were made, and the Secretary polled the vote, which unanimously elected to the offices indicated above those persons so nominated, to serve until their respective successors shall be elected and qualify.

Upon motion duly made, seconded, and approved, the annual salaries of the officers, payable in 12 equal monthly installments in arrears, were individually approved, unanimously.

President	$	_65,000.00_
Vice President	$	_55,000.00_
Secretary/Treasurer	$	_50,000.00_

Upon motion duly made, seconded, and approved, the directors approved the form of stock certificate and corporate seal as adopted by the subscribers and directed the Secretary to include an imprint of the corporate seal at the end of these minutes.

Upon motion duly made, seconded, and approved, it was

RESOLVED, that the Board of Directors be and it hereby is authorized in its discretion to issue the capital stock of this corporation to the full amount or number of shares authorized by the Articles of Incorporation, in such amounts and for such considerations in cash, property, or services as may from time to time be determined by the Board of Directors and as may be permitted by law.

Upon motion duly made, seconded, and approved, it was

RESOLVED, that the president be authorized and directed to open an account with the _First City_ bank.

Upon motion duly made, seconded, and approved, the meeting was adjourned.

Ed Jones
Secretary of the Meeting

Approved

Steve Ponder

Ed Jones

Cathy Kline
Signatures of all present

Minutes of the Organizational Meeting of the Board of Directors

_____

Name of Corporation

The organizational meeting of the Board of Directors of _____ was held at _____ o'clock A.M. on the _____ day of _____ , 199 ___ , at _____ in the city of _____ , state of _____ .

The following directors were present in person at the meeting:

Name	Address	Number of Shares
_____	_____	_____
_____	_____	_____
_____	_____	_____

The above members constitute all of the directors of the corporation.

By majority vote, _____ was elected Chairman of the Board, and _____ was elected Secretary of the meeting.

The Secretary presented the written Waiver of Notice of the First Meeting of the Board of Directors signed by all of the directors.

The Secretary next presented and read to the meeting the Minutes of the First Meeting of the Incorporators, which were then, upon motion duly made, seconded and unanimously approved and ratified.

The Secretary next presented and read to the meeting the bylaws, which were then, upon motion duly made, seconded, and unanimously approved and ratified.

The Chairman then accepted as nominations for the appointment of officers the following persons, said officers to serve until their respective successors should be appointed and qualify.

President	_____
Vice President	_____
Secretary	_____
Treasurer	_____

No other nominations were made, and the Secretary polled the vote, which unanimously elected to the offices indicated above those persons so nominated, to serve until their respective successors shall be elected and qualify.

Upon motion duly made, seconded, and approved, the annual salaries of the officers, payable in 12 equal monthly installments in arrears, were individually approved, unanimously.

President $ _____
Vice President $ _____
Secretary/Treasurer $ _____

Upon motion duly made, seconded, and approved, the directors approved the form of stock certificate and corporate seal as adopted by the subscribers and directed the Secretary to include an imprint of the corporate seal at the end of these minutes.

Upon motion duly made, seconded, and approved, it was
RESOLVED, that the Board of Directors be and it hereby is authorized in its discretion to issue the capital stock of this corporation to the full amount or number of shares authorized by the Articles of Incorporation, in such amounts and for such considerations in cash, property, or services as may from time to time be determined by the Board of Directors and as may be permitted by law.

Upon motion duly made, seconded, and approved, it was
RESOLVED, that the president be authorized and directed to open an account with the _____ bank.

Upon motion duly made, seconded, and approved, the meeting was adjourned.

_____
Secretary of the Meeting

Approval of minutes

_____

_____

_____
Signatures of all present

Shareholders' Agreement—Voting

AGREEMENT, made this _1st_ day of _November_ , 199 _5_ , by and between shareholders of _Comtel, Inc._ , a _Virginia_ corporation, hereinafter referred to as the Corporation, the said shareholder parties being as follows:

Name	Address	Number of Shares
Steve Ponder	_62 Winter Dr., Annandale, VA 22003_	_100_
Ed Jones	_1421 Park Cr., Annandale, VA 22003_	_100_
Cathy Kline	_21 E. Marks Pl., Annandale, VA 22003_	_100_

WHEREAS, each of the above individuals owns stock in the corporation, and

WHEREAS, the parties wish to promote their mutual interests and those of the Corporation through the adoption of certain voting and other provisions,

NOW THEREFORE, in consideration of the mutual promises herein contained and other good and valuable consideration, the parties hereto agree to legally bind themselves as follows:

1. During the duration of his ownership of stock, each shareholder party to this agreement agrees that he will vote his shares of stock in the Corporation for the following persons as directors of the Corporation.

Director	_Ed Jones_
Director	_Cathy Kline_

2. During the duration of his ownership of stock, each of the shareholders party to this agreement agrees that he will vote, when elected as a director, to elect the following persons to the stipulated office.

President	_Cathy Kline_
Vice President	_____
Secretary	_Ed Jones_
Treasurer	_____

3. In the event that any of the persons elected as directors of the Corporation shall resign, die, become incapacitated, or otherwise be unable or refuse to serve as a director of the Corporation, the remaining directors shall fill such vacancies by electing persons as directors who are designated by a majority of the shareholders who are parties to this agreement.

4. In the event that any of the persons elected as officers of the Corporation shall resign, die, become incapacitated, or otherwise be unable or refuse to serve as an officer of the Corporation, the remaining directors shall fill such vacancies by electing persons as officers who are designated by a majority of the shareholders who are parties to this agreement.

IN WITNESS WHEREOF, the parties hereto have affixed their hand in the year and day first above written.

By *Cathy Kline*

By *Ed Jones*

Note: The above agreement relates to voting control aspects of a close corporation. These are often not the sole provisions of a shareholders' agreement, but are included with other provisions, such as transfer restrictions.

Shareholders' Agreement—Voting

AGREEMENT, made this _____ day of _____ , 199 ___ , by and between shareholders of _____ , a _____ corporation, hereinafter referred to as the Corporation, the said shareholder parties being as follows:

Name	Address	Number of Shares
_____	_____	_____
_____	_____	_____
_____	_____	_____

WHEREAS, each of the above individuals owns stock in the corporation, and

WHEREAS, the parties wish to promote their mutual interests and those of the Corporation through the adoption of certain voting and other provisions,

NOW THEREFORE, in consideration of the mutual promises herein contained and other good and valuable consideration, the parties hereto agree to legally bind themselves as follows:

1. During the duration of his ownership of stock, each shareholder party to this agreement agrees that he will vote his shares of stock in the Corporation for the following persons as directors of the Corporation.

    Director   _____
    Director   _____

2. During the duration of his ownership of stock, each of the shareholders party to this agreement agrees that he will vote, when elected as a director, to elect the following persons to the stipulated office.

    President   _____
    Vice President   _____
    Secretary   _____
    Treasurer   _____

3. In the event that any of the persons elected as directors of the Corporation shall resign, die, become incapacitated, or otherwise be unable or refuse to serve as a director of the Corporation, the remaining directors shall fill such vacancies by electing persons as directors who are designated by a majority of the shareholders who are parties to this agreement.

4. In the event that any of the persons elected as officers of the Corporation shall resign, die, become incapacitated, or otherwise be unable or refuse to serve as an officer of the Corporation, the remaining directors shall fill such vacancies by electing persons as officers who are designated by a majority of the shareholders who are parties to this agreement.

IN WITNESS WHEREOF, the parties hereto have affixed their hand in the year and day first above written.

By _____

By _____

Note: The above agreement relates to voting control aspects of a close corporation. These are often not the sole provisions of a shareholders' agreement, but are included with other provisions, such as transfer restrictions.

Notice of Annual Shareholders' Meeting of

Comtel, Inc.

Notice is hereby given that the Annual Meeting of the shareholders of the Corporation will be held at _1821 Central Avenue_ , city of _Annandale_ , state of _Virginia_ , at _9_ o'clock A.M., on the _15th_ day of _October_ , 199 _6_ for the purpose of:

1. Electing the directors of the Corporation to hold office until the following annual meeting or until their successors are elected and qualify.
2. Transacting such other business as may properly come before the meeting.

At this meeting all shareholders holding the Common Stock of this Corporation at the close of business on _September 30_ , 199 _6_ , shall be entitled to vote, said date being the lawfully established record date in accordance with the corporation law of _Virginia_ .

In the event you do not expect to be present at the meeting, please sign the enclosed proxy and return it to the Corporation in the envelope provided.

Dated _September 15_ , 199 _6_

Ed Jones
Secretary

Notice of Annual Shareholders' Meeting of

_____
Name of Corporation

Notice is hereby given that the Annual Meeting of the shareholders of the Corporation will be held at _____ , city of _____ , state of _____ , at _____ o'clock (A.M.) (P.M.), on the _____ day of _____ , 199 ___ , for the purpose of:

1. Electing the directors of the Corporation to hold office until the following annual meeting or until their successors are elected and qualify.
2. Transacting such other business as may properly come before the meeting.

At this meeting all shareholders holding the Common Stock of this Corporation at the close of business on _____ , 199 ___ , shall be entitled to vote, said date being the lawfully established record date in accordance with the corporation law of _____ .

In the event you do not expect to be present at the meeting, please sign the enclosed proxy and return it to the Corporation in the envelope provided.

Dated _____ , 199 ___

_____
Secretary

Waiver of Notice of the Annual Meeting of Shareholders of

Comtel, Inc.

THE UNDERSIGNED, being all of the shareholders of _Comtel, Inc._ , severally waive notice and call of the time, place, and purposes of the annual meeting of the shareholders of the said corporation, and do hereby consent that the time and place for holding said meeting shall be _9_ o'clock A.M. on the _15th_ day of _October_ , 199 _6_ , at _1821 Central Avenue_ , city of _Annandale_ , state of _Virginia_ , and do hereby further consent to the transaction of such business as may lawfully come before said meeting, including the election of the directors.

    Dated _October 15_ , 199 _6_

                              Steve Ponder
                              Shareholder

                              Ed Jones
                              Shareholder

                              Cathy Kline
                              Shareholder

Waiver of Notice of the Annual Meeting of Shareholders of

_____

Name of Corporation

THE UNDERSIGNED, being all of the shareholders of _____ , severally waive notice and call of the time, place, and purposes of the annual meeting of the shareholders of the said corporation, and do hereby consent that the time and place for holding said meeting shall be _____ o'clock (A.M.) (P.M.) on the _____ day of _____ , 199 ___ , at _____ , city of _____ , state of _____ , and do hereby further consent to the transaction of such business as may lawfully come before said meeting, including the election of the directors.

Dated _____ , 199 ___

_____

_____

_____

Signatures

Minutes of the Annual Meeting of Shareholders of

Comtel, Inc.

The annual meeting of shareholders of _Comtel, Inc._ was held at _9_ o'clock, A.M. on the _15th_ day of _October_ , 199 _6_ , at _1821 Central Avenue_ in the city of _Annandale_ , state of _Virginia_ , pursuant to a Notice of Annual Shareholders' Meeting.

The following shareholders were present in person or by proxy at the meeting:

Name	Address	Number of Shares
Steve Ponder	*62 Winter Dr., Annandale, VA 22003*	*100*
Ed Jones	*1421 Park Cr., Annandale, VA 22003*	*100*
Cathy Kline	*21 E. Marks Pl., Annandale, VA 22003*	*100*

The President called the meeting to order and presided at the meeting.

The Secretary presented the minutes of the previous meeting of the corporation, held on the _15_ day of _October_ , 199 _5_ . The minutes were read and approved.

The chairman of the board of directors read a report of the business of the corporation during the previous period, including a statement of the financial condition of the corporation. Upon motion duly made and seconded, the report was unanimously approved.

The following were nominated as directors of the corporation

Name	Address
Steve Ponder	*62 Winter Dr., Annandale, VA 22003*
Ed Jones	*1421 Park Cr., Annandale, VA 22003*
Cathy Kline	*21 E. Marks Pl., Annandale, VA 22003*

to serve from the date of election until their respective successors shall be elected and qualify. No further nominations were made. The shareholders then unanimously elected the slate of directors as proposed.

The following old business was discussed: _none_ .

The following new business was discussed: _The purchase of a new office building. The shareholders unanimously elected the Board of Directors to make the decision_ .

No other business coming before the meeting, it was, upon motion duly made, seconded, and unanimously approved, adjourned.

Ed Jones
Secretary of Meeting

Steve Ponder
Shareholder

Ed Jones
Shareholder

Cathy Kline
Shareholder

Minutes of the Annual Meeting of Shareholders of

_____
Name of Corporation

The annual meeting of shareholders of _____ was held at _____ o'clock, A.M. on the _____ day of _____ , 199 ___ , at _____ in the city of _____ , state of _____ , pursuant to a Notice of Annual Shareholders' Meeting.

The following shareholders were present in person or by proxy at the meeting:

Name	Address	Number of Shares
_____	_____	_____
_____	_____	_____
_____	_____	_____

The President called the meeting to order and presided at the meeting.

The Secretary presented the minutes of the previous meeting of the corporation, held on the _____ day of _____ , 199 ___ . The minutes were read and approved.

The chairman of the board of directors read a report of the business of the corporation during the previous period, including a statement of the financial condition of the corporation. Upon motion duly made and seconded, the report was unanimously approved.

The following were nominated as directors of the corporation

Name	Address
_____	_____
_____	_____
_____	_____

to serve from the date of election until their respective successors shall be elected and qualify. No further nominations were made. The shareholders then unanimously elected the slate of directors as proposed.

The following old business was discussed: _____

_____

_____

_____.

The following new business was discussed: _____

_____

_____

_____.

No other business coming before the meeting, it was, upon motion duly made, seconded, and unanimously approved, adjourned.

_____
Secretary of Meeting

_____
Shareholder

_____
Shareholder

_____
Shareholder

Notice of Special Shareholders' Meeting of

Comtel, Inc.

Notice is hereby given that a Special Meeting of the Shareholders of the Corporation will be held at *1821 Central Avenue* , city of *Annandale* , state of *Virginia* , at *9* o'clock A.M., on the *5th* day of *February* , 199 *7* , for the purpose of:

1. *Electing a new director to replace a resigning director* .

At this meeting all shareholders holding the Common Stock of this Corporation at the close of business on *January 15* , 199 *7* , shall be entitled to vote.

In the event you do not expect to be present at the meeting, please sign the enclosed proxy and return it to the Corporation in the envelope provided.

Dated *January 15* , 199 *7*

Ed Jones
Secretary

Waiver of Notice of Special Meeting of Shareholders of

Comtel, Inc.

THE UNDERSIGNED, being all the shareholders of *Comtel, Inc.* , waive notice of a special meeting of the shareholders of the said corporation, and do hereby consent that the time and place for holding said meeting shall be *9* o'clock A.M. on the *5th* day of *February* , 199 *7* , at *1821 Central Avenue* , city of *Annandale* , state of *Virginia* , and do hereby further consent to the transaction of the following business:

1. *Electing a new director to replace a resigning director* .

Dated *February 5* , 199 *7*

Steve Ponder
Shareholder

Ed Jones
Shareholder

Cathy Kline
Shareholder

Notice of Special Shareholders' Meeting of

_____
Name of Corporation

Notice is hereby given that a Special Meeting of the Shareholders of the Corporation will be held at _____ , city of _____ , state of _____ , at _____ o'clock (A.M.) (P.M.), on the _____ day of _____ , 199 ___ , for the purpose of:

1. _____
2. _____
3. _____

At this meeting all shareholders holding the Common Stock of this Corporation at the close of business on _____ , 199 ___ , shall be entitled to vote.

In the event you do not expect to be present at the meeting, please sign the enclosed proxy and return it to the Corporation in the envelope provided.

Dated _____ , 199 ___

_____
Secretary

Waiver of Notice of Special Meeting of Shareholders of

_____
Name of Corporation

THE UNDERSIGNED, being all the shareholders of _____ , waive notice of a special meeting of the shareholders of the said corporation, and do hereby consent that the time and place for holding said meeting shall be _____ o'clock (A.M.) (P.M.) on the _____ day of _____ , 199 ___ , at _____ , city of _____ , state of _____ , and do hereby further consent to the transaction of the following business:

1. _____
2. _____
3. _____

Dated _____ , 199 ___

_____
Shareholders

_____
Shareholders

_____
Shareholders

Proxy to Vote Corporate Shares

THE UNDERSIGNED, being the owner of _100_ shares of voting common stock of _Comtel, Inc._ , do hereby grant to _Cathy Kline_ of _21 E. Marks Place_ , city of _Annandale_ , state of _Virginia_ , a proxy and appoint her my attorney-in-fact to vote _100_ shares of said stock at any meeting of the stockholders of the Corporation. Said Proxy holder is entitled to attend said meetings and act on my behalf and vote said shares personally or through mail proxy, all to the same extent as if I voted said shares personally.

During the pendency of this proxy, all rights to vote said shares shall be held by the Proxy holder with full power of substitution or revocation, provided that the undersigned may revoke this proxy at any time, upon written notice of termination by certified mail, return receipt to both the Proxy holder and the Corporation.

This agreement shall be binding upon and inure to the benefit of the parties, their successors, assigns, and personal representatives.

IN WITNESS WHEREOF, I have executed this proxy this _10th_ day of _November_ , 199 _6_ .

Accepted:

Cathy Kline   _Ed Jones_
Proxy holder   Stockholder

State of _Virginia_
County of _Arlington_

Then personally appeared _Ed Jones_ , who acknowledged the foregoing before me and is personally known to me or has produced _Virginia Driver's License_ as identification.

                              Debi Cade
                              Notary Public, state of _Virginia_

My Commission Expires: _October 31, 1997_

Proxy to Vote Corporate Shares

THE UNDERSIGNED, being the owner of _____ shares of voting common stock of _____ (Corporation), do hereby grant to _____ of _____ , city of _____ , state of _____ , a proxy and appoint him my attorney-in-fact to vote _____ shares of said stock at any meeting of the stockholders of the Corporation. Said Proxy holder is entitled to attend said meetings and act on my behalf and vote said shares personally or through mail proxy, all to the same extent as if I voted said shares personally.

During the pendency of this proxy, all rights to vote said shares shall be held by the Proxy holder with full power of substitution or revocation, provided that the undersigned may revoke this proxy at any time, upon written notice of termination by certified mail, return receipt to both the Proxy holder and the Corporation.

This agreement shall be binding upon and inure to the benefit of the parties, their successors, assigns, and personal representatives.

IN WITNESS WHEREOF, I have executed this proxy this _____ day of _____ , 199 ___ .

Accepted:

_____   _____

Proxy holder   Stockholder

State of _____
County of _____

Then personally appeared _____ , who acknowledged the foregoing before me and is personally known to me or has produced _____ as identification.

                                     _____

                                     Notary Public, state of _____

My Commission Expires: _____

Notice of Directors' Meeting of

Comtel, Inc.

To all members of the Board of Directors:

Notice is hereby given that a regular meeting of the Board of Directors of *Comtel, Inc.* will be held at *1821 Central Avenue* , city of *Annandale* , state of *Virginia* , at *9* o'clock A.M. on the *10th* day of *February* , 199 *7* , for the conduct of the regular business of the Board of Directors.

Dated *January 30* , 199 *7*

Ed Jones
Secretary

Waiver of Notice of the Regular Meeting of Directors of

Comtel, Inc.

THE UNDERSIGNED, being all of the directors of *Comtel, Inc.* , waive notice of the meeting of the Board of Directors of said corporation, and do hereby consent that the time and place for holding said meeting shall be *9* o'clock A.M. on the *10th* day of *February* , 199 *7* at *1821 Central Avenue* , in the city of *Annandale* , state of *Virginia* , and do hereby further consent to the transaction of such business as may lawfully come before said meeting.

Dated *January 31* , 199 *7*

Steve Ponder
Director

Ed Jones
Director

Cathy Kline
Director

Notice of Directors' Meeting of

_____
Name of Corporation

To all members of the Board of Directors:

Notice is hereby given that a regular meeting of the Board of Directors _____ of will be held at _____ , city of _____ , state of _____ , at _____ o'clock (A.M.) (P.M.) on the _____ day of _____ , 199 ___ , for the conduct of the regular business of the Board of Directors.

Dated _____ , 199 ___

_____
Secretary

Waiver of Notice of the Regular Meeting of Directors of

_____
Name of Corporation

THE UNDERSIGNED, being all of the directors of _____ , waive notice of the meeting of the Board of Directors of said corporation, and do hereby consent that the time and place for holding said meeting shall be _____ o'clock (A.M.) (P.M.) on the _____ day of _____ , 199 ___ , at _____ , in the city of _____ , state of _____ , and do hereby further consent to the transaction of such business as may lawfully come before said meeting.

Dated _____ , 199 ___

_____
Director

_____
Director

_____
Director

Minutes of the Meeting of Directors of

Comtel, Inc.

A meeting of the Board of Directors of _Comtel, Inc._ was held at _9_ o'clock A.M. on the _10th_ day of _February_ , 199 _7_ , at _1821 Central Ave._ in the city of _Annandale_ , state of _Virginia_ .

The following directors were present in person at the meeting:

Steve Ponder
Ed Jones
Cathy Kline

The Chairman of the Board called the meeting to order.

The Secretary of the Board of Directors presented the minutes of the previous meeting of the directors of the corporation, held on the _15th_ day of _June_ , 199 _6_ . The minutes were read and approved.

The following items of old business were discussed:
1. None
The following items of new business were discussed:
1. _Purchase of a new office building._
The following resolutions were made and approved:
1. _The President of the corporation shall be authorized to enter into a purchase agreement for the building at 1821 Central Avenue, Annandale, Virginia, for an amount no greater than $400,000. A thirty-year mortgage may be used as payment for up to 75% of the purchase price._

No other business coming before the meeting, it was, upon motion duly made, seconded, and unanimously approved, adjourned.

Dated _February 10_ , 199 _7_

Ed Jones
Secretary

Minutes of the Meeting of Directors of

_____
Name of Corporation

A meeting of the Board of Directors of _____ was held at _____ o'clock (A.M.) (P.M.) on the _____ day of _____ , 199 ___ , at _____ in the city of _____ , state of _____ .

The following directors were present in person at the meeting:

_____

_____

_____

The Chairman of the Board called the meeting to order.

The Secretary of the Board of Directors presented the minutes of the previous meeting of the directors of the corporation, held on the _____ day of _____ , 199 ___ . The minutes were read and approved.

The following items of old business were discussed:

1. _____
_____

2. _____
_____

3. _____
_____

The following items of new business were discussed:

1. _____
_____

2. _____
_____

3. _____
_____

The following resolutions were made and approved:

1. _____
_____

2. _____
_____

3. _____
_____

No other business coming before the meeting, it was, upon motion duly made, seconded, and unanimously approved, adjourned.

Dated _____ , 199 ___

_____
Secretary

Chapter 9
Real Estate

All entrepreneurs get involved in real estate at one time or another, even if only to get space in which to conduct a business. The forms I have included in this chapter deal primarily with leasing. Absent are a real estate sales contract and mortgage. I have elected to omit these forms because I think there are many clauses in a sales contract that are state-specific. If you want a good basic real estate contract, I recommend that you find a Realtor friend and get a copy of the purchase contract approved by your local board of Realtors and state Bar Association.

I have omitted the mortgage and mortgage note forms because several states use deeds of trust, and providing both might be confusing. To find which is appropriate for your state and to get a copy of a good form, I would contact a local title insurance company for a copy of one it uses.

Real estate and I have a special love/hate relationship. Over my twenty-five-year business career, I have made a lot of money in real estate, and I have lost a lot. I am convinced that people who have an estate at the end of their life can attribute much of it to real estate they buy somewhere along the way. Be cautious, but don't be afraid to buy real estate as an adjunct to your business. You've got to work somewhere, and you might as well own the property. Who knows, some day the real estate may be worth more than your business.

Commentary

An office-sharing agreement should be used when different business entities share common office space. Such an agreement helps you to clarify who will pay what expense or portion of that expense. It is easy to become confused about issues involving common area cost. In this day of great concern about liability, clause 6 reminds everyone of the importance of keeping separation between the businesses. The last thing you want is to find that you are being sued under some sort of quasi-partnership theory and becoming liable for something the other business did.

Note that clause 7 attempts to reaffirm that leaving the premises does not get you or the other party off the hook for payment. There are ongoing responsibilities that all of the parties are accountable for.

Office-Sharing Agreement

THIS AGREEMENT, entered into this the _1st_ day of _September_ , 199 _5_ , by and between _John Johnson_ (_Johnson_) of _125 West Street_ , city of _Longwood_ , state of _Florida_ , and _Frank Bones_ (_Bones_) of _754 Elias Street_ , city of _Longwood_ , state of _Florida_ .

WHEREAS the parties desire to lease space together in order to reduce the overall cost of having separate facilities, and

WHEREAS the parties wish to set down in writing their agreement regarding the sharing of cost associated with such space.

NOW THEREFORE, in consideration of the mutual promises and benefits to be derived by the parties, they do hereby agree to the following:

1. The parties shall jointly lease space at _1487 Maitland Circle, Longwood, Florida_ .

2. The space shall be divided according to the floor plan attached. The floor plan shall indicate by color code which space is to be occupied by which party and which space is common area.

3. The parties agree to be responsible for all cost associated with such space in proportion to the area they occupy compared to the total area. Common area cost shall be calculated the same way. Cost shall include but not be limited to rent, electricity, telephone service (but not long distance), answering service, repairs, supplies, postage, and similar items.

4. The parties agree to use the same for the following purpose and no other:

Name	Use
Johnson Consulting	_Business Advice_
Bone Real Estate	_Real Estate Sales_

5. The parties shall carry their own liability and personal property insurance.

6. The parties agree to post separate signs and make evident wherever possible that they are separate entities. Nothing in this agreement shall be construed in any way to form a partnership between the parties.

7. If either party shall vacate the premises prior to the expiration of the term of this lease, he shall nevertheless be bound by the lease and this agreement. The vacating party may assign this agreement subject to approval of the remaining party, which approval shall not be unreasonably withheld.

8. This agreement shall be effective during the initial lease period signed by the parties as well as all subsequent extensions and shall bind all heirs, successors, and assigns.

9. This agreement shall be construed under the laws of the state of _Florida_ . Should any disagreement arise out of this agreement, the prevailing party shall be awarded attorneys' fees and costs.

10. Time is of the essence.

The parties have set their hands and seals on the day first above written.

John Johnson

Frank Bones

Office-Sharing Agreement

THIS AGREEMENT, entered into this the _____ day of _____ , 199 ___ , by and between _____ (_____) of _____ , city of _____ , state of _____ , and _____ (_____) of _____ , city of _____ , state of _____ .

WHEREAS the parties desire to lease space together in order to reduce the overall cost of having separate facilities, and

WHEREAS the parties wish to set down in writing their agreement regarding the sharing of cost associated with such space.

NOW THEREFORE, in consideration of the mutual promises and benefits to be derived by the parties, they do hereby agree to the following:

1. The parties shall jointly lease space at _____ _____ .

2. The space shall be divided according to the floor plan attached. The floor plan shall indicate by color code which space is to be occupied by which party and which space is common area.

3. The parties agree to be responsible for all cost associated with such space in proportion to the area they occupy compared to the total area. Common area cost shall be calculated the same way. Cost shall include but not be limited to rent, electricity, telephone service (but not long distance), answering service, repairs, supplies, postage, and similar items.

4. The parties agree to use the same for the following purpose and no other:

Name	Use
_____	_____
_____	_____
_____	_____

5. The parties shall carry their own liability and personal property insurance.

6. The parties agree to post separate signs and make evident wherever possible that they are separate entities. Nothing in this agreement shall be construed in any way to form a partnership between the parties.

7. If either party shall vacate the premises prior to the expiration of the term of this lease, he shall nevertheless be bound by the lease and this agreement. The vacating party may assign this agreement subject to approval of the remaining party, which approval shall not be unreasonably withheld.

8. This agreement shall be effective during the initial lease period signed by the parties as well as all subsequent extensions and shall bind all heirs, successors, and assigns.

9. This agreement shall be construed under the laws of the state of _____ . Should any disagreement arise out of this agreement, the prevailing party shall be awarded attorneys' fees and costs.

10. Time is of the essence.

The parties have set their hands and seals on the day first above written.

_____
Signature

_____
Signature

Commentary

This residential rental agreement has been used by my clients and for my own properties. It is simple, yet it has numerous clauses that are advantageous for management. If you own real estate, you will find it extremely helpful in controlling potential problems with tenants.

The Discount clause, while unique, is the single most helpful thing we have ever used to get people to honor their commitments and pay on time. For complying with the contract terms in a timely fashion, we give them a discount. Lest you think this costs you money, you must remember that you have set the rent in the first place, and you are now offering a discount off of that. You may also note that the first sentence of the paragraph shifts all minor maintenance of the property to the tenant. We find that a deductible on all repairs helps keep down calls for repairs.

Note the Appliance clause (clause 4). If you have managed property, you know that appliances can present management problems because they are always breaking down. This is not a problem with this lease because appliances aren't a part of the lease. In fact, they are there at the option of the tenant, and if the tenant doesn't want them, management will remove them and lower the rent.

Clause 8, the Option clause, is a way of making a little extra money, or you may think of it as additional security that you do not have to account for or keep in a trust account. If your tenant doesn't want to put up the extra money, no problem. Just strike the clause and initial it. Don't leave the clause out because it may be helpful if you ever want to lease to someone else and the tenant argues that he or she should have some right of first refusal. A clause like this would help you persuade a judge that the tenant had the choice and gave up the right.

Note the Termination clause (clause 13). This contract is a month-to-month tenancy. I happen to be strongly of the opinion that annual leases overly favor the tenant, especially with the prevalence today of strong landlord/tenant laws. If you have a tenant who is hard to get along with, and he or she has a long-term lease, you have a problem. Some of you may feel you want a long-term lease; if so, just change the paragraph.

The Bonus clause (clause 22) is a preferred way of handling the end of a lease. Under most statutes, it is hard to keep security deposits. However, bonuses are options. If the tenant complies, he or she gets cash. This is an effective and useful method of handling the normal problems associated with the end of the lease.

You will note that this lease has some unusual provisions. Consequently, I have added a very bold disclaimer that puts the tenant on notice. You want the tenant to read and understand everything, so you give an extra warning. I also encourage you to have the lease reviewed by an attorney. Landlord/tenant laws are so local and change so often that such a review is worth the cost. Remember, you aren't paying the attorney to write the lease, just review it.

Rental Agreement

THIS AGREEMENT entered into this the _1st_ day of _October_ , 199 _6_ , by and between _Jeff Holt_ , hereinafter referred to as Management, and _Marcia Burrows_ of _1432 Olson Street_ , city of _Tampa_ , state of _Florida_ , hereinafter referred to as Occupant.

For and in consideration of the mutual benefits to be derived by each party, the Management hereby agrees to rent to the Occupant that dwelling located at _106 2nd Avenue North, Belleair, Florida_ , for a term commencing on the _1st_ day of _October_ , 199 _4_ , and monthly thereafter until the last day of _October_ , 199 _5_ , after which time this agreement is terminated without further notice. In consideration of the management permitting him to occupy the above property, the Occupant hereby agrees to the following terms and conditions:

```
Initial Payment                          $     0.00
Rent for Period  October 1, 1994         $   650.00
    to  November 1, 1994
Option Fees                              $   100.00
Clean-up Deposit                         $    50.00
Security Deposit                         $   650.00
Key Deposit                              $    10.00
                           Total   $  1460.00
```

1. **RENT:** To pay as rental the sum of $ _650.00_ per month due and payable monthly in advance from the First Day of every month. Occupant agrees to pay a late charge of $ _25.00_ for each and every time rent is not received by Management prior to 5:00 P.M. on the date due, regardless of the cause, including dishonored checks, time being of the essence.

2. **DISCOUNT:** As incentive to the Occupant to pay his rent Ahead of Time, **and being responsible for all minor maintenance of the premises** not to exceed $ _50.00_ (exclusive of labor charges) in any month, a DISCOUNT in the amount of $ _50.00_ may be deducted from the above rental sum each month. SUCH DISCOUNT WILL BE FORFEITED IF THE OCCUPANT FAILS TO PERFORM AS STATED HEREIN.

3. **USE:** To use the premises as **living quarters only** for _two (2)_ adults named _Marcia Burrows and Sue Evans_ , and _0_ children named _— — — — —_ , and to pay $ _200.00_ each month for each other person who shall occupy the premises in any capacity. Further, this Agreement is not assignable, nor shall the Occupant sublet any part of this premises.

4. **APPLIANCES:** Rental payments specifically exclude all appliances of any kind. Such appliances as are on the property are there solely at the convenience of the Management, who assumes no responsibility for their operation. AT THE REQUEST OF THE RESIDENT, PRIOR TO TAKING OCCUPANCY, they will be removed and the monthly rental discount will be increased by $ _5.00_ for each appliance so removed. In the event any of the appliances become unsatisfactory after occupancy has started, the Occupant may have them repaired at no cost to Management, or request Management to remove them with no increase in discount.

5. **UTILITIES:** To be responsible for payment of all utilities, garbage, sewer, water, telephone, gas, or other charges incurred during occupancy.

6. **ACCEPTANCE:** To accept said dwelling and all furnishings and appliances therein as being in good and satisfactory condition UNLESS A WRITTEN STATEMENT OF ANY OBJECTIONS is delivered to Management within THREE (3) DAYS AFTER TAKING POSSESSION. Resident agrees that failure to file such a statement shall be conclusive proof that there were no defects of note in the property. An inspection sheet· is provided for this purpose.

7. **MAINTENANCE:** Occupant agrees not to permit any deterioration (other than normal wear and tear) of the premises during the term of this Agreement. This clause includes, but is not limited to, woodwork, floors, walls, furnishings, fixtures, appliances, windows, screens, doors, plumbing, electrical, air conditioning, heating, and mechanical systems.

Exterior: Management shall at its own expense maintain and repair the roof, foundation, and exterior walls of the building, except repair necessitated by nuisance or neglect of the property by the Occupant.

Interior: Occupant shall at his own expense maintain and repair the interior of the building and fixtures belonging thereto. Occupant further agrees to pay for damage caused by rain or wind resulting from leaving windows open; or by overflow of water or stoppage thereof.

Lawn/Landscaping: Occupant agrees to maintain the lawns and shrubbery. Should, in Management's sole discretion, the lawn or shrubbery need mowing, trimming, or watering, Management will hire professional services and charge the Occupant. If within three (3) days the Occupant has not remedied the situation, Management will hire professional services and charge the Occupant an additional fee on the next month's rent. Occupant agrees that any vehicles found parked on unpaved areas may be towed away at the Occupant's expense.

Alterations: Occupant shall not paint, paper, or otherwise redecorate or make alterations to the premises without the prior written consent of Management.

8. **OPTION:** Occupant elects to pay the sum of $ _100.00_ for an option to renew this Agreement. THIS IS PAID IN SEPARATE LIEU OF ANY SECURITY DEPOSIT AND IS NONREFUNDABLE. IT IS NOT A DEPOSIT OF ANY KIND. SAID OPTION MAY BE EXERCISED ONLY IF THE OCCUPANT HAS LIVED UP TO ALL PROVISIONS OF THIS CONTRACT. Failure of the Occupant to exercise the option for any reason will terminate all parties' obligations under the Agreement.

9. **CHECKS AND CREDIT CARDS:** The initial payment of rent and the option consideration under the terms of this contract must be paid in cash, MasterCard, or Visa card. Thereafter, the rent may be paid by check until the first check is dishonored and returned unpaid regardless of cause. Afterwards, NO ADDITIONAL PAYMENTS MAY BE MADE BY CHECK! At the option of the Occupant, rent may be paid automatically by credit card, provided he agrees to pay an additional three percent (3%) processing charge. CREDIT CARD NUMBERS AND EXPIRATION DATES ARE:

MasterCard ,   _3714-264-2127 Exp. 6/95_

The above credit cards are specifically authorized to be used by the owner to pay rent any time it has not been paid prior to 5:00 P.M. when due. _Marcia Burrows_

(authorized signature of credit card holder).

10. **PAYMENT:** Checks sent through the mail are done so at the sender's own risk. Lost rents will be considered as unpaid until actually received by Management. To be certain of receiving full credit for timely payments, **rents should be delivered to** _122 Pine Street, Belleair, Florida_ . If payment is mailed, it is recommended that it be mailed at least one week prior to the due date to assure that Occupant retains the discount for the month.

11. **ENTRY AND INSPECTION:** Occupant agrees to give Management or its agent within reasonable hours the right of entry in order to show said premises for rent, sale, repair, or inspection as well as access to repairmen for the purpose of maintaining and repairing said property, which shall be done at the discretion of Management.

12. **PETS:** To pay a NONREFUNDABLE PET FEE OF $ _100.00_ per month for EACH PET. All pets on the property not registered under this Agreement will be presumed to be strays and will be disposed of by the appropriate agency as prescribed by law at Management's option. In the case of a dog, the Occupant will pay a nonrefundable deposit in advance of $ _150.00_ .

13. **TERMINATION:** In accordance with state statutes, after one month's rental payment has been received, this Agreement may be terminated by mutual consent of the parties; or by either party giving written notice at least _15_ days prior to the end of any monthly period. Any provision of this agreement may be reasonably changed by Management in like manner; thus THIS RENTAL CONTRACT ESTABLISHES A MONTH-TO-MONTH TENANCY ONLY! Termination of this contract prior to the ending date of the Agreement, regardless of cause, will constitute abandonment of any renewal, option rights, or entitlement to any performance bonus.

14. **DEFAULT:** In case of default on any of the covenants herein, Management may enforce the performance of this Agreement in any modes provided by law, and the Occupant hereby waives any statutory notice of such default. This Agreement may be forfeited at the Management's discretion if such default continues for a period of three (3) days, and thereupon this Agreement shall cease and come to an end as if that were the day originally fixed herein for the expiration of the term and Management and/or its agents shall have the right, without further notice or demand, to reenter and remove all persons and property therefrom without being guilty in any manner of trespass, or without any prejudices to any remedies for arrears of rent or breach of covenants. Management may resume possession of the premises and relet the same through the remainder of the term at the best rent Management may obtain for account of the Occupant, who shall make good any deficiency, including the cost of reletting. In the event of cancellation or termination of this Agreement by Management under the option provided herein, Management shall deduct from the Occupant's security deposit (if any) all unpaid rentals and damages and charges for which the Occupant is liable hereunder; any balance shall be returned to the Occupant.

15. **LEGAL RECOURSE/ATTORNEYS' FEES:** Occupant agrees to pay all court costs and attorneys' fees incurred by Management in enforcing legal action or in any of Management's other rights under this Agreement or any law of this state. All rights given to the Management by this Agreement shall be cumulative in addition to any other laws which might exist or become into being.

16. **WAIVER:** The acceptance by Management of partial payments of rent due shall not, under any circumstances, constitute a waiver of Management, or affect any notice or legal proceedings in unlawful detainers therefore given or commenced under the state statutes.

17. **INDEMNIFICATION:** Management shall not be liable to the Occupant or any other person for any damages to person or property occasioned by any defects in the dwelling, or by any other cause, or by an act, omission, or neglect of the Occupant or any other occupant of said dwelling, and Occupant agrees to hold Management and its agents harmless from any and all claims from any such damages, whether the injury occurs on or off the premises.

18. **HOLDOVER:** Any holding over by the Occupant of these premises after the expiration or other termination of this Agreement shall operate and be construed as a tenancy at sufferance at double the rental rate provided above, prorated by the day, and the Occupant agrees to surrender the premises upon 24 hours oral or written notice.

19. **CHANGES:** The provisions of this Agreement may be changed or added to by Management by giving notice to the tenant in writing.

20. **COMPETENCE:** In the event repairs are needed beyond the competence of the Occupant, he or she is urged to arrange for professional assistance. The Occupant warrants that any work or repairs performed by the Occupant will be undertaken only if he or she is competent and qualified to perform it, and the person performing the work will be totally responsible for all activities to assure that they are done in a safe manner which meets all the applicable statutes. The Occupant further warrants that he or she will be accountable for any mishaps or accidents resulting from such work and will hold the Management free from harm, litigation, or other claims of any other person.

21. **SPECIAL CLAUSE:** The Occupant understands that he is entering into a special rental agreement whereby the Management will be unable to offer the normal range of support provided to occupants. This is the reason for the rental discount, which is given to compensate the Occupant for taking the initiative required without involving the Management. **Therefore, any time the Management is contacted, this will result in the loss of the discount for that month.**

22. **BONUS:** As an incentive to the Occupant to perform all the covenants contained in this contract, a bonus will be paid in the amount of $ _100.00_ fifteen (15) days following the termination of the tenancy after all keys have been returned, bills paid, and premises inspected. In addition, the following conditions must be met:

- A. A formal written notice was given fifteen (15) days previous of intent to vacate, and the Occupant has cooperated and let Management show the property.
- B. No damage or deterioration to the property has occurred (other than reasonable wear and tear).
- C. The entire dwelling, appliances, closets, cupboards, garage, and outbuildings have been cleaned and are free of insects, carpets vacuumed, refrigerator defrosted, and all rubbish removed from premises.
- D. The provisions of the state statute have been complied with.
- E. A valid forwarding address and telephone number has been left with Management so that unpaid bills and charges can be directed to the Occupant.
- F. The Occupant does not exercise his option to renew.

Once the management has been satisfied that all conditions have been met in his sole opinion, the bonus check will be sent to the resident at his address.

THIS IS A SPECIAL RENTAL ARRANGEMENT REQUIRING A HIGHER LEVEL OF TENANT RESPONSIBILITY THAN IS REQUIRED IN OTHER RENTAL AGREEMENTS. A SPECIFIC DISCOUNT FROM MARKET RENT IS GIVEN IN ORDER TO COMPENSATE THE OCCUPANT FOR EXTRA EFFORT HE WILL BE PROVIDING IN MEETING CERTAIN OBLIGATIONS IMPOSED ON HIM BY THIS CONTRACT. BY SIGNING THIS DOCUMENT, YOU WARRANT THAT YOU UNDERSTAND ALL THE TERMS AND CONDITIONS UNDER WHICH THE MANAGEMENT HAS AGREED TO RENT THE PREMISES AND YOU ARE PREPARED TO PERFORM THE NORMAL DUTIES OF MANAGEMENT YOURSELF, OR HAVE THEM DONE BY SOMEONE ELSE AT YOUR EXPENSE. IN THE EVENT YOU FEEL IT IS NECESSARY, YOU ARE ADVISED TO SEEK THE ADVICE OF LEGAL COUNSEL PRIOR TO THE SIGNING OF THIS CONTRACT. THE OCCUPANT FURTHER STATES THAT ALL QUESTIONS HAVE BEEN ANSWERED BY MANAGEMENT TO THE OCCUPANT'S SATISFACTION AND THAT HE THOROUGHLY UNDERSTANDS ALL THE PROVISIONS AND OBLIGATIONS OUTLINED IN THIS CONTRACT.

Accepted this _1st_ day of _October_ , 199 _6_ .

Jeff Holt
Management

Marcia Burrows
Occupant

Rental Agreement

THIS AGREEMENT entered into this the _____ day of _____ , 199 ___ , by and between _____ , hereinafter referred to as Management, and _____ of _____ , city of _____ , state of _____ , hereinafter referred to as Occupant.

For and in consideration of the mutual benefits to be derived by each party, the Management hereby agrees to rent to the Occupant that dwelling located at _____ , for a term commencing on the _____ day of _____ , 199 ___ , and monthly thereafter until the last day of _____ , 199 ___ , after which time this agreement is terminated without further notice. In consideration of the management permitting him to occupy the above property, the Occupant hereby agrees to the following terms and conditions:

Initial Payment	$ _____
Rent for Period _____	$ _____
to _____	
Option Fees	$ _____
Clean-up Deposit	$ _____
Security Deposit	$ _____
Key Deposit	$ _____
Total	$ _____

1. **RENT:** To pay as rental the sum of $ _____ per month due and payable monthly in advance from the First Day of every month. Occupant agrees to pay a late charge of $ _____ for each and every time rent is not received by Management prior to 5:00 P.M. on the date due, regardless of the cause, including dishonored checks, time being of the essence.

2. **DISCOUNT:** As incentive to the Occupant to pay his rent Ahead of Time, **and being responsible for all minor maintenance of the premises** not to exceed $ _____ (exclusive of labor charges) in any month, a DISCOUNT in the amount of $ _____ may be deducted from the above rental sum each month. SUCH DISCOUNT WILL BE FORFEITED IF THE OCCUPANT FAILS TO PERFORM AS STATED HEREIN.

3. **USE:** To use the premises as **living quarters only** for _____ adults named _____ , and _____ children named _____, and to pay $ _____ each month for each other person who shall occupy the premises in any capacity. Further, this Agreement is not assignable, nor shall the Occupant sublet any part of this premises.

4. **APPLIANCES:** Rental payments specifically exclude all appliances of any kind. Such appliances as are on the property are there solely at the convenience of the Management, who assumes no responsibility for their operation. AT THE REQUEST OF THE RESIDENT, PRIOR TO TAKING OCCUPANCY, they will be removed and the monthly rental discount will be increased by $ _____ for each appliance so removed. In the event any of the appliances become unsatisfactory after occupancy has started, the Occupant may have them repaired at no cost to Management, or request Management to remove them with no increase in discount.

5. **UTILITIES:** To be responsible for payment of all utilities, garbage, sewer, water, telephone, gas, or other charges incurred during occupancy.

6. **ACCEPTANCE:** To accept said dwelling and all furnishings and appliances therein as being in good and satisfactory condition UNLESS A WRITTEN STATEMENT OF ANY OBJECTIONS is delivered to Management within THREE (3) DAYS AFTER TAKING POSSESSION. Resident agrees that failure to file such a statement shall be conclusive proof that there were no defects of note in the property. An inspection sheet is provided for this purpose.

7. **MAINTENANCE:** Occupant agrees not to permit any deterioration (other than normal wear and tear) of the premises during the term of this Agreement. This clause includes, but is not limited to, woodwork, floors, walls, furnishings, fixtures, appliances, windows, screens, doors, plumbing, electrical, air conditioning, heating, and mechanical systems.

Exterior: Management shall at its own expense maintain and repair the roof, foundation, and exterior walls of the building, except repair necessitated by nuisance or neglect of the property by the Occupant.

Interior: Occupant shall at his own expense maintain and repair the interior of the building and fixtures belonging thereto. Occupant further agrees to pay for damage caused by rain or wind resulting from leaving windows open; or by overflow of water or stoppage thereof.

Lawn/Landscaping: Occupant agrees to maintain the lawns and shrubbery. Should, in Management's sole discretion, the lawn or shrubbery need mowing, trimming, or watering, Management will hire professional services and charge the Occupant. If within three (3) days the Occupant has not remedied the situation, Management will hire professional services and charge the Occupant an additional fee on the next month's rent. Occupant agrees that any vehicles found parked on unpaved areas may be towed away at the Occupant's expense.

Alterations: Occupant shall not paint, paper, or otherwise redecorate or make alterations to the premises without the prior written consent of Management.

8. **OPTION:** Occupant elects to pay the sum of $ _____ for an option to renew this Agreement. THIS IS PAID IN SEPARATE LIEU OF ANY SECURITY DEPOSIT AND IS NONREFUNDABLE. IT IS NOT A DEPOSIT OF ANY KIND. SAID OPTION MAY BE EXERCISED ONLY IF THE OCCUPANT HAS LIVED UP TO ALL PROVISIONS OF THIS CONTRACT. Failure of the Occupant to exercise the option for any reason will terminate all parties' obligations under the Agreement.

9. **CHECKS AND CREDIT CARDS:** The initial payment of rent and the option consideration under the terms of this contract must be paid in cash, MasterCard, or Visa card. Thereafter, the rent may be paid by check until the first check is dishonored and returned unpaid regardless of cause. Afterwards, NO ADDITIONAL PAYMENTS MAY BE MADE BY CHECK! At the option of the Occupant, rent may be paid automatically by credit card, provided he agrees to pay an additional three percent (3%) processing charge. CREDIT CARD NUMBERS AND EXPIRATION DATES ARE:

_____ , _____

The above credit cards are specifically authorized to be used by the owner to pay rent any time it has not been paid prior to 5:00 P.M. when due. _____

(authorized signature of credit card holder).

10. **PAYMENT:** Checks sent through the mail are done so at the sender's own risk. Lost rents will be considered as unpaid until actually received by Management. To be certain of receiving full credit for timely payments, **rents should be delivered to** _____ . If payment is mailed, it is recommended that it be mailed at least one week prior to the due date to assure that Occupant retains the discount for the month.

11. **ENTRY AND INSPECTION:** Occupant agrees to give Management or its agent within reasonable hours the right of entry in order to show said premises for rent, sale, repair, or inspection as well as access to repairmen for the purpose of maintaining and repairing said property, which shall be done at the discretion of Management.

12. **PETS:** To pay a NONREFUNDABLE PET FEE OF $ _____ per month for EACH PET. All pets on the property not registered under this Agreement will be presumed to be strays and will be disposed of by the appropriate agency as prescribed by law at Management's option. In the case of a dog, the Occupant will pay a nonrefundable deposit in advance of $ _____ .

13. **TERMINATION:** In accordance with state statutes, after one month's rental payment has been received, this Agreement may be terminated by mutual consent of the parties; or by either party giving written notice at least _____ days prior to the end of any monthly period. Any provision of this agreement may be reasonably changed by Management in like manner; thus THIS RENTAL CONTRACT ESTABLISHES A MONTH-TO-MONTH TENANCY ONLY! Termination of this contract prior to the ending date of the Agreement, regardless of cause, will constitute abandonment of any renewal, option rights, or entitlement to any performance bonus.

14. **DEFAULT:** In case of default on any of the covenants herein, Management may enforce the performance of this Agreement in any modes provided by law, and the Occupant hereby waives any statutory notice of such default. This Agreement may be forfeited at the Management's discretion if such default continues for a period of three (3) days, and thereupon this Agreement shall cease and come to an end as if that were the day originally fixed herein for the expiration of the term and Management and/or its agents shall have the right, without further notice or demand, to reenter and remove all persons and property therefrom without being guilty in any manner of trespass, or without any prejudices to any remedies for arrears of rent or breach of covenants. Management may resume possession of the premises and relet the same through the remainder of the term at the best rent Management may obtain for account of the Occupant, who shall make good any deficiency, including the cost of reletting. In the event of cancellation or termination of this Agreement by Management under the option provided herein, Management shall deduct from the Occupant's security deposit (if any) all unpaid rentals and damages and charges for which the Occupant is liable hereunder; any balance shall be returned to the Occupant.

15. **LEGAL RECOURSE/ATTORNEYS' FEES:** Occupant agrees to pay all court costs and attorneys' fees incurred by Management in enforcing legal action or in any of Management's other rights under this Agreement or any law of this state. All rights given to the Management by this Agreement shall be cumulative in addition to any other laws which might exist or become into being.

16. **WAIVER:** The acceptance by Management of partial payments of rent due shall not, under any circumstances, constitute a waiver of Management, or affect any notice or legal proceedings in unlawful detainers therefore given or commenced under the state statutes.

17. **INDEMNIFICATION:** Management shall not be liable to the Occupant or any other person for any damages to person or property occasioned by any defects in the dwelling, or by any other cause, or by an act, omission, or neglect of the Occupant or any other occupant of said dwelling, and Occupant agrees to hold Management and its agents harmless from any and all claims from any such damages, whether the injury occurs on or off the premises.

18. **HOLDOVER:** Any holding over by the Occupant of these premises after the expiration or other termination of this Agreement shall operate and be construed as a tenancy at sufferance at double the rental rate provided above, prorated by the day, and the Occupant agrees to surrender the premises upon 24 hours oral or written notice.

19. **CHANGES:** The provisions of this Agreement may be changed or added to by Management by giving notice to the tenant in writing.

20. **COMPETENCE:** In the event repairs are needed beyond the competence of the Occupant, he or she is urged to arrange for professional assistance. The Occupant warrants that any work or repairs performed by the Occupant will be undertaken only if he or she is competent and qualified to perform it, and the person performing the work will be totally responsible for all activities to assure that they are done in a safe manner which meets all the applicable statutes. The Occupant further warrants that he or she will be accountable for any mishaps or accidents resulting from such work and will hold the Management free from harm, litigation, or other claims of any other person.

21. **SPECIAL CLAUSE:** The Occupant understands that he is entering into a special rental agreement whereby the Management will be unable to offer the normal range of support provided to occupants. This is the reason for the rental discount, which is given to compensate the Occupant for taking the initiative required without involving the Management. **Therefore, any time the Management is contacted, this will result in the loss of the discount for that month.**

22. **BONUS:** As an incentive to the Occupant to perform all the covenants contained in this contract, a bonus will be paid in the amount of $ _____ fifteen (15) days following the termination of the tenancy after all keys have been returned, bills paid, and premises inspected. In addition, the following conditions must be met:

    A.   A formal written notice was given fifteen (15) days previous of intent to vacate, and the Occupant has cooperated and let Management show the property.

    B.   No damage or deterioration to the property has occurred (other than reasonable wear and tear).

    C.   The entire dwelling, appliances, closets, cupboards, garage, and outbuildings have been cleaned and are free of insects, carpets vacuumed, refrigerator defrosted, and all rubbish removed from premises.

    D.   The provisions of the state statute have been complied with.

    E.   A valid forwarding address and telephone number has been left with Management so that unpaid bills and charges can be directed to the Occupant.

    F.   The Occupant does not exercise his option to renew.

Once the management has been satisfied that all conditions have been met in his sole opinion, the bonus check will be sent to the resident at his address.

THIS IS A SPECIAL RENTAL ARRANGEMENT REQUIRING A HIGHER LEVEL OF TENANT RESPONSIBILITY THAN IS REQUIRED IN OTHER RENTAL AGREEMENTS. A SPECIFIC DISCOUNT FROM MARKET RENT IS GIVEN IN ORDER TO COMPENSATE THE OCCUPANT FOR EXTRA EFFORT HE WILL BE PROVIDING IN MEETING CERTAIN OBLIGATIONS IMPOSED ON HIM BY THIS CONTRACT. BY SIGNING THIS DOCUMENT, YOU WARRANT THAT YOU UNDERSTAND ALL THE TERMS AND CONDITIONS UNDER WHICH THE MANAGEMENT HAS AGREED TO RENT THE PREMISES AND YOU ARE PREPARED TO PERFORM THE NORMAL DUTIES OF MANAGEMENT YOURSELF, OR HAVE THEM DONE BY SOMEONE ELSE AT YOUR EXPENSE. IN THE EVENT YOU FEEL IT IS NECESSARY, YOU ARE ADVISED TO SEEK THE ADVICE OF LEGAL COUNSEL PRIOR TO THE SIGNING OF THIS CONTRACT. THE OCCUPANT FURTHER STATES THAT ALL QUESTIONS HAVE BEEN ANSWERED BY MANAGEMENT TO THE OCCUPANT'S SATISFACTION AND THAT HE THOROUGHLY UNDERSTANDS ALL THE PROVISIONS AND OBLIGATIONS OUTLINED IN THIS CONTRACT.

Accepted this _____ day of _____ , 199 ___ .

_____
Management

_____
Occupant

Commercial Lease Agreement

THIS LEASE AGREEMENT, is made and entered into as of this _1st_ day of _November_ , 199 _6_ , by and between _High Point Management, Inc._ (Lessor) of _332 Forest Drive_ , city of _Orlando_ , state of _Florida_ , and _Creative Marketing, Inc._ (Lessee) of _21 E. Nova Street_ , city of _Orlando_ , state of _Florida_ . The aforementioned shall hereinafter jointly be referred to as the "PARTIES."

WITNESSETH:

Article 1
Leased Premises

In consideration of the rents herein provided and the terms, provisions and covenants hereof, Lessor hereby leases, lets and demises to Lessee the following described premises (hereinafter referred to as the "Leased Premises"): _14 High Point Center_

Approximately _2500_ square feet of gross rentable area, and more particularly described in Exhibit "B" attached. Lessee hereby unequivocally acknowledges by execution of this Lease Agreement that the aforementioned square feet of gross rentable area may include Lessee's pro rata share of common areas shared by other tenants. In such event, Lessee may be actually occupying less than _2500_ square feet; however, it shall not be construed that Lessee is in any way relieved of paying rent pursuant to Article 3 herein.

Exhibits

Exhibit A describes and incorporates in this Lease Agreement a Floor Plan locating the portion of the Building to be leased by Lessee; Exhibit B describes and incorporates in this Lease Agreement a Site Plan .

Article 2
Term

Subject to and upon the conditions set forth herein, and in any exhibit or addendum hereto, the term of this Lease (hereinafter referred to as the "Lease Term") shall commence on _November 1_ , 199 _6_ (hereinafter referred to as the "Commencement Date"), and shall continue for _36_ months until _October 31_ , 199 _9_ , at which time this lease shall expire. Immediately upon said date of termination of this Lease, Lessee shall voluntarily surrender the Leased Premises to Lessor.

Article 3
Rent

Lessee agrees to pay in advance to Lessor during the Term hereof, without deduction, setoff, prior notice, or demand, monthly rental (hereinafter referred to as the "Base Monthly Rental") for the Leased Premises in the amount of: _Two thousand five hundred_ dollars, which amount shall be payable in advance on the first business day of each month of the Lease Term. Payment of such rent shall be accompanied by all sales tax levied by any federal, state, county, or city government or by any agency authorized to levy and collect rent tax, and shall be payable in lawful money of the United States of America to Lessor at the address of Lessor set forth below. The amount of the monthly installments set forth above shall be subject to escalation, and additional rent shall be due and payable from Lessee to Lessor, as hereinafter provided. Other remedies for nonpayment of rent under this Lease notwithstanding, if the rental payment is not received by Lessor on or before _ten_ (_10_) days after such rent is due, a service charge of _five_ percent (_5_ %) of the rent then due shall become due and payable on demand in addition to the rent owed under this Lease as remuneration for the additional expense for handling late rentals.

Article 4
Rental Adjustment: Consumer Price Index

On the first day of the second lease year (which "lease year" shall commence on the first anniversary of the Commencement Date if the Commencement Date is the first day of a calendar month, or on the first day of the first calendar month following the anniversary of the Commencement Date if the Commencement Date is other than the first day of a calendar month), and on the first day of each lease year (including renewals of this Lease Agreement, if any) thereafter until this Lease is terminated as set forth herein, the Base Annual Rent shall be adjusted and changed, on a cumulative basis, as follows:

The Base Annual Rent and the monthly rental installments payable for each lease year during the Lease Term (other than the first lease year) shall be computed by multiplying the Base

Annual Rental (and the monthly rental installment) as set forth in Article 3 above by a fraction, the numerator of which shall be the Consumer Price Index ("Urban," the United States city average for urban wage earners, all items [Base 1982-84 = 100], issued by the Bureau of Labor Statistics of the United States Department of Labor) for the second (2nd) full month prior to the Commencement Date of this Lease; provided, however, that in no event shall such increase in Annual Rent be less than _four_ percent (_4_ %) throughout the Lease Term.

In the event that the Consumer Price Index ceases to use the 1982-84 average of one hundred (100) as the basis of calculation, or if a change is made in the terms of particular items contained in the Consumer Price Index, then the Consumer Price Index shall, at the discretion of the Lessor, be adjusted to the figure that would have been arrived at had the change in the manner of computing the Consumer Price Index in effect at the commencement of the Lease Term not been affected. In the event that such Consumer Price Index (or successor or substitute Consumer Price Index) is not available, a reliable governmental or other nonpartisan publication evaluating the purchasing power of money may be used at the discretion of Lessor.

Article 5
Security Deposit

The Lessee agrees to pay a security deposit equal to _Two thousand dollars_ ($ _2,000_) upon the beginning of the lease. Unless required under state law, the security deposit will be released to the Lessor, who shall not be required to maintain it in a separate account nor be charged interest thereon.

The security deposit shall be used by the lessor to pay for any damage caused by the Lessee during his occupancy, reasonable wear and tear excepted. In addition, the security deposit may also be used to offset monetary damage of unpaid rent or unpaid late fees.

Article 6
Quiet Enjoyment

The Lessor covenants and agrees that Lessee, on paying said monthly rent and performing all the covenants of this Lease on the part of Lessee to be performed herein, shall and may peaceably and quietly hold and enjoy the said Leased Premises.

Article 7
Operating Expense Adjustments

It is understood that the Annual Rent specified in Articles 3 and 4 is in anticipation of Lessor incurring certain expenses for taxes, operations, and maintenance costs. Therefore, the Lessor and Lessee agree to the definitions and terms set forth below:

A. Real Estate Taxes: Lessor shall pay real estate taxes imposed on the Leased Premises. Lessee shall reimburse Lessor for any increase in real estate taxes imposed on the Leased Premises over and above the amount of these taxes for the calendar year _1996_ . Said increase shall be payable on or before _thirty_ (_30_) days after receipt of notice of the amount from Lessor. The term "real estate taxes" shall include all ad valorem taxes and general and special assessments levied against the Leased Premises. Lessee shall be responsible for all taxes levied on Lessee's personal property.

B. Utility Service: Lessor shall provide the standard utility service connections for water, sewer, electricity, and telephone into the Leased Premises. Lessee shall pay the cost of all utility services for the Leased Premises, including but not limited to initial connection charges and/or deposits, all charges for water, sewer, telephone, and electricity, and all replacement of electric light lamps, tubes, and ballasts used on or in connection with the Leased Premises. The Lessee's pro rata share of the entire building is _50_ percent. Failure by the Lessor to make available these services, or any cessation thereof, resulting from causes beyond the control of the Lessor, shall neither render Lessor liable in any respect for damages to either person or property, nor relieve Lessee from fulfillment of any covenant of this Lease. Should any of the equipment or machinery, under the control of the Lessor, necessary to provide such services break down, or for any cause cease to function properly, Lessor shall use reasonable diligence to repair the same properly.

C. Repairs and Maintenance: The Lessor and Lessee shall maintain the Building and the Leased Premises in good repair and condition according to the following schedule:

Mechanical, Heating, Ventilation, and Air Conditioning: Lessor shall be responsible for all major maintenance and repairs to the mechanical, heating, air conditioning, and ventilation systems; provided, however, that Lessee shall pay the first $ _300_ per occurrence (for items not protected by service warranties) for all maintenance and repairs of such systems within the Leased Premises or Lessee's pro rata share of the total building if appropriate. Lessor shall supply and change all air conditioning filters as required. Lessee shall reimburse to Lessor the cost of supplying and changing such filters within thirty (30) days of receiving bill from Lessor.

Plumbing and Electrical: Lessor shall be responsible for all major repairs and maintenance of the plumbing and electrical systems; provided, however, that Lessee shall pay the first $ _300_ per occurrence (for items not protected by service contracts or warranties) for maintenance and repairs of such systems within the Leased Premises or Lessee's pro rata share of Building if the cost of such repair and maintenance shall be billed to the Building as a whole.

Interior Maintenance: Lessee shall clean, provide cleaning supplies, and maintain the Leased Premises in a clean, sanitary, and good condition. Lessee shall make all needed repairs, including but not limited to interior pest control, and replacements to the interior of the Leased Premises, except for those responsibilities expressly imposed upon Lessor above. Lessee shall maintain and repair all interior glass.

Common Area Maintenance Charges: Lessee shall pay its pro rata share of the common area charges. Said charges are assessed by Lessor to pay for maintenance, repairs, and replacements, as necessary, to include, but not be limited to, the maintenance of common streets, drives, street lighting, landscaping, swale and berm maintenance, common area irrigation, fountains, walls, parking lot maintenance, refuse service, building exteriors and roofs, et cetera. The Lessee's pro rata share of common area maintenance charges shall be computed by multiplying the total common area maintenance charges by a fraction, the numerator of which shall be the Lessee's _2,500_ square feet and the denominator of which shall be _5,000_ (the total number of square feet of office buildings for which certificates of occupancy have been issued in the building). Payment shall be made monthly by Lessee within _ten_ (_10_) days after Lessee receives notice from Lessor showing the sum due, which notice shall state in reasonable detail the manner in which Lessee's share of common area maintenance is computed. Lessee has the obligation to pay for any partial month at the commencement and expiration or termination of the Lease Term.

D. Insurance: Lessor shall pay for fire and extended coverage insurance for the Leased Premises. Lessee shall reimburse Lessor for any increase in the cost of insurance that Lessor is responsible to carry on the Leased Premises, over and above the insurance cost for the calendar year _1996_ . Reimbursement shall be made by Lessee within _ten_ (_10_) days after Lessee receives notice from Lessor showing the sum due, which notice shall state in reasonable detail the manner in which Lessee's share of insurance costs is computed. Lessee shall not be obligated to reimburse Lessor for any portion of any increase in the insurance premium caused by a particular use or activity of any other tenant in the Building in which the Leased

Premises is located. Lessee's obligation to pay the insurance costs shall be prorated for any partial year at the commencement and expiration or termination of the lease term. Lessee shall provide fire and extended coverage insurance on its personal property and contents.

Article 8
Alterations and Improvements

Lessee shall not make or allow to be made any alterations or physical additions in or to the Leased Premises without first obtaining the written consent of Lessor, which consent may be withheld at the sole discretion of Lessor for any reason. Any and all such alterations, physical additions, or improvements to the Leased Premises, when made by Lessee, shall at once become the property of Lessor and shall be surrendered to Lessor upon the termination of this Lease, by lapse of time or otherwise; provided, however, this clause shall not apply to movable equipment, partitions, or furniture owned by Lessee, which may be removed by Lessee at the end of the term of this Lease if Lessee is not then in default and if such equipment, partitions, and furniture are not then subject to any other rights, liens, and interests of Lessor hereunder. All damages to the Leased Premises caused by or becoming evident by the removal of such movable equipment, furniture, or partitions or otherwise shall be repaired by Lessee at Lessee's cost prior to surrender of the Leased Premises.

Article 9
Liens

It is expressly covenanted and agreed by and between the Parties hereto that nothing contained in this Lease shall authorize Lessee to do any act which shall in any way encumber the title of Lessor in and to the Building or the land upon which the Building is situated, nor shall the interest or estate of Lessor in the Leased Premises be in any way subject to any claim by way of lien or encumbrance, whether by operation of law or by virtue of any express or implied contract by Lessee, and any claim to or lien upon the Leased Premises arising from any act or omission of Lessee shall accrue only against the leasehold estate of Lessee and shall in all respects be subject and subordinate to the paramount title and right of Lessor in and to the Leased Premises. Lessee will not permit the Leased Premises to become subject to any mechanics', laborers', or materialmen's lien on account of labor or material furnished to Lessee or any sublessee in connection with work of any character performed or claimed to have been performed on the Leased Premises by or at the direction or sufferance of Lessee; provided, however, that Lessee shall have the right to contest in good faith and with reasonable diligence the validity of any such lien or claimed lien if Lessee shall give to Lessor such reasonable security as may be demanded by Lessor to ensure payment to prevent any sale, foreclosure, or forfeiture of the Leased Premises by reason of nonpayment thereof. On final determination of the lien or claim for lien, Lessee will immediately pay any judgment rendered with all proper costs and charges and will at its own expense have the lien released and any judgment satisfied. In case Lessee shall fail to contest the validity of any lien or claimed lien and give security to Lessor to ensure payment thereof, or having commenced to contest the same, and having given such security, shall fail to prosecute such contest with diligence, or shall fail to have the same released and satisfy any judgment rendered thereon, then Lessor may, at its election and without any requirement that it do so, remove or discharge such lien or claim for lien (with the right in its discretion to settle or compromise the same), and any amounts advanced by Lessor for such purposes shall be so much additional rental due from Lessee to Lessor on demand, with interest at the highest rate allowed by law from the date of payment thereof by Lessor until the repayment thereof by Lessee to Lessor.

Article 10
Fire and Casualty

If the Leased Premises shall be injured or damaged by fire or other causes and should Lessor elect to make repairs to the Leased Premises and complete said repairs within _one hundred eighty_ (_180_) days of the damage, then this Lease shall not be terminated. Should Lessor elect not to rebuild, it may terminate this Lease by written notice to Lessee. In either event, Lessor shall give Lessee written notice of its intention to rebuild or terminate this Lease within _thirty_ (_30_) days after the event that causes said injury or damage. In no event shall Lessor be liable to Lessee in any respect whatsoever for Lessee's inability to operate its business as a result of any casualty, including but not limited to injury or damage to the Leased Premises caused by fire or other causes.

Lessee shall carry a work/rental interruption insurance policy covering risk of loss due to casualty in an amount not less than the aggregate amount to be paid by Lessee to Lessor or to a third party under the terms and provisions of this Lease, including but not limited to rent, real property taxes, and common area maintenance charges, for a period of _six_ (_6_) months following any occurrence of the said casualty.

Article 11
Liability Insurance

Lessee agrees to carry at its own expense a Lessor/Lessee's Liability Insurance policy from a company satisfactory to Lessor, with minimum limits for general public liability insurance for personal injury including death in the amount of _Three hundred thousand and no/100_ dollars ($ _300,000_) and _Five hundred thousand and no/100_ dollars ($ _500,000_) for each occurrence, with _One million and no/100_ dollars ($ _1,000,000_) umbrella coverage, and for property damage insurance a single limit of not less than _One hundred thousand and no/100_ dollars ($ _100,000_) for each occurrence; such insurance shall be for the joint benefit of Lessor and Lessee and shall name Lessor as an additional insured.

Irrespective of the adequacy of said insurance, Lessee shall indemnify and save Lessor free and harmless from any and all claims, actions, damages, expenses (including without limitation reasonable attorneys' fees), and liability whatsoever arising out of or in any way connected with injury (including death) or property damage to any person, firm, corporation, or other entity, including Lessor, arising directly or indirectly from being on the Leased Premises or the use or occupancy of said Leased Premises.

Copies of all the Lessee's required insurance policies shall be delivered to Lessor prior to occupancy of the Leased Premises. On an annual basis, the Lessee shall provide Lessor with a Certificate of Insurance reflecting the types of policies held, their amounts, and the Lessor's interest as loss payee. Lessee agrees that every insurer shall agree by endorsement upon the policy(ies) issued by it, that it will give Lessor _ten_ (_10_) days written notice at the address where rental is paid before the policy(ies) is question shall be altered or canceled.

Article 12
Waiver of Subrogation

Anything in this Lease to the contrary notwithstanding, the Lessee hereby waives any and all rights of recovery, claim, action, or cause of action against Lessor, his agents, offices, and employees, for any loss or damage that may occur to the Leased Premises hereby demised, or any improvements thereto, or personal property located therein, or said Building of which the Leased Premises are part, or any other cause which could be insured against under the terms of standard fire and extended coverage insurance policies, regardless of cause or origin, including negligence of the Parties hereto, their agents, officers, and employees. Lessee agrees to make best efforts to have its insurance company waive its subrogation rights under all policies.

Article 13
Condemnation

Lessee agrees that if the said Leased Premises, or any part thereof, shall be taken or condemned for public or quasi-public use or purpose by any authority, Lessee shall have no claim against the Lessor and shall not have any claim or right to any portion of the amount that may be awarded to the Lessee as damages or paid as a result of such condemnation; all the rights of the Lessee to damages thereof, if any, are hereby assigned by the Lessee to the Lessor. If the condemnation or taking is for the entire Leased Premises, the term of the Lease shall cease and terminate from the date of such governmental taking or condemnation, and the Lessee shall have no claim against the Lessor for the value of any unexpired term of this Lease. Should the taking or condemnation be for a part of the Leased Premises, then at the sole option of the Lessor, this Lease shall not cease and terminate, but continue in full force and effect.

Article 14
Usage of Leased Premises

The Leased Premises are to be occupied and used by the Lessee for office(s) and for no other purpose. Use for any other purpose shall constitute a breach of this Lease. Lessee shall not occupy or use, or permit any portion of the Leased Premises to be occupied or used, for any business or purpose which is unlawful, disreputable, or deemed by Lessor to be extrahazardous, or permit anything to be done which in any way will increase the rate of insurance coverage on said Leased Premises, and in the event that, by reason of such acts of Lessee, there shall be any increase in the insurance rates for the building or contents above normal rates, Lessee agrees to pay to Lessor upon receipt of notice, as additional rental, an amount equal to all such increase. Lessee shall conduct its business and control its agents, employees, invitees, and visitors in such a manner as not to create any nuisance, or interfere with, annoy, or disturb any other Lessee, Lessor, or any other party involved in the management of the Building.

Article 15
Compliance with Laws, Regulations, and Restrictions

Lessee shall comply with all laws, ordinances, orders, rules, and regulations (state, federal, municipal and other agencies, or bodies having any jurisdiction thereof) relating to the use, condition, or occupancy of the Leased Premises. Lessee shall indemnify and save and hold Lessor harmless from Lessee's violation of any laws and ordinances. Lessee shall comply with all Building Rules and Regulations of the Building.

Article 16
Lessor's Right of Entry

Lessee shall permit Lessor or its agents or representatives to enter into and upon any part of the Leased Premises, at all reasonable hours, to inspect the same, to clean or make repairs, alterations, or additions thereto, as Lessor in its opinion may deem necessary or desirable, or for the purpose of determining Lessee's use thereof or whether an act of default under this Lease has occurred.

Article 17
Parking

Lessor shall provide nonexclusive parking for the benefit of Lessee, its employees, customers, and visitors and for the benefit of other owners and tenants, in the areas shown on the Site Plan attached hereto as Exhibit _B_. Lessor has provided and Lessee exclusively designated for certain owners and Lessees. _2_ exclusive parking spaces per One Thousand (1,000) square feet of leasable area (within the Leased Premises) throughout the term of this lease.

Article 18
Signs and Advertising

The Lessee shall have sign space on the following signs (see Exhibit _A_, Sign Site Plan, for location of signs):

A. Building (Lessee) Identification Sign located near the Building.

B. Sign at the entrance to the Leased Premises.

All of the signs are to be in conformity with the building Sign Regulations and the county of _Seminole_ Sign Regulations. No other advertising or signs shall be placed by Lessee so as to be visible from the exterior of the Leased Premises without the prior consent and design approval of the Lessor. Any such signs and advertising shall be placed where designated by the Lessor and installed by Lessor at Lessee's expense. The cost of constructing and placing any exterior sign or signs shall be at Lessee's expense.

Article 19
Assignment or Sublease

The Lessee covenants and agrees not to encumber or assign this Lease or sublet all or any part (including desk space or mailing privileges) of the Leased Premises without the written consent of the Lessor, which consent may be withheld by Lessor. Such assignment shall in no way relieve the Lessee from any obligations, covenants, and provisions of this Lease. If Lessor grants its consent to an assignment or subletting, rent under this Lease shall thereafter be the greater of (a) the rent payable as per terms and conditions of this Lease, or (b) the rent payable by the Assignee or Subtenant (including any consideration paid by Assignee or Subtenant).

In no event shall Lessee assign or sublet the Leased Premises for any terms, conditions, and covenants other than those contained herein. In no event shall this Lease be assigned or be assignable by operation of Law or by voluntary or involuntary bankruptcy proceedings or otherwise, and in no event shall this lease or any rights or privileges hereunder be an asset of Lessee under any bankruptcy, insolvency, or reorganizational proceedings. Lessor shall not be liable nor shall the Leased Premises be subject to any mechanics', materialmen's, or other type liens, and Lessee shall keep the Leased Premises and land on which the Leased Premises are situated free from any such liens which may occur because of acts of Lessee, notwithstanding any foregoing provision.

Any consent to any subletting or assignment shall not be deemed a consent to any subsequent subletting or assignment. Any assignee, transferee, or purchaser shall agree in writing to be bound by and comply with the provisions of this Lease.

Article 20
Mortgaging of Lessor's Estate

The Lessor shall have the right, at any time or from time to time during the continuance of this Lease, as security for any indebtedness owed by it, to create an encumbrance against its estate in the Leased Premises or any part thereof, and Lessee hereby agrees that this Lease and Lessee's estate hereunder shall be junior, inferior, subject, and subordinate in all respects to the rights and interests of the party to whom such security is granted. Lessee agrees that, upon written request of Lessor so to do, it shall execute such instruments as may be required from time to time to confirm the subordinate interest of Lessee under this Lease to such encumbrance of the fee estate of Lessor.

Article 21
Transfer by Lessor

If the interest of Lessor under this Lease shall be transferred, whether voluntarily or by reason of foreclosure, voluntary sale, or other proceedings for enforcement of any mortgage on the Leased Premises, Lessee shall be bound to such transferee (herein sometimes called the "Purchaser") under the terms, covenants, and conditions of this Lease for the balance of the term hereof remaining and any extensions or renewal hereof which may be effected in accordance with the terms and provisions hereof, with the same force and effect as if the Purchaser were the Lessor under this Lease, and Lessee does hereby agree to attorn to the Purchaser, including the mortgagee under any such mortgage, if it be the Purchaser, as its Lessor, said attornment to be effective and self-operative without the execution of any further instruments upon the Purchaser succeeding to the interest of the Lessor under this Lease. The respective rights and obligations of Lessee and the Purchaser upon such attornment, to the extent of the then remaining balance of the term of this Lease and any such extensions and renewals, shall be and are the same as those set forth herein.

Article 22
Default by Lessee

It shall be an event of default and shall be considered a breach of this Lease by Lessee if one or any of the following shall occur:

A. Lessee shall make default in the payment of rent or other payment when due as herein provided; and such default shall continue for a period of _ten_ (_10_) days or more; or default shall be made in any of the other covenants, agreements, conditions, or undertakings herein required to be kept, observed, and performed by Lessee, and such other default shall continue for _ten_ (_10_) days after notice thereof in writing to Lessee; or,

B. Lessee shall file a petition in voluntary or reorganization bankruptcy or under applicable Chapters of the Federal Bankruptcy Act or similar law, state or federal, whether now or hereafter existing, or an answer admitting insolvency or inability to pay its debts, or fail to obtain a vacation or stay of involuntary bankruptcy proceedings within _thirty_ (_30_) days as hereinafter provided; or,

C. Lessee shall be adjudicated a bankrupt, or a trustee or receiver shall be appointed for all of its property or the major part thereof in any involuntary proceedings, or any court shall have taken jurisdiction of the property of Lessee or the major part thereof in any involuntary proceedings for the reorganization, dissolution, liquidation, or winding up of Lessee, and such jurisdiction is not relinquished or vacated or stayed on appeal or otherwise within _thirty_ (_30_) days; or,

D. Lessee shall make an assignment for the benefit of its creditors, or shall vacate or abandon the Leased Premises.

Article 23
Remedies upon Default

If any one or more of the events of default set forth in Article 22 occurs, then Lessor may, at its election:

Give Lessee written notice of its intention to terminate this Lease on the date of such notice or on any later date specified in such notice, and, on the date specified in such notice, Lessee's right to possession of the Leased Premises will cease and the Lease will be terminated (except as to Lessee's liability set forth in this Article 23), as if the date fixed in such notice were the end of the term of this Lease. If this Lease is terminated pursuant to the provisions of this Article, Lessee will remain liable to Lessor for damages in an amount equal to the rent and other sums which would have been owing by Lessee under this Lease for the balance of the term if this Lease had not been terminated, less the net proceeds, if any, of any reletting of the premises by the Lessor subsequent to such termination, and after deduction of all Lessor's expenses set forth in the Lease. Lessor will be entitled to collect such damages from Lessee monthly on the days on which the rent and other amounts would have been payable under this Lease if this Lease had not been terminated, and Lessor will be entitled to receive such damages from Lessee on each such day. Alternatively, at the option of the Lessor, if this Lease is terminated, Lessor will be entitled to recover from Lessee.

i.   The worth at the time of award of the amount by which the unpaid rent that would have been earned after termination until the time of award exceeds the amount of such rent loss that Lessee proves could reasonably have been avoided;

ii. The worth at the time of award of the amount by which the unpaid rent for the balance of the term of this Lease after the time of award exceeds the amount of such rent loss that Lessee proves could reasonably be avoided; and

iii. Any other amount necessary to compensate Lessor for all the detriment proximately caused by Lessee's failure to perform its obligations under this Lease or which in the ordinary course of things would be likely to result from such failure. The "worth at the time of award" of the amount referred to in clauses (i) and (ii) is computed by allowing interest at the highest rate permitted by law. The worth at the time of award of the amount referred to in clause (iii) is computed by discounting such amount at the discount rate of the Federal Reserve Bank of Atlanta at the time of award,

iv. If Lessor elects to take possession of the premises according to this Lease paragraph without terminating this Lease, Lessee will pay Lessor the rent and other sums which would be payable under this Lease as if such repossession had not occurred, less the net proceeds, if any, of the reletting of the premises after deducting all of Lessor's expenses incurred in connection with such reletting, including, without limitation, all repossession costs, brokerage commissions, legal expenses, attorneys' fees, expenses of employees, alterations, remodeling and repair costs, and expenses of preparation for such reletting. If, in connection with any reletting, the new Lease term extends beyond the existing term, or the premises covered by such reletting include areas which are not part of the premises, a fair

apportionment of the rent received from such
reletting and the expenses incurred in connection
with such reletting will be made in determining the
net proceeds received from such reletting. In
addition, in determining the net proceeds from such
reletting, any rent concessions will be apportioned
over the term of the new Lease. Lessee will pay such
amounts to Lessor monthly on the days on which the
rent and all other amounts owing under this Lease
would have been payable if possession had not been
retaken, and Lessor will be entitled to receive the
rent and other amounts from Lessee on each such day.

Article 24
Waiver of Breach

Failure of Lessor to declare any default immediately upon
occurrence thereof, or delay in taking any action in connection
therewith, shall not waive such default, but Lessor shall have
the right to declare any such default at any time and take such
action as might be lawful or authorized hereunder, either in law
or in equity.

Article 25
Abandonment

In the event the Lease Premises are abandoned by Lessee,
Lessor shall have the right, but not the obligation, to relet the
same for the remainder of the term provided for herein and if the
rent received through such reletting does not at least equal the
rent provided for herein, Lessee shall pay and satisfy any
deficiency between the amount of the rent so provided for and
that received through reletting, and, in addition thereto, shall
pay all expenses incurred in connection with any such reletting,
including, but not limited to, the cost of renovation, altering,
and decorating for a new occupant. Nothing herein shall be
construed as in any way denying Lessor the right in the event of
abandonment of said Leased Premises or other breach of this
Agreement by Lessee to treat the same as an entire breach and, at
Lessor's option, to immediately sue for the entire breach of this
Agreement and any and all damages that Lessor suffers thereby.

Article 26
Holding Over

In the event of holding over by Lessee after the expiration or
termination of this Lease, such holdover shall be as a tenant at
will, and all of the terms and provisions of this Lease shall be
applicable during such period, except that Lessee shall pay
Lessor as rental for the period of such holdover an amount equal
to twice the rent which would have been payable by Lessee had
such holdover period been a part of the original term of this

Lease, and Lessee will vacate the Leased Premises and deliver the same to Lessor upon Lessee's receipt of notice from Lessor to vacate said Premises. The rental payable during such holdover period shall be payable to Lessor on demand. No holding over by Lessee shall operate to extend this Lease except as herein provided. Lessee agrees to pay Lessor's costs and reasonable attorneys' fees should Lessor expend monies for the removal of Lessee or any of Lessee's property.

Article 27
Attorneys' Fees

In the event Lessee makes default in the performance of any of the terms, covenants, agreements, or conditions contained in this Lease and Lessor places the enforcement of this Lease, or any part thereof, or the collection of any rent due or to become due hereunder, or recovery of the possession of the Leased Premises, in the hands of an attorney, or files suit upon the same, Lessee agrees to pay Lessor's costs and reasonable attorneys' fees for the services of such attorneys. The obligation of Lessee to pay such costs of collections including reasonable attorneys' fees shall apply whether or not suit be brought, and if suit be brought, then at both trial and appellate levels.

Article 28
Hold Harmless

Lessee agrees to defend, indemnify, and hold Lessor harmless against any and all claims, damages, accidents, and injuries to persons or property caused by or resulting from or in connection with anything in or pertaining to or upon the Leased Premises.

As a material part of the consideration to be rendered to Lessor under this Lease, Lessor shall not be liable for damage to property of Lessee or of others located on the Leased Premises or Building, nor for the loss of or damage to any property of Lessee or of others by theft, casualty loss, or otherwise, nor shall Lessor be liable to Lessee for losses arising from the inability of Lessee to operate its business for any reason whatsoever, and Lessee hereby waives all such claims against Lessor and will hold Lessor exempt and harmless for or on account of such damage or injury. Lessor shall not be liable for any injury or damage to persons or property resulting from (but not limited to) fire or explosion on any part of the Leased Premises or Building or from the pipes, appliances, or plumbing works or from the roof, street, or subsurface or from any place or by dampness or any other cause of whatsoever nature. Lessor shall not be liable for any such damage caused by other tenants or persons in the building, occupants of adjacent property, or the public, or caused by operations in construction of any private, public, or quasi-public work. All property of the Lessee kept or stored on the Leased Premises shall be so kept or stored at the risk of

Lessee, and Lessee shall hold Lessor harmless from any claims arising out of damage to the same, including subrogation claims by Lessee's insurance carriers.

Article 29
Lessor's Liability

The term "Lessor" as used in this Lease means only the owner from time to time of the Leased Premises. Lessor shall be under no personal liability with respect to any of the provisions of this Lease, and if Lessor is in default with respect to its obligations hereunder, Lessee shall look solely to the equity of the Lessor in the Leased Premises and Building for the satisfaction of the Lessee's remedies. It is expressly understood and agreed that the Lessor's liability under this Lease shall in no event exceed the loss of its equity interest in the Leased Premises.

Article 30
Force Majeure

Lessor shall be excused for the period of any delay in the performance of any obligation when the delay is a result of any cause or causes beyond its control, which includes but is not limited to all labor disputes, governmental regulations or control, fire or other casualty, or inability to obtain any material, services, or financing.

Article 31
Notice

All rent and other payments required to be made by Lessee to Lessor hereunder shall be payable to Lessor at the address set forth below, or such other address as Lessor may specify from time to time, by written notice delivered in accordance herewith. Unless otherwise provided to the contrary herein, any notice or document required or permitted to be delivered hereunder shall be deemed to be delivered (whether or not actually received) when deposited in the United States mail, postage prepaid, Certified Mail, Return Receipt Requested, addressed to the Parties hereto at the respective addresses set out opposite their names below, or at such other address as they have theretofore specified by written notice delivered in accordance herewith:

Lessor: *High Point Management*
332 Forest Drive
Orlando, FL 32804

Lessee: *Jeff Parks*
21 E. Nova Street
Orlando, FL 32858L

Article 32
Estoppel Certificates

Lessee accepts this Lease subject and subordinate to any mortgage now or at any time hereafter constituting a lien or charge upon the Leased Premises. Lessee shall, on demand, execute any instrument which may be required by any mortgagee for the purpose of subjecting and subordinating this Lease to the lien of any such mortgage or deed of trust.

Upon three (3) days prior written notice from Lessor, Lessee shall execute and deliver to Lessor a statement in writing (1) certifying that this Lease is unmodified and in full force and effect, and dates to which the rent and other charges are paid in advance, if any, and (2) acknowledging that to Lessee's knowledge there are not any uncured defaults on the part of Lessor hereunder and that Lessee has no right of offset, counterclaim, or deduction in rent or specifying such defaults, if any, or claim, together with the amount of any offset, counterclaim, or deduction alleged by Lessee. Any such statement may be relied upon by any prospective purchaser or lender upon the security of the real property of which the Leased Premises are a part. Lessee's failure to deliver said statement within such time shall constitute agreement by Lessee (1) that this Lease is in full force and effect without modification except as may be represented by Lessor, (2) that there are no uncured defaults in Lessor's performance and that Lessee has no right of offset, counterclaim, or deduction against rent, and (3) that no more than one month's rent has been paid in advance.

Article 33
Liens for Rents

As security for Lessee's payment of rent and all other payments required to be made by Lessee hereunder (including, by way of illustration only, excess taxes, damage to the Leased Premises, court costs, and attorneys' fees), Lessee hereby grants to Lessor a lien upon all property of Lessee now or hereafter located upon the Leased Premises. If default is made by Lessee in the payment of any sum which may become due hereunder and said sum is not paid within _ten_ (_10_) days after written notice is given by Lessor to Lessee for Lessee's default, Lessor may enter upon the Leased Premises and take possession of said property, or any part thereof, and may sell all or part of such property at public or private sale in one or successive sales, with or without notice, to the highest bidder for cash and on behalf of Lessee. Lessor may sell and convey such property, or any part thereof, to such bidder, delivering to such bidder all of Lessee's title and interest in such property sold to him. The proceeds of such sale shall be applied by Lessor toward the costs thereof and then toward the payment of all sums then due by Lessee to Lessor hereunder.

Article 34
Security Agreement

As additional security for the performance of the covenants and obligations herein contained by the Lessee to be performed, the Lessee hereby grants to the Lessor a security interest in all of Lessee's personal property, tangible and intangible. This security interest shall be subordinate to the lien of any chattel mortgage, collateral assignment, or security interest given by Lessee to any such Uniform Commercial Code forms as may be requested by Lessor, and that all remedies afforded by the Uniform Commercial Code in the event of default shall be available to Lessor. If Lessee is in default under this Lease, such personal property shall not be removed from the Leased Premises (except to the extent such property is replaced with an item of equal or greater value) without the written consent of Lessor. It is intended by the parties hereto that this instrument shall have the effect of a security agreement covering such personal property, and the Lessor, upon the occurrence of an event of default, may exercise any rights of a secured party under the Uniform Commercial Code of the state of _Florida_ , including the right to take possession of such personal property and to sell the same at public or private sale, and out of the money derived therefrom, pay the amount due Lessor and all costs arising out of the execution of the provisions of this section, paying the surplus, if any, to Lessee. If such personal property, or any portion thereof, shall be offered at a public sale, Lessor may become a purchaser thereof.

Article 35
Common Area Usage

Should Lessee purchase or lease security, telephone, communications, electronic, or any other kind of equipment, then said equipment shall not be installed, placed, or stored in any common areas of the Park or Building. Should Lessee place any such equipment or any kind of personal property in said common areas, then Lessor, at his election, may remove said personal property at Lessee's expense.

Article 36
Floor Loads

Lessee shall not place a load upon the floor of the Leased Premises which exceeds the floor load per square foot which such floor was designed to carry. Floor load is stipulated to be _70_ pounds per square foot. Lessor and Lessee will determine jointly the approximate weight and the position of all safes and heavy installations which the Lessee wishes to place in the Leased Premises so as to distribute properly the weight thereof.

Business machines and mechanical equipment belonging to Lessee which cause noise and/or vibration that may be transmitted to the structure of the Building or to any leased space to such a degree as to be objectionable to Lessor or to any tenants in the Building shall be placed and maintained by the party owning the machines or equipment, at such party's expense, in a setting of cork, rubber, or springs-type noise and/or vibration eliminators sufficient to eliminate vibration and/or noise.

Article 37
General

A. This Lease shall be binding and inure to the benefit of the Parties hereto and their respective heirs, personal representatives, successors, and assigns.

B. This Lease shall create the relationship of Lessor and Lessee. No estate shall pass out of the Lessor, and the Lessee shall have only a right of use which shall not be subject to levy and sale.

C. The submission of this instrument for examination or signature by the Lessee does not constitute a reservation of or an option for lease, and it is not effective as a lease or otherwise until execution and delivery by both Lessor and Lessee.

D. Lessor shall have the right to transfer and assign, in whole or in part, all of its rights and obligations hereunder in the Building and/or Leased Premises referred to herein.

E. The captions or headings of the various Articles in this Lease Agreement are for convenience only, and are not to be construed as part of this Lease, and shall not be construed as defining or limiting in any way the scope or intent of the provisions hereof.

F. Time is of the essence of this Lease Agreement.

G. Any pronouns used in the Lease shall be deemed to include the masculine, feminine, neuter, singular, and plural as appropriate.

H. This instrument embodies the whole agreement between the Parties, and there are no promises, terms, conditions, or obligations other than those herein contained. This agreement shall supersede all previous communications, representations, proposals, or agreements, either verbal or written, between the parties hereto and not herein contained. This agreement shall not be modified or canceled unless reduced in writing and signed by both parties, properly witnessed, and by direct reference therein made a part hereof.

I. If any term, covenant, condition, or provision of the Lease or the application thereof to any person or circumstance shall, at any time or to any extent, be invalid or unenforceable, the remainder of this Lease shall not be affected thereby, and each term, covenant, condition, and provision of this Lease shall be valid and be enforced to the fullest extent of the law. This Lease and the performance thereof shall be governed, interpreted, construed, and regulated by the laws of the state of _Florida_ , and the venue of any action shall lie in _Orange_ County, _Florida_ .

J. The Parties hereto further understand and agree that this Lease shall not be recorded in any Public Records of _Orange_ County, _Florida_ , except at the option of the Lessor. The Parties also agree, at the option of the Lessor, to execute a short-form lease for recording, containing the names of the parties and such other terms and conditions of the Lease as may be requested by the Lessor.

K. To the extent permitted by applicable law, Lessor and Lessee hereby waive trial by jury in any action, proceeding, or counterclaim brought by either against the other on any matter whatsoever arising out of or in any way connected with this Lease, the relationship of Lessor and Lessee, or Lessee's use or occupancy of the Leased Premises, or any emergency or other statutory remedy with respect hereto.

Article 39
Signature Page

IN WITNESS WHEREOF, the Parties hereto have executed this Lease Agreement on the day and year first above written.

Signed, sealed, and delivered in the presence of:

High Point Management, Inc.
Lessor

Kathleen Shuman   By _Bart Thomas_
Witness   Authorized Representative

Sarah Barrett
Witness

Greg Taylor   _Creative Marketing, Inc._
Witness   Lessee

Chris Johnson   By _Jeff Parks, President_
Witness   Authorized Representative

Exhibit A   Sign Site Plan
Exhibit B   Site Plan

Building Rules and Regulations

The following Rules and Regulations have been adopted by the owners for the care and protection of the building located in _High Point Center_ , and for the general comfort and welfare of all occupants.

1. Wherever Tenant is obligated under these Rules and Regulations to do or refrain from doing an act or thing, such obligation shall include the exercise by Tenant of its best efforts to secure compliance with such obligation by the servants, employees, contractors, jobbers, agents, invitees, licensees, guests, sublessees, and visitors of Lessee. The term "Building" shall include the structure within which the Leased Premises is located, and any obligations of Tenant hereunder with regard to the Building shall apply with equal force to the Leased Premises and to other parts of the Building.

2. Tenant shall not obstruct or interfere with the rights of other occupants in the Building, or of persons having business in the Building in which the Leased Premises are located, or in any way injure or annoy such persons.

3. Tenant shall not use the Leased Premises or the Building for lodging, sleeping, cooking, or any immoral or illegal purposes, or for any purpose that will damage the building, or the reputation thereof, or for any purpose other than those specified in the Lease.

4. Canvassing, soliciting, and peddling in the Building are prohibited, and Tenant shall cooperate to prevent such activities.

5. Tenant shall not bring or keep within the Building any animal or motorcycle.

6. Tenant shall not conduct mechanical or manufacturing operations, cook or prepare food, or place in use any inflammable, combustible, explosive, or hazardous fluid, chemical device, substance, or material in or about the Leased Premises or the Building without the prior written consent of Landlord. Tenant shall comply with all rules, orders, regulations, and requirements of the applicable Fire Rating Bureau, or any other similar body, and Tenant shall not commit any act or permit any object to be brought or kept in Leased Premises or the Building which shall increase the rate of fire insurance on the Building or on property located therein.

7. Tenant shall not use the Leased Premises or Building for the storage of goods, wares, or merchandise, except as such storage may be incidental to the use of the Leased Premises for general office purposes. Tenant shall not occupy the Leased Premises or permit any portion of the Leased Premises to be occupied for the manufacture or direct sale of liquor, narcotics, or tobacco in any form.

Tenant shall not conduct in or about the Leased Premises or Building any auction, public or private, without the prior written approval of Landlord.

8. Tenant shall not install or use in the Leased Premises or Building any engine, boiler, generator, heating unit, air conditioning unit (other than the air conditioning and heating unit Landlord provides), stove, water cooler, ventilator, radiator, or any other similar apparatus without the prior written consent of Landlord.

9. Tenant shall not use in the Leased Premises or Building any machines, other than standard office machines such as typewriters, calculators, copying machines, computers, and similar machines, without prior written approval of the Landlord. All office equipment and any other device of any electrical or mechanical nature shall be placed by Landlord in the Leased Premises in settings so as to absorb or prevent any vibration, noise, or annoyance. Tenant shall not cause improper noises, vibrations, or odors within the Building.

10. Tenant shall not install, place, or store any security, telephone, or communication equipment in any common areas of the Project or Building. Should Tenant place such equipment or any kind of personal property in the common areas in the Project or Building without the prior written consent of Landlord, then Landlord, at his election, may remove said personal property at Tenant's expense.

11. Tenant shall move all freight, supplies, furniture, fixtures, and other personal property into, within, and out of the Building only at such times and through such entrances as may be designated by Landlord, and such movement of such items shall be under the supervision of Landlord. Landlord reserves the right to inspect all such freight, supplies, furniture, fixtures, and other personal property to be brought into the Building and to exclude from the Building all such objects which violate any of these Rules and Regulations. Tenant shall not move or install such objects in or about the Building in such a fashion as to unreasonably obstruct the activities of the other occupants, and all such moving shall be at the sole expense, risk, and responsibility of Tenant. Tenant shall not use in the delivery, receipt, or other movement of freight, supplies, furniture, fixtures, and other personal property to, from, or within the Building, any hand trucks other than those equipped with rubber tires and side guards.

12. Tenant shall not place within the Building any safes, copying machines, computer equipment, or other objects of unusual size or weight without the prior written consent of Landlord. The placement and positioning of all such

objects within the Building shall be prescribed by Landlord, and such objects shall, in all cases, be placed upon plates or footings of such size as shall be prescribed by Landlord.

13. Tenant shall not deposit any trash, refuge, cigarettes, or other substances of any kind within or out of the Building except in the refuse containers provided therefor. Tenant shall not introduce into the Building any substance which might add an undue burden to the cleaning or maintenance of the Leased Premises or the Building. Tenant shall exercise its best efforts to keep the sidewalks, entrances, passages, courts, lobby areas, parking areas, stairways, vestibules, public corridors, and halls in and about the Building (hereinafter referred to as "Common Areas") clean and free from rubbish.

14. Tenant shall use the Common Areas only as a means of ingress and egress, and Tenant shall permit no loitering by any persons upon Common Areas. Common Areas and the roof of the Building are not for the use of the general public, and Landlord shall in all cases retain the right to control or prevent access thereto by all persons whose presence, in the judgment of Landlord, shall be detrimental to the Building and/or its tenants. Tenant shall not enter the mechanical room, air conditioning rooms, electrical closets, janitorial closets, or similar areas or go upon the roof of the Building without the prior written consent of Landlord, unless such areas shall have been designated as part of the Leased Premises.

15. Tenant shall not use the washrooms, rest rooms, and plumbing fixtures of the Building, if any, and appurtenances thereto, for any purpose other than the purposes for which they were constructed, and Tenants shall not deposit any sweepings, rubbish, rags, or other improper substances therein. Tenant shall not waste water by interfering or tampering with the faucets or otherwise. If Tenant or Tenant's servants, employees, agents, contractors, jobbers, licensees, invitees, guests, or visitors cause any damage to such washrooms, rest rooms, plumbing fixtures, or appurtenances, such damage shall be repaired at Tenant's expense and Landlord shall not be responsible therefor.

16. Tenant shall not mark, paint, drill into, cut, string wires, or in any way deface any part of the Building without the prior written consent of Landlord. Upon removal of any wall decorations or installations of floor coverings by Tenant, any damage to the walls or floors shall be repaired by Tenant at Tenant's sole cost and expense. Tenant shall refer all contractors, representatives, installations technicians, and other

mechanics, artisans, and laborers rendering any service in connection with the repair, maintenance, or improvement of the Leased Premises to Landlord for Landlord's supervision, approval, and control before performance of any such service. This Paragraph 16 shall apply to all work performed in the building, including, without limitation, installation of the telephones, telegraph equipment, electrical devices, and attachments and installations of any nature affecting floor, walls, woodwork, trim, windows, ceilings, equipment, or any structural portion of the Building. Plans and specifications for such work, prepared at Tenant's sole expense, shall be submitted to Landlord for its prior written approval in each instance before commencement of work. All installations, alterations, and additions shall be constructed by Tenant in a good and workmanlike manner, and only good grades of material shall be used in connection therewith. The means by which telephone, telegraph, and similar wires are to be introduced to the Leased Premises and the location of telephones, call boxes, and other office equipment affixed to the Leased Premises shall be subject to the prior written approval of Landlord.

17. Tenant shall not obstruct, alter, or in any way impair the efficient operation of the Leased Premises' heating, ventilating, air conditioning, electrical, fire, safety, or lighting systems.

18. Subject to applicable fire or other safety regulations, all doors opening onto Common Areas and all doors upon the perimeters of the Leased Premises shall be kept closed and, during nonbusiness hours, locked, except when in use for ingress or egress. If Tenant uses the Leased Premises after regular business hours or on nonbusiness days, Tenant shall lock any entrance doors to the Building used by Tenant immediately after using such doors.

19. Employees of the Landlord or the Building Association ("Association") shall not receive or carry messages for or to Tenant or any other person, nor contact with nor render free or paid services to Tenant or Tenant's servants, employees, contractors, jobbers, agents, invitees, licensees, guests, or visitors. In the event that any of Landlord's or Association's employees perform any such services, such employees shall be deemed to be the agents of Tenant regardless of whether or how payment is arranged for such services, and Tenant hereby indemnifies and holds Landlord or Association harmless from any and all liability in connection with any such services and any associated injury or damage to property or injury or death to personal resulting therefrom.

20. No radio or television aerial or other similar device shall be installed without first obtaining Landlord's consent in writing on each separate instance. No aerial shall be erected on the roof or exterior walls of the Building, or on the grounds, without in each instance the written consent of Landlord. Any aerial so installed without such written consent shall be subject to removal without notice at any time.
21. No loudspeaker, televisions, phonographs, radios, or other devices shall be used in a manner so as to be heard or seen outside of the Leased Premises without prior written consent of Landlord.

Acknowledgment of Receipt

The undersigned hereby acknowledges receipt of a complete copy of the foregoing Rules and Regulations.

By *Jeff Parks, President*
Authorized Representative for
Creative Marketing, Inc.

Commercial Lease Agreement

THIS LEASE AGREEMENT, is made and entered into as of this
_____ day of _____ , 199 ___ , by and between
_____ (Lessor) of _____ , city of _____ , state of
_____ , and _____ (Lessee) of _____ , city of
_____ , state of _____ . The aforementioned shall
hereinafter jointly be referred to as the "PARTIES."

WITNESSETH:

Article 1
Leased Premises

In consideration of the rents herein provided and the terms,
provisions and covenants hereof, Lessor hereby leases, lets and
demises to Lessee the following described premises (hereinafter
referred to as the "Leased Premises"): _____

Approximately _____ square feet of gross rentable area,
and more particularly described in Exhibit "B" attached. Lessee
hereby unequivocally acknowledges by execution of this Lease
Agreement that the aforementioned square feet of gross rentable
area may include Lessee's pro rata share of common areas shared
by other tenants. In such event, Lessee may be actually occupying
less than _____ square feet; however, it shall not be
construed that Lessee is in any way relieved of paying rent
pursuant to Article 3 herein.

Exhibits

_____
_____
_____
_____ .

Article 2
Term

Subject to and upon the conditions set forth herein, and in
any exhibit or addendum hereto, the term of this Lease
(hereinafter referred to as the "Lease Term") shall commence on
_____ , 199 ___ (hereinafter referred to as the
"Commencement Date"), and shall continue for _____ months
until _____ , 199 ___ , at which time this lease shall
expire. Immediately upon said date of termination of this Lease,
Lessee shall voluntarily surrender the Leased Premises to Lessor.

Article 3
Rent

Lessee agrees to pay in advance to Lessor during the Term hereof, without deduction, setoff, prior notice, or demand, monthly rental (hereinafter referred to as the "Base Monthly Rental") for the Leased Premises in the amount of: _____ dollars, which amount shall be payable in advance on the first business day of each month of the Lease Term. Payment of such rent shall be accompanied by all sales tax levied by any federal, state, county, or city government or by any agency authorized to levy and collect rent tax, and shall be payable in lawful money of the United States of America to Lessor at the address of Lessor set forth below. The amount of the monthly installments set forth above shall be subject to escalation, and additional rent shall be due and payable from Lessee to Lessor, as hereinafter provided. Other remedies for nonpayment of rent under this Lease notwithstanding, if the rental payment is not received by Lessor on or before _____ (_____) days after such rent is due, a service charge of _____ percent (_____ %) of the rent then due shall become due and payable on demand in addition to the rent owed under this Lease as remuneration for the additional expense for handling late rentals.

Article 4
Rental Adjustment: Consumer Price Index

On the first day of the second lease year (which "lease year" shall commence on the first anniversary of the Commencement Date if the Commencement Date is the first day of a calendar month, or on the first day of the first calendar month following the anniversary of the Commencement Date if the Commencement Date is other than the first day of a calendar month), and on the first day of each lease year (including renewals of this Lease Agreement, if any) thereafter until this Lease is terminated as set forth herein, the Base Annual Rent shall be adjusted and changed, on a cumulative basis, as follows:

The Base Annual Rent and the monthly rental installments payable for each lease year during the Lease Term (other than the first lease year) shall be computed by multiplying the Base Annual Rental (and the monthly rental installment) as set forth in Article 3 above by a fraction, the numerator of which shall be the Consumer Price Index ("Urban," the United States city average for urban wage earners, all items [Base 1982-84 = 100], issued by the Bureau of Labor Statistics of the United States Department of Labor) for the second (2nd) full month prior to the Commencement Date of this Lease; provided, however, that in no event shall such increase in Annual Rent be less than _____ percent (_____ %) throughout the Lease Term.

In the event that the Consumer Price Index ceases to use the 1982-84 average of one hundred (100) as the basis of calculation, or if a change is made in the terms of particular items contained in the Consumer Price Index, then the Consumer Price Index shall, at the discretion of the Lessor, be adjusted to the figure that would have been arrived at had the change in the manner of computing the Consumer Price Index in effect at the commencement of the Lease Term not been affected. In the event that such Consumer Price Index (or successor or substitute Consumer Price Index) is not available, a reliable governmental or other nonpartisan publication evaluating the purchasing power of money may be used at the discretion of Lessor.

Article 5
Security Deposit

The Lessee agrees to pay a security deposit equal to _____ ($ _____) upon the beginning of the lease. Unless required under state law, the security deposit will be released to the Lessor, who shall not be required to maintain it in a separate account nor be charged interest thereon.

The security deposit shall be used by the lessor to pay for any damage caused by the Lessee during his occupancy, reasonable wear and tear excepted. In addition, the security deposit may also be used to offset monetary damage of unpaid rent or unpaid late fees.

Article 6
Quiet Enjoyment

The Lessor covenants and agrees that Lessee, on paying said monthly rent and performing all the covenants of this Lease on the part of Lessee to be performed herein, shall and may peaceably and quietly hold and enjoy the said Leased Premises.

Article 7
Operating Expense Adjustments

It is understood that the Annual Rent specified in Articles 3 and 4 is in anticipation of Lessor incurring certain expenses for taxes, operations, and maintenance costs. Therefore, the Lessor and Lessee agree to the definitions and terms set forth below:

A. Real Estate Taxes: Lessor shall pay real estate taxes imposed on the Leased Premises. Lessee shall reimburse Lessor for any increase in real estate taxes imposed on the Leased Premises over and above the amount of these taxes for the calendar year _____ . Said increase shall be payable on or before _____ (_____) days after receipt of notice of the amount from Lessor. The term "real estate taxes" shall include all ad valorem taxes and general and special assessments levied against the Leased Premises. Lessee shall be responsible for all taxes levied on Lessee's personal property.

B. Utility Service: Lessor shall provide the standard utility service connections for water, sewer, electricity, and telephone into the Leased Premises. Lessee shall pay the cost of all utility services for the Leased Premises, including but not limited to initial connection charges and/or deposits, all charges for water, sewer, telephone, and electricity, and all replacement of electric light lamps, tubes, and ballasts used on or in connection with the Leased Premises. The Lessee's pro rata share of the entire building is _____ percent. Failure by the Lessor to make available these services, or any cessation thereof, resulting from causes beyond the control of the Lessor, shall neither render Lessor liable in any respect for damages to either person or property, nor relieve Lessee from fulfillment of any covenant of this Lease. Should any of the equipment or machinery, under the control of the Lessor, necessary to provide such services break down, or for any cause cease to function properly, Lessor shall use reasonable diligence to repair the same properly.

C. Repairs and Maintenance: The Lessor and Lessee shall maintain the Building and the Leased Premises in good repair and condition according to the following schedule:

Mechanical, Heating, Ventilation, and Air Conditioning: Lessor shall be responsible for all major maintenance and repairs to the mechanical, heating, air conditioning, and ventilation systems; provided, however, that Lessee shall pay the first $ _____ per occurrence (for items not protected by service warranties) for all maintenance and repairs of such systems within the Leased Premises or Lessee's pro rata share of the total building if appropriate. Lessor shall supply and change all air conditioning filters as required. Lessee shall reimburse to Lessor the cost of supplying and changing such filters within thirty (30) days of receiving bill from Lessor.

Plumbing and Electrical: Lessor shall be responsible for all major repairs and maintenance of the plumbing and electrical systems; provided, however, that Lessee shall pay the first $ _____ per occurrence (for items not protected by service contracts or warranties) for maintenance and repairs of such systems within the Leased Premises or Lessee's pro rata share of Building if the cost of such repair and maintenance shall be billed to the Building as a whole.

Interior Maintenance: Lessee shall clean, provide cleaning supplies, and maintain the Leased Premises in a clean, sanitary, and good condition. Lessee shall make all needed repairs, including but not limited to interior pest control, and replacements to the interior of the Leased Premises, except for those responsibilities expressly imposed upon Lessor above. Lessee shall maintain and repair all interior glass.

Common Area Maintenance Charges: Lessee shall pay its pro rata share of the common area charges. Said charges are assessed by Lessor to pay for maintenance, repairs, and replacements, as necessary, to include, but not be limited to, the maintenance of common streets, drives, street lighting, landscaping, swale and berm maintenance, common area irrigation, fountains, walls, parking lot maintenance, refuse service, building exteriors and roofs, et cetera. The Lessee's pro rata share of common area maintenance charges shall be computed by multiplying the total common area maintenance charges by a fraction, the numerator of which shall be the Lessee's _____ square feet and the denominator of which shall be _____ (the total number of square feet of office buildings for which certificates of occupancy have been issued in the building). Payment shall be made monthly by Lessee within _____ (_____) days after Lessee receives notice from Lessor showing the sum due, which notice shall state in reasonable detail the manner in which Lessee's share of common area maintenance is computed. Lessee has the obligation to pay for any partial month at the commencement and expiration or termination of the Lease Term.

D. Insurance: Lessor shall pay for fire and extended coverage insurance for the Leased Premises. Lessee shall reimburse Lessor for any increase in the cost of insurance that Lessor is responsible to carry on the Leased Premises, over and above the insurance cost for the calendar year _____ . Reimbursement shall be made by Lessee within _____ (_____) days after Lessee receives notice from Lessor showing the sum due, which notice shall state in reasonable detail the manner in which Lessee's share of insurance costs is computed. Lessee shall not be obligated to reimburse Lessor for any portion of any increase in the insurance premium caused by a particular use or activity of any other tenant in the Building in which the Leased Premises is located. Lessee's obligation to pay the insurance costs shall be prorated for any partial year at the commencement and expiration or termination of the lease term. Lessee shall provide fire and extended coverage insurance on its personal property and contents.

Article 8
Alterations and Improvements

Lessee shall not make or allow to be made any alterations or physical additions in or to the Leased Premises without first obtaining the written consent of Lessor, which consent may be withheld at the sole discretion of Lessor for any reason. Any and all such alterations, physical additions, or improvements to the Leased Premises, when made by Lessee, shall at once become the property of Lessor and shall be surrendered to Lessor upon the termination of this Lease, by lapse of time or otherwise; provided, however, this clause shall not apply to movable equipment, partitions, or furniture owned by Lessee, which may be removed by Lessee at the end of the term of this Lease if Lessee is not then in default and if such equipment, partitions, and furniture are not then subject to any other rights, liens, and interests of Lessor hereunder. All damages to the Leased Premises caused by or becoming evident by the removal of such movable equipment, furniture, or partitions or otherwise shall be repaired by Lessee at Lessee's cost prior to surrender of the Leased Premises.

Article 9
Liens

It is expressly covenanted and agreed by and between the Parties hereto that nothing contained in this Lease shall authorize Lessee to do any act which shall in any way encumber the title of Lessor in and to the Building or the land upon which the Building is situated, nor shall the interest or estate of Lessor in the Leased Premises be in any way subject to any claim by way of lien or encumbrance, whether by operation of law or by virtue of any express or implied contract by Lessee, and any claim to or lien upon the Leased Premises arising from any act or omission of Lessee shall accrue only against the leasehold estate of Lessee and shall in all respects be subject and subordinate to the paramount title and right of Lessor in and to the Leased Premises. Lessee will not permit the Leased Premises to become subject to any mechanics', laborers', or materialmen's lien on account of labor or material furnished to Lessee or any sublessee in connection with work of any character performed or claimed to have been performed on the Leased Premises by or at the direction or sufferance of Lessee; provided, however, that Lessee shall have the right to contest in good faith and with reasonable diligence the validity of any such lien or claimed lien if Lessee shall give to Lessor such reasonable security as may be demanded by Lessor to ensure payment to prevent any sale, foreclosure, or forfeiture of the Leased Premises by reason of nonpayment thereof. On final determination of the lien or claim for lien, Lessee will immediately pay any judgment rendered with all proper costs and charges and will at its own expense have the lien released and any judgment satisfied. In case Lessee shall fail to contest the validity of any lien or claimed lien and give security to Lessor to ensure payment thereof, or having commenced to contest the same, and having given such security, shall fail to prosecute such contest with diligence, or shall fail to have the same released and satisfy any judgment rendered thereon, then

Lessor may, at its election and without any requirement that it do so, remove or discharge such lien or claim for lien (with the right in its discretion to settle or compromise the same), and any amounts advanced by Lessor for such purposes shall be so much additional rental due from Lessee to Lessor on demand, with interest at the highest rate allowed by law from the date of payment thereof by Lessor until the repayment thereof by Lessee to Lessor.

Article 10
Fire and Casualty

If the Leased Premises shall be injured or damaged by fire or other causes and should Lessor elect to make repairs to the Leased Premises and complete said repairs within _____ (_____) days of the damage, then this Lease shall not be terminated. Should Lessor elect not to rebuild, it may terminate this Lease by written notice to Lessee. In either event, Lessor shall give Lessee written notice of its intention to rebuild or terminate this Lease within _____ (_____) days after the event that causes said injury or damage. In no event shall Lessor be liable to Lessee in any respect whatsoever for Lessee's inability to operate its business as a result of any casualty, including but not limited to injury or damage to the Leased Premises caused by fire or other causes.

Lessee shall carry a work/rental interruption insurance policy covering risk of loss due to casualty in an amount not less than the aggregate amount to be paid by Lessee to Lessor or to a third party under the terms and provisions of this Lease, including but not limited to rent, real property taxes, and common area maintenance charges, for a period of _____ (_____) months following any occurrence of the said casualty.

Article 11
Liability Insurance

Lessee agrees to carry at its own expense a Lessor/Lessee's Liability Insurance policy from a company satisfactory to Lessor, with minimum limits for general public liability insurance for personal injury including death in the amount of
_____ dollars ($ _____) and
_____ dollars ($ _____) for each occurrence, with _____ dollars ($ _____) umbrella coverage, and for property damage insurance a single limit of not less than _____ dollars ($ _____) for each occurrence; such insurance shall be for the joint benefit of Lessor and Lessee and shall name Lessor as an additional insured.

Irrespective of the adequacy of said insurance, Lessee shall indemnify and save Lessor free and harmless from any and all claims, actions, damages, expenses (including without limitation reasonable attorneys' fees), and liability whatsoever arising out of or in any way connected with injury (including death) or property damage to any person, firm, corporation, or other entity, including Lessor, arising directly or indirectly from being on the Leased Premises or the use or occupancy of said Leased Premises.

Copies of all the Lessee's required insurance policies shall be delivered to Lessor prior to occupancy of the Leased Premises. On an annual basis, the Lessee shall provide Lessor with a Certificate of Insurance reflecting the types of policies held, their amounts, and the Lessor's interest as loss payee. Lessee agrees that every insurer shall agree by endorsement upon the policy(ies) issued by it, that it will give Lessor _____ (_____) days written notice at the address where rental is paid before the policy(ies) is question shall be altered or canceled.

Article 12
Waiver of Subrogation

Anything in this Lease to the contrary notwithstanding, the Lessee hereby waives any and all rights of recovery, claim, action, or cause of action against Lessor, his agents, offices, and employees, for any loss or damage that may occur to the Leased Premises hereby demised, or any improvements thereto, or personal property located therein, or said Building of which the Leased Premises are part, or any other cause which could be insured against under the terms of standard fire and extended coverage insurance policies, regardless of cause or origin, including negligence of the Parties hereto, their agents, officers, and employees. Lessee agrees to make best efforts to have its insurance company waive its subrogation rights under all policies.

Article 13
Condemnation

Lessee agrees that if the said Leased Premises, or any part thereof, shall be taken or condemned for public or quasi-public use or purpose by any authority, Lessee shall have no claim against the Lessor and shall not have any claim or right to any portion of the amount that may be awarded to the Lessee as damages or paid as a result of such condemnation; all the rights of the Lessee to damages thereof, if any, are hereby assigned by the Lessee to the Lessor. If the condemnation or taking is for the entire Leased Premises, the term of the Lease shall cease and terminate from the date of such governmental taking or condemnation, and the Lessee shall have no claim against the Lessor for the value of any unexpired term of this Lease. Should the taking or condemnation be for a part of the Leased Premises, then at the sole option of the Lessor, this Lease shall not cease and terminate, but continue in full force and effect.

Article 14
Usage of Leased Premises

The Leased Premises are to be occupied and used by the Lessee for office(s) and for no other purpose. Use for any other purpose shall constitute a breach of this Lease. Lessee shall not occupy or use, or permit any portion of the Leased Premises to be occupied or used, for any business or purpose which is unlawful, disreputable, or deemed by Lessor to be extrahazardous, or permit anything to be done which in any way will increase the rate of insurance coverage on said Leased Premises, and in the event that, by reason of such acts of Lessee, there shall be any increase in the insurance rates for the building or contents above normal rates, Lessee agrees to pay to Lessor upon receipt of notice, as additional rental, an amount equal to all such increase. Lessee shall conduct its business and control its agents, employees, invitees, and visitors in such a manner as not to create any nuisance, or interfere with, annoy, or disturb any other Lessee, Lessor, or any other party involved in the management of the Building.

Article 15
Compliance with Laws, Regulations, and Restrictions

Lessee shall comply with all laws, ordinances, orders, rules, and regulations (state, federal, municipal and other agencies, or bodies having any jurisdiction thereof) relating to the use, condition, or occupancy of the Leased Premises. Lessee shall indemnify and save and hold Lessor harmless from Lessee's violation of any laws and ordinances. Lessee shall comply with all Building Rules and Regulations of the Building as shown in Exhibit _____.

Article 16
Lessor's Right of Entry

Lessee shall permit Lessor or its agents or representatives to enter into and upon any part of the Leased Premises, at all reasonable hours, to inspect the same, to clean or make repairs, alterations, or additions thereto, as Lessor in its opinion may deem necessary or desirable, or for the purpose of determining Lessee's use thereof or whether an act of default under this Lease has occurred.

Article 17
Parking

Lessor shall provide nonexclusive parking for the benefit of Lessee, its employees, customers, and visitors and for the benefit of other owners and tenants, in the areas shown on the Site Plan attached hereto as Exhibit _____ . Lessor has provided and Lessee exclusively designated for certain owners and Lessees. _____ exclusive parking spaces per One Thousand (1,000) square feet of leasable area (within the Leased Premises) throughout the term of this lease.

Article 18
Signs and Advertising

The Lessee shall have sign space on the following signs (see Exhibit _____ , Sign Site Plan, for location of signs):

A. Building (Lessee) Identification Sign located near the Building.

B. Sign at the entrance to the Leased Premises.

All of the signs are to be in conformity with the building Sign Regulations (see Exhibit _____) and the county of _____ Sign Regulations. No other advertising or signs shall be placed by Lessee so as to be visible from the exterior of the Leased Premises without the prior consent and design approval of the Lessor. Any such signs and advertising shall be placed where designated by the Lessor and installed by Lessor at Lessee's expense. The cost of constructing and placing any exterior sign or signs shall be at Lessee's expense.

Article 19
Assignment or Sublease

The Lessee covenants and agrees not to encumber or assign this Lease or sublet all or any part (including desk space or mailing privileges) of the Leased Premises without the written consent of the Lessor, which consent may be withheld by Lessor. Such assignment shall in no way relieve the Lessee from any obligations, covenants, and provisions of this Lease. If Lessor grants its consent to an assignment or subletting, rent under this Lease shall thereafter be the greater of (a) the rent payable as per terms and conditions of this Lease, or (b) the rent payable by the Assignee or Subtenant (including any consideration paid by Assignee or Subtenant).

In no event shall Lessee assign or sublet the Leased Premises for any terms, conditions, and covenants other than those contained herein. In no event shall this Lease be assigned or be assignable by operation of Law or by voluntary or involuntary bankruptcy proceedings or otherwise, and in no event shall this lease or any rights or privileges hereunder be an asset of Lessee under any bankruptcy, insolvency, or reorganizational proceedings. Lessor shall not be liable nor shall the Leased Premises be subject to any mechanics', materialmen's, or other type liens, and Lessee shall keep the Leased Premises and land on which the Leased Premises are situated free from any such liens which may occur because of acts of Lessee, notwithstanding any foregoing provision.

Any consent to any subletting or assignment shall not be deemed a consent to any subsequent subletting or assignment. Any assignee, transferee, or purchaser shall agree in writing to be bound by and comply with the provisions of this Lease.

Article 20
Mortgaging of Lessor's Estate

The Lessor shall have the right, at any time or from time to time during the continuance of this Lease, as security for any indebtedness owed by it, to create an encumbrance against its estate in the Leased Premises or any part thereof, and Lessee hereby agrees that this Lease and Lessee's estate hereunder shall be junior, inferior, subject, and subordinate in all respects to the rights and interests of the party to whom such security is granted. Lessee agrees that, upon written request of Lessor so to do, it shall execute such instruments as may be required from time to time to confirm the subordinate interest of Lessee under this Lease to such encumbrance of the fee estate of Lessor.

Article 21
Transfer by Lessor

If the interest of Lessor under this Lease shall be transferred, whether voluntarily or by reason of foreclosure, voluntary sale, or other proceedings for enforcement of any mortgage on the Leased Premises, Lessee shall be bound to such transferee (herein sometimes called the "Purchaser") under the terms, covenants, and conditions of this Lease for the balance of the term hereof remaining and any extensions or renewal hereof which may be effected in accordance with the terms and provisions hereof, with the same force and effect as if the Purchaser were the Lessor under this Lease, and Lessee does hereby agree to attorn to the Purchaser, including the mortgagee under any such mortgage, if it be the Purchaser, as its Lessor, said attornment to be effective and self-operative without the execution of any further instruments upon the Purchaser succeeding to the interest of the Lessor under this Lease. The respective rights and obligations of Lessee and the Purchaser upon such attornment, to the extent of the then remaining balance of the term of this Lease and any such extensions and renewals, shall be and are the same as those set forth herein.

Article 22
Default by Lessee

It shall be an event of default and shall be considered a breach of this Lease by Lessee if one or any of the following shall occur:

A. Lessee shall make default in the payment of rent or other payment when due as herein provided; and such default shall continue for a period of _____ (_____) days or more; or default shall be made in any of the other covenants, agreements, conditions, or undertakings herein required to be kept, observed, and performed by Lessee, and such other default shall continue for _____

(_____) days after notice thereof in writing to Lessee; or,

B. Lessee shall file a petition in voluntary or reorganization bankruptcy or under applicable Chapters of the Federal Bankruptcy Act or similar law, state or federal, whether now or hereafter existing, or an answer admitting insolvency or inability to pay its debts, or fail to obtain a vacation or stay of involuntary bankruptcy proceedings within _____ (_____) days as hereinafter provided; or,

C. Lessee shall be adjudicated a bankrupt, or a trustee or receiver shall be appointed for all of its property or the major part thereof in any involuntary proceedings, or any court shall have taken jurisdiction of the property of Lessee or the major part thereof in any involuntary proceedings for the reorganization, dissolution, liquidation, or winding up of Lessee, and such jurisdiction is not relinquished or vacated or stayed on appeal or otherwise within _____ (_____) days; or,

D. Lessee shall make an assignment for the benefit of its creditors, or shall vacate or abandon the Leased Premises.

Article 23
Remedies upon Default

If any one or more of the events of default set forth in Article 22 occurs, then Lessor may, at its election:

Give Lessee written notice of its intention to terminate this Lease on the date of such notice or on any later date specified in such notice, and, on the date specified in such notice, Lessee's right to possession of the Leased Premises will cease and the Lease will be terminated (except as to Lessee's liability set forth in this Article 23), as if the date fixed in such notice were the end of the term of this Lease. If this Lease is terminated pursuant to the provisions of this Article, Lessee will remain liable to Lessor for damages in an amount equal to the rent and other sums which would have been owing by Lessee under this Lease for the balance of the term if this Lease had not been terminated, less the net proceeds, if any, of any reletting of the premises by the Lessor subsequent to such termination, and after deduction of all Lessor's expenses set forth in the Lease. Lessor will be entitled to collect such damages from Lessee monthly on the days on which the rent and other amounts would have been payable under this Lease if this Lease had not been terminated, and Lessor will be entitled to receive such damages from Lessee on each such day. Alternatively, at the option of the Lessor, if this Lease is terminated, Lessor will be entitled to recover from Lessee.

i. The worth at the time of award of the amount by which the unpaid rent that would have been earned after termination until the time of award exceeds the amount of such rent loss that Lessee proves could reasonably have been avoided;

ii. The worth at the time of award of the amount by which the unpaid rent for the balance of the term of this Lease after the time of award exceeds the amount of such rent loss that Lessee proves could reasonably be avoided; and

iii. Any other amount necessary to compensate Lessor for all the detriment proximately caused by Lessee's failure to perform its obligations under this Lease or which in the ordinary course of things would be likely to result from such failure. The "worth at the time of award" of the amount referred to in clauses (i) and (ii) is computed by allowing interest at the highest rate permitted by law. The worth at the time of award of the amount referred to in clause (iii) is computed by discounting such amount at the discount rate of the Federal Reserve Bank of Atlanta at the time of award,

iv. If Lessor elects to take possession of the premises according to this Lease paragraph without terminating this Lease, Lessee will pay Lessor the rent and other sums which would be payable under this Lease as if such repossession had not occurred, less the net proceeds, if any, of the reletting of the premises after deducting all of Lessor's expenses incurred in connection with such reletting, including, without limitation, all repossession costs, brokerage commissions, legal expenses, attorneys' fees, expenses of employees, alterations, remodeling and repair costs, and expenses of preparation for such reletting. If, in connection with any reletting, the new Lease term extends beyond the existing term, or the premises covered by such reletting include areas which are not part of the premises, a fair apportionment of the rent received from such reletting and the expenses incurred in connection with such reletting will be made in determining the net proceeds received from such reletting. In addition, in determining the net proceeds from such reletting, any rent concessions will be apportioned over the term of the new Lease. Lessee will pay such amounts to Lessor monthly on the days on which the rent and all other amounts owing under this Lease would have been payable if possession had not been retaken, and Lessor will be entitled to receive the rent and other amounts from Lessee on each such day.

Article 24
Waiver of Breach

Failure of Lessor to declare any default immediately upon occurrence thereof, or delay in taking any action in connection therewith, shall not waive such default, but Lessor shall have the right to declare any such default at any time and take such action as might be lawful or authorized hereunder, either in law or in equity.

Article 25
Abandonment

In the event the Lease Premises are abandoned by Lessee, Lessor shall have the right, but not the obligation, to relet the same for the remainder of the term provided for herein and if the rent received through such reletting does not at least equal the rent provided for herein, Lessee shall pay and satisfy any deficiency between the amount of the rent so provided for and that received through reletting, and, in addition thereto, shall pay all expenses incurred in connection with any such reletting, including, but not limited to, the cost of renovation, altering, and decorating for a new occupant. Nothing herein shall be construed as in any way denying Lessor the right in the event of abandonment of said Leased Premises or other breach of this Agreement by Lessee to treat the same as an entire breach and, at Lessor's option, to immediately sue for the entire breach of this Agreement and any and all damages that Lessor suffers thereby.

Article 26
Holding Over

In the event of holding over by Lessee after the expiration or termination of this Lease, such holdover shall be as a tenant at will, and all of the terms and provisions of this Lease shall be applicable during such period, except that Lessee shall pay Lessor as rental for the period of such holdover an amount equal to twice the rent which would have been payable by Lessee had such holdover period been a part of the original term of this Lease, and Lessee will vacate the Leased Premises and deliver the same to Lessor upon Lessee's receipt of notice from Lessor to vacate said Premises. The rental payable during such holdover period shall be payable to Lessor on demand. No holding over by Lessee shall operate to extend this Lease except as herein provided. Lessee agrees to pay Lessor's costs and reasonable attorneys' fees should Lessor expend monies for the removal of Lessee or any of Lessee's property.

Article 27
Attorneys' Fees

In the event Lessee makes default in the performance of any of the terms, covenants, agreements, or conditions contained in this Lease and Lessor places the enforcement of this Lease, or any part thereof, or the collection of any rent due or to become due hereunder, or recovery of the possession of the Leased Premises, in the hands of an attorney, or files suit upon the same, Lessee agrees to pay Lessor's costs and reasonable attorneys' fees for the services of such attorneys. The obligation of Lessee to pay such costs of collections including reasonable attorneys' fees shall apply whether or not suit be brought, and if suit be brought, then at both trial and appellate levels.

Article 28
Hold Harmless

Lessee agrees to defend, indemnify, and hold Lessor harmless against any and all claims, damages, accidents, and injuries to persons or property caused by or resulting from or in connection with anything in or pertaining to or upon the Leased Premises.

As a material part of the consideration to be rendered to Lessor under this Lease, Lessor shall not be liable for damage to property of Lessee or of others located on the Leased Premises or Building, nor for the loss of or damage to any property of Lessee or of others by theft, casualty loss, or otherwise, nor shall Lessor be liable to Lessee for losses arising from the inability of Lessee to operate its business for any reason whatsoever, and Lessee hereby waives all such claims against Lessor and will hold Lessor exempt and harmless for or on account of such damage or injury. Lessor shall not be liable for any injury or damage to persons or property resulting from (but not limited to) fire or explosion on any part of the Leased Premises or Building or from the pipes, appliances, or plumbing works or from the roof, street, or subsurface or from any place or by dampness or any other cause of whatsoever nature. Lessor shall not be liable for any such damage caused by other tenants or persons in the building, occupants of adjacent property, or the public, or caused by operations in construction of any private, public, or quasi-public work. All property of the Lessee kept or stored on the Leased Premises shall be so kept or stored at the risk of Lessee, and Lessee shall hold Lessor harmless from any claims arising out of damage to the same, including subrogation claims by Lessee's insurance carriers.

Article 29
Lessor's Liability

The term "Lessor" as used in this Lease means only the owner from time to time of the Leased Premises. Lessor shall be under no personal liability with respect to any of the provisions of this Lease, and if Lessor is in default with respect to its obligations hereunder, Lessee shall look solely to the equity of the Lessor in the Leased Premises and Building for the satisfaction of the Lessee's remedies. It is expressly understood and agreed that the Lessor's liability under this Lease shall in no event exceed the loss of its equity interest in the Leased Premises.

Article 30
Force Majeure

Lessor shall be excused for the period of any delay in the performance of any obligation when the delay is a result of any cause or causes beyond its control, which includes but is not limited to all labor disputes, governmental regulations or control, fire or other casualty, or inability to obtain any material, services, or financing.

Article 31
Notice

All rent and other payments required to be made by Lessee to Lessor hereunder shall be payable to Lessor at the address set forth below, or such other address as Lessor may specify from time to time, by written notice delivered in accordance herewith. Unless otherwise provided to the contrary herein, any notice or document required or permitted to be delivered hereunder shall be deemed to be delivered (whether or not actually received) when deposited in the United States mail, postage prepaid, Certified Mail, Return Receipt Requested, addressed to the Parties hereto at the respective addresses set out opposite their names below, or at such other address as they have theretofore specified by written notice delivered in accordance herewith:

Lessor: _____
               _____
               _____

Lessee: _____
               _____
               _____

Article 32
Estoppel Certificates

Lessee accepts this Lease subject and subordinate to any mortgage now or at any time hereafter constituting a lien or charge upon the Leased Premises. Lessee shall, on demand, execute any instrument which may be required by any mortgagee for the purpose of subjecting and subordinating this Lease to the lien of any such mortgage or deed of trust.

Upon three (3) days prior written notice from Lessor, Lessee shall execute and deliver to Lessor a statement in writing (1) certifying that this Lease is unmodified and in full force and effect, and dates to which the rent and other charges are paid in advance, if any, and (2) acknowledging that to Lessee's knowledge there are not any uncured defaults on the part of Lessor hereunder and that Lessee has no right of offset, counterclaim, or deduction in rent or specifying such defaults, if any, or claim, together with the amount of any offset, counterclaim, or deduction alleged by Lessee. Any such statement may be relied upon by any prospective purchaser or lender upon the security of the real property of which the Leased Premises are a part. Lessee's failure to deliver said statement within such time shall constitute agreement by Lessee (1) that this Lease is in full force and effect without modification except as may be represented by Lessor, (2) that there are no uncured defaults in Lessor's performance and that Lessee has no right of offset, counterclaim, or deduction against rent, and (3) that no more than one month's rent has been paid in advance.

Article 33
Liens for Rents

As security for Lessee's payment of rent and all other payments required to be made by Lessee hereunder (including, by way of illustration only, excess taxes, damage to the Leased Premises, court costs, and attorneys' fees), Lessee hereby grants to Lessor a lien upon all property of Lessee now or hereafter located upon the Leased Premises. If default is made by Lessee in the payment of any sum which may become due hereunder and said sum is not paid within _____ (_____) days after written notice is given by Lessor to Lessee for Lessee's default, Lessor may enter upon the Leased Premises and take possession of said property, or any part thereof, and may sell all or part of such property at public or private sale in one or successive sales, with or without notice, to the highest bidder for cash and on behalf of Lessee. Lessor may sell and convey such property, or any part thereof, to such bidder, delivering to such bidder all of Lessee's title and interest in such property sold to him. The proceeds of such sale shall be applied by Lessor toward the costs thereof and then toward the payment of all sums then due by Lessee to Lessor hereunder.

Article 34
Security Agreement

As additional security for the performance of the covenants and obligations herein contained by the Lessee to be performed, the Lessee hereby grants to the Lessor a security interest in all of Lessee's personal property, tangible and intangible. This security interest shall be subordinate to the lien of any chattel mortgage, collateral assignment, or security interest given by Lessee to any such Uniform Commercial Code forms as may be requested by Lessor, and that all remedies afforded by the Uniform Commercial Code in the event of default shall be available to Lessor. If Lessee is in default under this Lease, such personal property shall not be removed from the Leased Premises (except to the extent such property is replaced with an item of equal or greater value) without the written consent of Lessor. It is intended by the parties hereto that this instrument shall have the effect of a security agreement covering such personal property, and the Lessor, upon the occurrence of an event of default, may exercise any rights of a secured party under the Uniform Commercial Code of the state of _____ , including the right to take possession of such personal property and to sell the same at public or private sale, and out of the money derived therefrom, pay the amount due Lessor and all costs arising out of the execution of the provisions of this section, paying the surplus, if any, to Lessee. If such personal property, or any portion thereof, shall be offered at a public sale, Lessor may become a purchaser thereof.

Article 35
Common Area Usage

Should Lessee purchase or lease security, telephone, communications, electronic, or any other kind of equipment, then said equipment shall not be installed, placed, or stored in any common areas of the Park or Building. Should Lessee place any such equipment or any kind of personal property in said common areas, then Lessor, at his election, may remove said personal property at Lessee's expense.

Article 36
Floor Loads

Lessee shall not place a load upon the floor of the Leased Premises which exceeds the floor load per square foot which such floor was designed to carry. Floor load is stipulated to be _____ pounds per square foot. Lessor and Lessee will determine jointly the approximate weight and the position of all safes and heavy installations which the Lessee wishes to place in the Leased Premises so as to distribute properly the weight thereof.

Business machines and mechanical equipment belonging to Lessee which cause noise and/or vibration that may be transmitted to the structure of the Building or to any leased space to such a degree as to be objectionable to Lessor or to any tenants in the Building shall be placed and maintained by the party owning the machines or equipment, at such party's expense, in a setting of cork, rubber, or springs-type noise and/or vibration eliminators sufficient to eliminate vibration and/or noise.

Article 37
General

A. This Lease shall be binding and inure to the benefit of the Parties hereto and their respective heirs, personal representatives, successors, and assigns.

B. This Lease shall create the relationship of Lessor and Lessee. No estate shall pass out of the Lessor, and the Lessee shall have only a right of use which shall not be subject to levy and sale.

C. The submission of this instrument for examination or signature by the Lessee does not constitute a reservation of or an option for lease, and it is not effective as a lease or otherwise until execution and delivery by both Lessor and Lessee.

D. Lessor shall have the right to transfer and assign, in whole or in part, all of its rights and obligations hereunder in the Building and/or Leased Premises referred to herein.

E. The captions or headings of the various Articles in this Lease Agreement are for convenience only, and are not to be construed as part of this Lease, and shall not be construed as defining or limiting in any way the scope or intent of the provisions hereof.

F. Time is of the essence of this Lease Agreement.

G. Any pronouns used in the Lease shall be deemed to include the masculine, feminine, neuter, singular, and plural as appropriate.

H. This instrument embodies the whole agreement between the Parties, and there are no promises, terms, conditions, or obligations other than those herein contained. This agreement shall supersede all previous communications, representations, proposals, or agreements, either verbal or written, between the parties hereto and not herein contained. This agreement shall not be modified or canceled unless reduced in writing and signed by both parties, properly witnessed, and by direct reference therein made a part hereof.

I. If any term, covenant, condition, or provision of the Lease or the application thereof to any person or circumstance shall, at any time or to any extent, be invalid or unenforceable, the remainder of this Lease shall not be affected thereby, and each term, covenant, condition, and provision of this Lease shall be valid and be enforced to the fullest extent of the law. This Lease and the performance thereof shall be governed, interpreted, construed, and regulated by the laws of the state of _____ , and the venue of any action shall lie in _____ County, _____ .

J. The Parties hereto further understand and agree that this Lease shall not be recorded in any Public Records of _____ County, _____ , except at the option of the Lessor. The Parties also agree, at the option of the Lessor, to execute a short-form lease for recording, containing the names of the parties and such other terms and conditions of the Lease as may be requested by the Lessor.

K. To the extent permitted by applicable law, Lessor and Lessee hereby waive trial by jury in any action, proceeding, or counterclaim brought by either against the other on any matter whatsoever arising out of or in any way connected with this Lease, the relationship of Lessor and Lessee, or Lessee's use or occupancy of the Leased Premises, or any emergency or other statutory remedy with respect hereto.

Article 39
Signature Page

IN WITNESS WHEREOF, the Parties hereto have executed this Lease Agreement on the day and year first above written. Signed, sealed, and delivered in the presence of:

_____
Lessor

_____   By _____
Witness   Authorized Representative

_____
Witness

_____   _____
Witness   Lessee

_____   By _____
Witness   Authorized Representative

Exhibit A   Sign Site Plan
Exhibit B   Site Plan

Building Rules and Regulations

The following Rules and Regulations have been adopted by the owners for the care and protection of the building located in _____ , and for the general comfort and welfare of all occupants.

1. Wherever Tenant is obligated under these Rules and Regulations to do or refrain from doing an act or thing, such obligation shall include the exercise by Tenant of its best efforts to secure compliance with such obligation by the servants, employees, contractors, jobbers, agents, invitees, licensees, guests, sublessees, and visitors of Lessee. The term "Building" shall include the structure within which the Leased Premises is located, and any obligations of Tenant hereunder with regard to the Building shall apply with equal force to the Leased Premises and to other parts of the Building.

2. Tenant shall not obstruct or interfere with the rights of other occupants in the Building, or of persons having business in the Building in which the Leased Premises are located, or in any way injure or annoy such persons.

3. Tenant shall not use the Leased Premises or the Building for lodging, sleeping, cooking, or any immoral or illegal purposes, or for any purpose that will damage the building, or the reputation thereof, or for any purpose other than those specified in the Lease.

4. Canvassing, soliciting, and peddling in the Building are prohibited, and Tenant shall cooperate to prevent such activities.

5. Tenant shall not bring or keep within the Building any animal or motorcycle.

6. Tenant shall not conduct mechanical or manufacturing operations, cook or prepare food, or place in use any inflammable, combustible, explosive, or hazardous fluid, chemical device, substance, or material in or about the Leased Premises or the Building without the prior written consent of Landlord. Tenant shall comply with all rules, orders, regulations, and requirements of the applicable Fire Rating Bureau, or any other similar body, and Tenant shall not commit any act or permit any object to be brought or kept in Leased Premises or the Building which shall increase the rate of fire insurance on the Building or on property located therein.

7. Tenant shall not use the Leased Premises or Building for the storage of goods, wares, or merchandise, except as such storage may be incidental to the use of the Leased Premises for general office purposes. Tenant shall not occupy the Leased Premises or permit any portion of the Leased Premises to be occupied for the manufacture or direct sale of liquor, narcotics, or tobacco in any form.

Tenant shall not conduct in or about the Leased Premises or Building any auction, public or private, without the prior written approval of Landlord.

8. Tenant shall not install or use in the Leased Premises or Building any engine, boiler, generator, heating unit, air conditioning unit (other than the air conditioning and heating unit Landlord provides), stove, water cooler, ventilator, radiator, or any other similar apparatus without the prior written consent of Landlord.

9. Tenant shall not use in the Leased Premises or Building any machines, other than standard office machines such as typewriters, calculators, copying machines, computers, and similar machines, without prior written approval of the Landlord. All office equipment and any other device of any electrical or mechanical nature shall be placed by Landlord in the Leased Premises in settings so as to absorb or prevent any vibration, noise, or annoyance. Tenant shall not cause improper noises, vibrations, or odors within the Building.

10. Tenant shall not install, place, or store any security, telephone, or communication equipment in any common areas of the Project or Building. Should Tenant place such equipment or any kind of personal property in the common areas in the Project or Building without the prior written consent of Landlord, then Landlord, at his election, may remove said personal property at Tenant's expense.

11. Tenant shall move all freight, supplies, furniture, fixtures, and other personal property into, within, and out of the Building only at such times and through such entrances as may be designated by Landlord, and such movement of such items shall be under the supervision of Landlord. Landlord reserves the right to inspect all such freight, supplies, furniture, fixtures, and other personal property to be brought into the Building and to exclude from the Building all such objects which violate any of these Rules and Regulations. Tenant shall not move or install such objects in or about the Building in such a fashion as to unreasonably obstruct the activities of the other occupants, and all such moving shall be at the sole expense, risk, and responsibility of Tenant. Tenant shall not use in the delivery, receipt, or other movement of freight, supplies, furniture, fixtures, and other personal property to, from, or within the Building, any hand trucks other than those equipped with rubber tires and side guards.

12. Tenant shall not place within the Building any safes, copying machines, computer equipment, or other objects of unusual size or weight without the prior written consent of Landlord. The placement and positioning of all such

objects within the Building shall be prescribed by Landlord, and such objects shall, in all cases, be placed upon plates or footings of such size as shall be prescribed by Landlord.

13. Tenant shall not deposit any trash, refuge, cigarettes, or other substances of any kind within or out of the Building except in the refuse containers provided therefor. Tenant shall not introduce into the Building any substance which might add an undue burden to the cleaning or maintenance of the Leased Premises or the Building. Tenant shall exercise its best efforts to keep the sidewalks, entrances, passages, courts, lobby areas, parking areas, stairways, vestibules, public corridors, and halls in and about the Building (hereinafter referred to as "Common Areas") clean and free from rubbish.

14. Tenant shall use the Common Areas only as a means of ingress and egress, and Tenant shall permit no loitering by any persons upon Common Areas. Common Areas and the roof of the Building are not for the use of the general public, and Landlord shall in all cases retain the right to control or prevent access thereto by all persons whose presence, in the judgment of Landlord, shall be detrimental to the Building and/or its tenants. Tenant shall not enter the mechanical room, air conditioning rooms, electrical closets, janitorial closets, or similar areas or go upon the roof of the Building without the prior written consent of Landlord, unless such areas shall have been designated as part of the Leased Premises.

15. Tenant shall not use the washrooms, rest rooms, and plumbing fixtures of the Building, if any, and appurtenances thereto, for any purpose other than the purposes for which they were constructed, and Tenants shall not deposit any sweepings, rubbish, rags, or other improper substances therein. Tenant shall not waste water by interfering or tampering with the faucets or otherwise. If Tenant or Tenant's servants, employees, agents, contractors, jobbers, licensees, invitees, guests, or visitors cause any damage to such washrooms, rest rooms, plumbing fixtures, or appurtenances, such damage shall be repaired at Tenant's expense and Landlord shall not be responsible therefor.

16. Tenant shall not mark, paint, drill into, cut, string wires, or in any way deface any part of the Building without the prior written consent of Landlord. Upon removal of any wall decorations or installations of floor coverings by Tenant, any damage to the walls or floors shall be repaired by Tenant at Tenant's sole cost and expense. Tenant shall refer all contractors, representatives, installations technicians, and other

mechanics, artisans, and laborers rendering any service in connection with the repair, maintenance, or improvement of the Leased Premises to Landlord for Landlord's supervision, approval, and control before performance of any such service. This Paragraph 16 shall apply to all work performed in the building, including, without limitation, installation of the telephones, telegraph equipment, electrical devices, and attachments and installations of any nature affecting floor, walls, woodwork, trim, windows, ceilings, equipment, or any structural portion of the Building. Plans and specifications for such work, prepared at Tenant's sole expense, shall be submitted to Landlord for its prior written approval in each instance before commencement of work. All installations, alterations, and additions shall be constructed by Tenant in a good and workmanlike manner, and only good grades of material shall be used in connection therewith. The means by which telephone, telegraph, and similar wires are to be introduced to the Leased Premises and the location of telephones, call boxes, and other office equipment affixed to the Leased Premises shall be subject to the prior written approval of Landlord.

17. Tenant shall not obstruct, alter, or in any way impair the efficient operation of the Leased Premises' heating, ventilating, air conditioning, electrical, fire, safety, or lighting systems.

18. Subject to applicable fire or other safety regulations, all doors opening onto Common Areas and all doors upon the perimeters of the Leased Premises shall be kept closed and, during nonbusiness hours, locked, except when in use for ingress or egress. If Tenant uses the Leased Premises after regular business hours or on nonbusiness days, Tenant shall lock any entrance doors to the Building used by Tenant immediately after using such doors.

19. Employees of the Landlord or the Building Association ("Association") shall not receive or carry messages for or to Tenant or any other person, nor contact with nor render free or paid services to Tenant or Tenant's servants, employees, contractors, jobbers, agents, invitees, licensees, guests, or visitors. In the event that any of Landlord's or Association's employees perform any such services, such employees shall be deemed to be the agents of Tenant regardless of whether or how payment is arranged for such services, and Tenant hereby indemnifies and holds Landlord or Association harmless from any and all liability in connection with any such services and any associated injury or damage to property or injury or death to personal resulting therefrom.

20. No radio or television aerial or other similar device shall be installed without first obtaining Landlord's consent in writing on each separate instance. No aerial shall be erected on the roof or exterior walls of the Building, or on the grounds, without in each instance the written consent of Landlord. Any aerial so installed without such written consent shall be subject to removal without notice at any time.
21. No loudspeaker, televisions, phonographs, radios, or other devices shall be used in a manner so as to be heard or seen outside of the Leased Premises without prior written consent of Landlord.

Acknowledgment of Receipt

The undersigned hereby acknowledges receipt of a complete copy of the foregoing Rules and Regulations.

By _____
Authorized Representative for

_____

Lease Modification

This lease modification is to be made a part of the lease dated the _1st_ day of _November_ , 199 _6_ , by and between _High Point Management, Inc._ of _332 Forest Drive_ , city of _Orlando_ , state of _Florida_ , as Lessor and _Creative Marketing, Inc._ of _21 E. Nova Street_ , city of _Orlando_ , state of _Florida_ , as Lessee, on the premises described as _14 High Point Center_ .

For value received and by mutual consent, the aforementioned lease is hereby modified by the following terms:

The lease shall be extended twelve (12) additional months ending October 31, 2000.

All other provisions shall remain the same.

It is expressly understood that in all respects, said terms and conditions of the lease shall be in full force and effect.

THIS modification agreement shall bind the heirs, executors, administrators, and assigns of the respective parties.

IN WITNESS WHEREOF, the parties hereto set their hands and seals on this _4th_ day of _April_ , 199 _7_ .

Kathleen Shuman
Witness

High Point Management, Inc.
Lessor

By _Bart Thomas, Agent_

Creative Marketing, Inc.
Lessee

By _Jeff Parks, President_

Lease Modification

    This lease modification is to be made a part of the lease
dated the _____ day of _____ , 199 ___ , by and between
of _____ , city of _____ , state of _____ , as
Lessor and _____ of _____ , city of _____ , state
of _____ , as Lessee, on the premises described as

_____

_____

_____ .

    For value received and by mutual consent, the aforementioned
lease is hereby modified by the following terms:

    It is expressly understood that in all respects, said terms
and conditions of the lease shall be in full force and effect.

    THIS modification agreement shall bind the heirs, executors,
administrators, and assigns of the respective parties.

    IN WITNESS WHEREOF, the parties hereto set their hands and
seals on this _____ day of _____ , 199 ___ .

_____   _____

Witness   Lessor

                                        By _____

                                        _____

                                        Lessor

                                        By _____

Rent Reminder

Date: _June 10_ , 199 _7_

To: _Creative Marketing Inc._

From: _High Point Management, Inc._

Please be advised that rent for the month of _June_ , 199 _7_ , is overdue on the property located at: _14 High Point Center_

A rental payment of $ _2,500_ was due on _June 1_ . According to our records, a payment has not been received. Please arrange to make payment at your earliest convenience. If you have already mailed your check, please disregard this notice.

High Point Management, Inc.

By _Bart Thomas, Management_

Rent Reminder

Date: _____ , 199 ___

To: _____

From: _____

Please be advised that rent for the month of _____ ,
199 ___ , is overdue on the property located at: _____
_____
_____
_____.

A rental payment of $ _____ was due on _____ .
According to our records, a payment has not been received. Please
arrange to make payment at your earliest convenience. If you have
already mailed your check, please disregard this notice.

_____

By _____

Rent Receipt

   RECEIPT is hereby acknowledged from _Creative Marketing Inc._
of _332 Forest Drive_ , city of _Orlando_ , state of _Florida_ of
the sum of _Two thousand five hundred 00/0_ dollars (_$2,500_),
being one month's rent in advance for property located at _14
High Point Center_ commencing _November 1_ , 199 _6_ , and ending
October 31 , 199 _9_ .

   Bart Thomas
   Authorized Agent

Rent Receipt

RECEIPT is hereby acknowledged from _____ of _____ ,
city of _____ , state of _____ of the sum of
_____ dollars ($ _____), being one month's
rent in advance for property located at _____

_____

_____

_____

commencing _____ , 199 ___ , and ending _____ , 199 ___ .

_____
Authorized Agent

Guaranty of Rents

FOR GOOD CONSIDERATION, and as an inducement for _High Point Management, Inc._ (Landlord) to enter into a lease or tenancy agreement with _Creative Marketing, Inc._ (Tenant) for premises at _14 High Point Center_ .

BE IT KNOWN, that the undersigned does hereby jointly and severally guaranty to the Landlord and his successors and assigns the prompt, punctual, and full payment of all rents and other charges that may become due and owing from Tenant to Landlord under said lease or tenancy agreement or any renewal or extension thereof. This guaranty, however, shall not extend to apply to any damages incurred by Landlord for any breach of lease other than the failure to pay rents or other charges due under the lease.

Signed under seal this _1st_ day of _November_ , 199 _6_ .

Top Printing, Inc.
Guarantor

By _Robert Top_

Guaranty of Rents

FOR GOOD CONSIDERATION, and as an inducement for _____ (Landlord) to enter into a lease or tenancy agreement with _____ (Tenant) for premises at _____

_____

_____

_____ .

BE IT KNOWN, that the undersigned does hereby jointly and severally guaranty to the Landlord and his successors and assigns the prompt, punctual, and full payment of all rents and other charges that may become due and owing from Tenant to Landlord under said lease or tenancy agreement or any renewal or extension thereof. This guaranty, however, shall not extend to apply to any damages incurred by Landlord for any breach of lease other than the failure to pay rents or other charges due under the lease.

Signed under seal this _____ day of _____ , 199 ___ .

_____
Guarantor

By _____

Sublease

Sublease Agreement entered into between _Creative Marketing, Inc._ (Tenant), _Advertising Alternatives, Inc._ (Subtenant), and _High Point Management, Inc._ (Landlord).

Sublease Period: The Subtenant agrees to sublease from Tenant, property known as _14 High Point Center_ , city of _Orlando_ , state of _Florida_ , from _September 3_ , 199 _7_ , to _October 31_ , 199 _9_ .

Terms of Sublease: The Subtenant agrees to comply with all terms and conditions of the lease entered into by the Tenant, including the prompt payment of all rents. The lease is attached and incorporated into this agreement by reference. The Subtenant agrees to pay the Landlord the monthly rent stated in that lease, and all other rental charges hereinafter due, and otherwise assume all of Tenant's obligations during the Sublease period and indemnify Tenant from same.

Security Deposit: The Subtenant agrees to pay to Tenant the sum of $ _2,500_ as a security deposit, to be promptly returned upon the termination of this sublease and compliance with all conditions.

Inventory: Attached to this agreement is an inventory of items or fixtures on the above described property on this day. The Subtenant agrees to replace or reimburse the Tenant for any of these items that are missing or damaged.

Landlord's Consent: The Landlord consents to this sublease and agrees to promptly notify the Tenant at _21 Nova Street_ , city of _Orlando_ , state of _Florida_ if the Subtenant is in breach of this agreement. Nothing herein shall constitute a release of Tenant, who shall remain bound under this lease. Nothing herein shall constitute a consent to any further Sublease or Assignment of Lease.

Date _September 3, 1997_   _High Point Management, Inc._
Landlord

By _Bart Thomas, Agent_

Advertising Alternatives, Inc.   _Creative Marketing, Inc._
Subtenant   Tenant

By _Jennifer Jones, President_ By _Jeff Parks, President_

Sublease

Sublease Agreement entered into between _____ (Tenant), _____ (Subtenant), and _____ (Landlord).

Sublease Period: The Subtenant agrees to sublease from Tenant, property known as _____ , city of _____ , state of _____ , from _____ , 199 ___ , to _____ , 199 ___ .

Terms of Sublease: The Subtenant agrees to comply with all terms and conditions of the lease entered into by the Tenant, including the prompt payment of all rents. The lease is attached and incorporated into this agreement by reference. The Subtenant agrees to pay the Landlord the monthly rent stated in that lease, and all other rental charges hereinafter due, and otherwise assume all of Tenant's obligations during the Sublease period and indemnify Tenant from same.

Security Deposit: The Subtenant agrees to pay to Tenant the sum of $ _____ as a security deposit, to be promptly returned upon the termination of this sublease and compliance with all conditions.

Inventory: Attached to this agreement is an inventory of items or fixtures on the above described property on this date. The Subtenant agrees to replace or reimburse the Tenant for any of these items that are missing or damaged.

Landlord's Consent: The Landlord consents to this sublease and agrees to promptly notify the Tenant at _____ , city of _____ , state of _____ if the Subtenant is in breach of this agreement. Nothing herein shall constitute a release of Tenant, who shall remain bound under this lease. Nothing herein shall constitute a consent to any further Sublease or Assignment of Lease.

Date: _____

_____
Landlord

By _____

_____
Subtenant

By _____

_____
Tenant

By _____

Notice to Exercise Option to Extend Lease

Date: _September 1, 1999_

To: _High Point Management, Inc._
          332 Forest Drive
          Orlando, FL 32804

We hereby refer to a certain lease between us dated _November 1_ , 199 _6_ , (Lease) for premises described as: _14 High Point Center_ .

Under the terms of said lease, we have the option to extend or renew said lease for a _3_ year term commencing on _October 31_ , 199 _9_ .

Pursuant to said lease option provisions, this notice is provided to advise you of our election to exercise the option to so renew or extend the lease on the terms therein contained.

                    Creative Marketing, Inc.
                    Lessee

                    By _Jeff Parks, President_

SENT CERTIFIED MAIL, RETURN RECEIPT REQUESTED.

Notice to Exercise Option to Extend Lease

Date: _____

To: _____
       Lessor

       _____
       Address

       _____
       City, State, Zip

We hereby refer to a certain lease between us dated _____ ,
199 ___ , (Lease) for premises described as: _____
_____
_____
_____ .
Under the terms of said lease, we have the option to extend or
renew said lease for a _____ year term commencing on
_____ , 199 ___ .
    Pursuant to said lease option provisions, this notice is
provided to advise you of our election to exercise the option to
so renew or extend the lease on the terms therein contained.

                        _____
                        Lessee

                        By _____

CERTIFIED MAIL, RETURN RECEIPT REQUESTED.

Extension of Lease

Agreement to extend lease made by and between _High Point Management, Inc._ (Landlord) and _Creative Marketing_ (Tenant) relative to a certain lease agreement for premises known as _14 High Point Center_ , said lease dated _November 1_ , 199 _6_ (Lease).

For good consideration, Landlord and Tenant each agree to extend the term of said Lease for a period of _3_ years commencing on _November 1_ , 199 _9_ , and terminating on _October 31_ , _2001_ , with no further right of renewal or extension beyond said extended termination date.

During the extended term, Tenant shall pay Landlord rent of $ _3,000_ per month in advance. Other modified terms of Lease during the extended term are as follows: _None_

It is further provided, however, that all other terms of the original Lease shall continue in full force during this extended term, which lease terms are fully incorporated herein by reference.

This agreement shall be binding upon and shall inure to the benefit of the parties, their successors, assigns, and personal representatives.

Signed under seal this _1st_ day of _September_ , 199 _9_ .

Sarah Barrett
Witness

Chris Johnson
Witness

High Point Management, Inc.
Landlord

By _Bart Thomas_

Creative Marketing, Inc.
Tenant

By _Jeff Parks, President_

Extension of Lease

Agreement to extend lease made by and between _____ (Landlord) and _____ (Tenant) relative to a certain lease agreement for premises known as _____ , said lease dated _____ , 199 ___ (Lease).

For good consideration, Landlord and Tenant each agree to extend the term of said Lease for a period of _____ years commencing on _____ , 199 ___ , and terminating on _____ , 199 ___ , with no further right of renewal or extension beyond said extended termination date.

During the extended term, Tenant shall pay Landlord rent of $ _____ per month in advance. Other modified terms of Lease during the extended term are as follows: _____

_____

_____

_____ .

It is further provided, however, that all other terms of the original Lease shall continue in full force during this extended term, which lease terms are fully incorporated herein by reference.

This agreement shall be binding upon and shall inure to the benefit of the parties, their successors, assigns, and personal representatives.

Signed under seal this _____ day of _____ , 199 ___ .

_____   _____
Witness   Landlord

                                 By _____

_____   _____
Witness   Tenant

                                 By _____

Tenant's Notice to Exercise Purchase Option

Date: *October 4, 1998*

To: *High Point Management, Inc.*
332 Forest Drive
Orlando, FL 32804

Notice is hereby provided that the undersigned as Lessee under a certain Lease dated *November 1* , 199 *6* , does hereby exercise its purchase option under said Lease to purchase the property described as *14 High Point Center* for the option price of $ *250,000 cash* .

As contained within the agreement, I enclose $ *25,000* as a deposit on said purchase option.

Creative Marketing, Inc.
Lessee

By *Jeff Parks, President*

SENT CERTIFIED MAIL, RETURN RECEIPT REQUESTED.

Tenant's Notice to Exercise Purchase Option

Date: _____

To: _____
      Lessor

      _____
      Address

      _____
      City, State, Zip

Notice is hereby provided that the undersigned as Lessee under a certain Lease dated _____ , 199 ___ , does hereby exercise its purchase option under said Lease to purchase the property described as _____
_____
_____
_____
for the option price of $ _____ .
As contained within the agreement, I enclose $ _____ as a deposit on said purchase option.

      _____
      Lessee

      By _____

SENT CERTIFIED MAIL, RETURN RECEIPT REQUESTED.

Lease Termination Agreement

FOR GOOD CONSIDERATION, be it acknowledged that _Creative Marketing, Inc._ (Lessee) and _High Point Management_ (Lessor) under a certain lease agreement between the parties under date of _November 1_ , 199 _6_ , (Lease) do mutually agree to terminate and cancel said Lease effective _November 1_ , 199 _7_ . All rights and obligations under said Lease shall thereupon be canceled, excepting only for any rents under the Lease accruing prior to the effective termination date which then remain unpaid or otherwise not satisfied, and which shall be paid by Lessee on or prior to termination date.

Lessee agrees to promptly surrender the premises to Lessor on or before the termination date and deliver same to Lessor in good condition free of Lessee's goods and effects, waiving all further rights to possession.

This agreement shall be binding upon the parties, their successors, assigns, and personal representatives.

Signed under seal this _1st_ day of _August_ , 199 _7_ .

Sarah Barrett
Witness

Creative Marketing, Inc.
Lessee

By _Jeff Parks, President_

Chris Johnson
Witness

High Point Management, Inc.
Lessor

By _Bart Thomas, Agent_

Lease Termination Agreement

FOR GOOD CONSIDERATION, be it acknowledged that _____ (Lessee) and _____ (Lessor) under a certain lease agreement between the parties under date of _____ , 199 ___ , (Lease) do mutually agree to terminate and cancel said Lease effective _____ , 199 ___ . All rights and obligations under said Lease shall thereupon be canceled, excepting only for any rents under the Lease accruing prior to the effective termination date which then remain unpaid or otherwise not satisfied, and which shall be paid by Lessee on or prior to termination date.

Lessee agrees to promptly surrender the premises to Lessor on or before the termination date and deliver same to Lessor in good condition free of Lessee's goods and effects, waiving all further rights to possession.

This agreement shall be binding upon the parties, their successors, assigns, and personal representatives.

Signed under seal this _____ day of _____ , 199 ___ .

_____

Witness

_____

Witness

_____

Lessee

By _____

_____

Landlord

By _____

Landlord's Notice to Vacate

Date: *March 10, 1997*

To: *Creative Marketing, Inc.*
         14 High Point Center
         Orlando, FL 32804

To the above Tenant and all others now in possession of the below described premises:

You are hereby notified to vacate the below premises you now occupy: *14 High Point Center*

You must deliver possession thereof to the undersigned on or before *March 20* , 199 *7* .

This notice to vacate is due to your following breach of tenancy *Failure to pay rent* .

If you fail, refuse, or neglect to pay your rent, cure the breach, or vacate said premises within *10* days from service of this notice, I will take such legal action as the law requires to evict you from the premises. You are to further understand that we shall in all instances hold you responsible for all present and future rents due under your tenancy agreement.

                    High Point Management, Inc.
                    Landlord

                    By *Bart Thomas, Agent*

SENT CERTIFIED MAIL, RETURN RECEIPT REQUESTED.

Landlord's Notice to Vacate

Date: _____

To: _____

Tenant

_____

Address

_____

City, State, Zip

To the above Tenant and all others now in possession of the below described premises:

You are hereby notified to vacate the below premises you now occupy: _____

_____

_____

_____.

You must deliver possession thereof to the undersigned on or before _____ , 199 ___ .

This notice to vacate is due to your following breach of tenancy _____

_____

_____

_____.

If you fail, refuse, or neglect to pay your rent, cure the breach, or vacate said premises within _____ days from service of this notice, I will take such legal action as the law requires to evict you from the premises. You are to further understand that we shall in all instances hold you responsible for all present and future rents due under your tenancy agreement.

_____

Landlord

By _____

SENT CERTIFIED MAIL, RETURN RECEIPT REQUESTED.

Landlord's and Tenant's Mutual Release

BE IT KNOWN THAT _High Point Management_ (Landlord) hereby acknowledges that _Creative Marketing, Inc._ (Tenant) duly delivered up possession of the premises known as _14 High Point Center_ and has fully paid all rents due and performed all obligations under said tenancy.

And Tenant acknowledges surrender of said premises as of this date and acknowledges return of any security deposit due.

Now, therefore, Landlord and Tenant release and discharge one and the other from any and all claims arising under said tenancy.

Signed under seal this _1st_ day of _November_ , 199 _7_ .

High Point Management, Inc.
Landlord

By _Bart Thomas, Agent_

Creative Marketing, Inc.
Tenant

By _Jeff Parks, President_

Landlord's and Tenant's Mutual Release

BE IT KNOWN THAT _____ (Landlord) hereby acknowledges that _____ (Tenant) duly delivered up possession of the premises known as _____

_____

_____

_____

and has fully paid all rents due and performed all obligations under said tenancy.

And Tenant acknowledges surrender of said premises as of this date and acknowledges return of any security deposit due.

Now, therefore, Landlord and Tenant release and discharge one and the other from any and all claims arising under said tenancy.

Signed under seal this _____ day of _____ , 199 ___ .

_____

Landlord

By _____

_____

Tenant

By _____

Warranty Deed

This WARRANTY DEED, made this _12th_ day of _June_ , 199 _5_ , by _Bob & Mary Yates_ of _102 6th Street_ , city of _Tampa_ , state of _Florida_ , hereinafter referred to as Grantor, to _Herb Abbott_ of _142 5th Street_ , city of _Altamonte Springs_ , state of _Florida_ , hereinafter referred to as Grantee.

WITNESSETH

For good and valuable consideration, the Grantor hereby grants, bargains, sells, aliens, remises, releases, conveys, and confirms unto the Grantee all that certain property located in the county of _Seminole_ , state of _Florida_ . Said land to be fully described as: _Lot 25, Blk B Newcastle Subdivision, Altamonte Springs, FL_

Together with all the tenements, hereditaments and appurtenances thereto belonging or in anywise appertaining.

To have and to hold the same in fee simple forever.

The Grantor hereby covenants to the Grantee that he is lawfully seized of said land in fee simple; that the Grantor has good right and lawful authority to sell and convey said land; that the Grantor hereby fully warrants the title to said land and will defend the same against the lawful claims of all persons; and that said land is free and clear of all encumbrances, except taxes occurring subsequent to December 31, 199 _5_ .

IN WITNESS WHEREOF, the said Grantor has signed and sealed these presents the day and year first above written.

Signed, sealed, and delivered in our presence.

Bob Yates	L.S.
Mary Yates	L.S.

State of _Florida_
County of _Seminole_

I hereby certify that on this day, before me, an officer duly authorized in the state aforesaid and in the county aforesaid to take acknowledgments, personally appeared: _Bob Yates and Mary Yates_ to me known to be the person(s) described in and who executed the foregoing instrument, and _they_ acknowledged to me that _they_ executed the same.

WITNESS my hand and official seal in the county and state last aforesaid this _12th_ day of _June_ , 199 _5_ .

Debi Cade
Notary Public, state of _Florida_
Debi Cade
Notary's Printed Name

My Commission Expires: _August 1, 1997_

Warranty Deed

This WARRANTY DEED, made this _____ day of _____ ,
199 ___ , by _____ of _____ , city of _____ ,
state of _____ , hereinafter referred to as Grantor, to
_____ of _____ ,city of _____ , state of
_____ , hereinafter referred to as Grantee.

WITNESSETH

For good and valuable consideration, the Grantor hereby
grants, bargains, sells, aliens, remises, releases, conveys, and
confirms unto the Grantee all that certain property located in
the county of _____ , state of _____ . Said land to be
fully described as: _____
_____ .

Together with all the tenements, hereditaments, and
appurtenances thereto belonging or in anywise appertaining.

To have and to hold the same in fee simple forever.

The Grantor hereby covenants to the Grantee that he is
lawfully seized of said land in fee simple; that the Grantor has
good right and lawful authority to sell and convey said land;
that the Grantor hereby fully warrants the title to said land and
will defend the same against the lawful claims of all persons;
and that said land is free and clear of all encumbrances, except
taxes occurring subsequent to December 31, 199 ___ .

IN WITNESS WHEREOF, the said Grantor has signed and sealed
these presents the day and year first above written.

Signed, sealed, and delivered in our presence.

_____ L.S.

_____ L.S.

State of _____
County of _____

I hereby certify that on this day, before me, an officer duly
authorized in the state aforesaid and in the county aforesaid to
take acknowledgments, personally appeared: _____ to
me known to be the person(s) described in and who executed the
foregoing instrument, and _____ acknowledged to me that
_____ executed the same.

WITNESS my hand and official seal in the county and state last
aforesaid this _____ day of _____ , 199 ___ .

_____
Notary Public, state of _____

_____
Notary's Printed Name

My Commission Expires: _____

Quitclaim Deed

This Quitclaim Deed, executed this _12th_ day of _June_ , 199 _5_ , by _Bob Yates_ (Grantor) of _102 6th Street_ , city of _Tampa_ , state of _Florida_ , to _Herb Abbott_ (Grantee) of _142 5th Street_ , city of _Altamonte Springs_ , state of _Florida_ .

WITNESS, that the Grantor, for good and valuable consideration, does hereby remise, release, and quitclaim unto the said Grantee forever, all the right, title, interest, claim, and demand which the Grantor has in and to the following described property, lying and being in the county of _Seminole_ , state of _Florida_ , to wit: _Lot 4, Blk K, Ellsworth Subdivision, Seminole County, Florida_

TO HAVE AND TO HOLD the same together with any and all appurtenances thereto, including the estate, right, title, interest, lien, equity, and claim whatsoever of Grantor, either in law or equity, to the complete benefit and use of the Grantee forever.

IN WITNESS WHEREOF, the Grantor has signed and sealed on the day and year first above written.

Signed, sealed, and delivered in the presence of:

Bob Yates   L.S.

_____   L.S.

State of _Florida_
County of _Seminole_

I hereby certify that on this day, before me, an officer duly authorized in the state aforesaid and in the county aforesaid to take acknowledgments, personally appeared: _Bob Yates_ to me known to be the person(s) described in and who executed the foregoing instrument, and _he_ acknowledged to me that _he_ executed the same.

WITNESS my hand and official seal in the county and state last aforesaid this _12th_ day of _June_ , 199 _5_ .

Debi Cade
Notary Public, state of _Florida_
Debi Cade
Notary's Printed Name

My Commission Expires: _August 1, 1997_

Quitclaim Deed

This Quitclaim Deed, executed this _____ day of _____ , 199 ___ , by _____ (Grantor) of _____ , city of _____ , state of _____ , to _____ (Grantee) of _____ , city of _____ , state of _____ .

WITNESS, that the Grantor, for good and valuable consideration, does hereby remise, release, and quitclaim unto the said Grantee forever, all the right, title, interest, claim, and demand which the Grantor has in and to the following described property, lying and being in the county of _____ , state of _____ , to wit: _____ _____ _____ _____ .

TO HAVE AND TO HOLD the same together with any and all appurtenances thereto, including the estate, right, title, interest, lien, equity, and claim whatsoever of Grantor, either in law or equity, to the complete benefit and use of the Grantee forever.

IN WITNESS WHEREOF, the Grantor has signed and sealed on the day and year first above written.

Signed, sealed, and delivered in the presence of:

_____ L.S.

_____ L.S.

State of _____
County of _____

I hereby certify that on this day, before me, an officer duly authorized in the state aforesaid and in the county aforesaid to take acknowledgments, personally appeared: _____ to me known to be the person(s) described in and who executed the foregoing instrument, and _____ acknowledged to me that _____ executed the same.

WITNESS my hand and official seal in the county and state last aforesaid this _____ day of _____ , 199 ___ .

_____
Notary Public, state of _____

_____
Notary's Printed Name

My Commission Expires: _____

Option Contract

THIS OPTION CONTRACT, made this __12th__ day of __June__ , 199 __6__ , by and between __Madison Stewart__ (Seller) of __210 Wind Cove__ , city of __Edisto__ , state of __South Carolina__ , and __B. J. Brandon__ (Purchaser) of __45 Eagle Nest Lane__ , city of __Edisto__ , state of __South Carolina__ .

WITNESSETH: That the Seller, for __One thousand ($1,000)__ dollars and other good and valuable consideration, hereby gives to the Purchaser the privilege of purchasing, on or before the __12th__ day of __June__ , 199 __8__ , the following described real estate: __Lot 14, Block A, Summer Subdivision, Edisto, South Carolina__

The terms for said option shall be:

Purchase price	$ __100,000__
Terms:	__Cash: the option fee shall be paid in full__

The Seller agrees to furnish title insurance showing good and marketable title to said real estate, in case the privilege of purchase hereby given is exercised upon the terms above written, to convey said property to the Purchaser by good and sufficient warranty deed, free and clear of all liens and encumbrances.

In the event the option to purchase is not exercised and the conditions hereof fully performed by the Purchaser and written notice of such exercise and performance given to the Seller on or before the __12__ day of __June__ , 199 __8__ , said option shall thereupon wholly cease (but no liability to refund the money paid therefor shall arise), and said title insurance shall be redelivered to the Seller, and this instrument shall at once be delivered to the Seller for cancellation. This Contract shall be binding upon and shall inure to the benefit of the heirs, personal representatives, and assigns of all the parties hereto.

IN WITNESS WHEREOF, the parties hereto have subscribed their names and affixed their seals the day and year above written.

Kathleen Shuman	Madison Stewart	(Seal)
Witness	Seller	

Sarah Barrett
Witness

Greg Taylor	B. J. Brandon	(Seal)
Witness	Purchaser	

Chris Johnson
Witness

State of _South Carolina_
County of _Edisto_

I hereby certify that on this day, before me, an officer duly authorized in the state aforesaid and in the county aforesaid to take acknowledgments, personally appeared: _Madison Stewart and B. J. Brandon_ to me known to be the person(s) described in and who executed the foregoing instrument, and _they_ acknowledged to me that _they_ executed the same.

WITNESS my hand and official seal in the county and state last aforesaid this _12th_ day of _June_ , 199 _6_ .

Debi Cade
Notary Public, State of _Florida_
Debi Cade
Notary's Printed Name

My Commission Expires: _August 1, 1997_

Option Contract

THIS OPTION CONTRACT, made this _____ day of _____ ,
199 ___ , by and between _____ (Seller) of _____ , city
of _____ , state of _____ , and _____ (Purchaser)
of _____ , city of _____ , state of _____ .

WITNESSETH: That the Seller, for _____ dollars and other
good and valuable consideration, hereby gives to the Purchaser
the privilege of purchasing, on or before the _____ day of
_____ , 199 ___ , the following described real estate: _____
_____
_____ .

The terms for said option shall be:

Purchase price $ _____
Terms: _____
                  _____

The Seller agrees to furnish title insurance showing good and
marketable title to said real estate, in case the privilege of
purchase hereby given is exercised upon the terms above written,
to convey said property to the Purchaser by good and sufficient
warranty deed, free and clear of all liens and encumbrances.

In the event the option to purchase is not exercised and the
conditions hereof fully performed by the Purchaser and written
notice of such exercise and performance given to the Seller on or
before the _____ day of _____ , 199 ___ , said option
shall thereupon wholly cease (but no liability to refund the
money paid therefor shall arise), and said title insurance shall
be redelivered to the Seller, and this instrument shall at once
be delivered to the Seller for cancellation. This Contract shall
be binding upon and shall inure to the benefit of the heirs,
personal representatives, and assigns of all the parties hereto.

IN WITNESS WHEREOF, the parties hereto have subscribed their
names and affixed their seals the day and year above written.

_____   _____ (Seal)
Witness   Seller

_____
Witness

_____   _____ (Seal)
Witness   Seller

_____
Witness

State of _____
County of _____

    I hereby certify that on this day, before me, an officer duly authorized in the state aforesaid and in the county aforesaid to take acknowledgments, personally appeared: _____
_____ to me known to be the person(s) described in and who executed the foregoing instrument, and _____ acknowledged to me that _____ executed the same.

    WITNESS my hand and official seal in the county and state last aforesaid this _____ day of _____ , 199 ___ .

                                 _____
                                 Notary Public, state of _____
                                 _____
                                 Notary's Printed Name

    My Commission Expires: _____

Exercise of Option

Date: _September 4_ , 199 _7_

To: _Madison Stewart_
1487 Sweet Bay Ct.
Altamonte Springs, FL 32714

This letter is to notify you that pursuant to the option agreement executed by us on the _12th_ day of _June_ , 199 _6_ , I hereby advise you of my intention to proceed with the purchase of the property.

Please contact me at your earliest convenience so that we can proceed with the consummation of this transaction.

B. J. Brandon
Buyer

45 Eagle Nest Lane
Edisto, SC
_(803) 869-2232_

Exercise of Option

Date: _____ , 199 ___

To: _____
    _____
    _____

This letter is to notify you that pursuant to the option agreement executed by us on the _____ day of _____ , 199 ___ , I hereby advise you of my intention to proceed with the purchase of the property.

Please contact me at your earliest convenience so that we can proceed with the consummation of this transaction.

_____
Buyer

_____
Address

_____
City, State, Zip
(___)_____
Telephone Number

Chapter 10
Special Forms

This chapter includes a group of miscellaneous forms that didn't fit into the other chapters. However, they solve specific problems or issues that come up in business, so I thought it was important to include them.

Affidavit

I, _Mark Stone_ , of _22 Live Oak Lane_ , city of _Portland_ , state of _Oregon_ , being of legal age, do hereby state under oath:

That the office furniture delivered to Creative Marketing, Inc. was damaged when the boxes were opened.

Signed and sealed under penalty of perjury this _14th_ day of _January_ , 199 _6_ .

State of _Oregon_
County of _Stuart_

Sworn to and subscribed before me this _14th_ day of _January_ , 199 _6_ , by _Mark Stone_ , who is personally known to me or who produced _his driver's license_ as identification.

Debi Cade
Notary Public, state of _Oregon_
Debi Cade
Notary's Printed Name

My Commission Expires: August 1, 1997

Affidavit

I, _____ , of _____ , city of _____ , state of _____ , being of legal age, do hereby state under oath: ____

_____

_____

_____

_____

_____

Signed and sealed under penalty of perjury this _____ day of _____ , 199 ___ .

State of _____
County of _____

Sworn to and subscribed before me this _____ day of _____ , 199 ___ , by _____ who is personally known to me or who produced _____ as identification.

_____
Notary Public, state of _____

_____
Notary's Printed Name

My Commission Expires: _____

Agreement to Share Litigation Expense

THIS AGREEMENT, entered into this the _3rd_ day of _May_ , 199 _6_ , by and between:

Name	Address
Joe Delany	_44 Easterly St., Phoenix, AZ 85013_
Berry Worth	_921 Wekiva Rd., Phoenix, AZ 85013_

WHEREAS, the parties are about to commence action against _First Bank_ of _14 Tower Center_ , city of _Phoenix_ , state of _Arizona_ , and,

WHEREAS, the parties feel it to be in their mutual interest to share expenses in said litigation.

NOW THEREFORE, in consideration of the mutual promises and benefits to be derived by the parties, they do hereby agree to the following:

1. Each of the parties shall pay a pro rata share of all expenses, costs, and charges in connection with the suit according to the proportion of their share in the amount of the judgment recovered by or against them. Until such amount can be determined, all expenses shall be advanced equally.

2. No settlement shall be made that would bind any party without their written consent.

3. Should any party fail to make any payment contemplated by this agreement, the remaining parties may proceed under the cause of action without the withdrawing party's participation.

4. The parties have agreed to open a mutual litigation account with _Western Savings_ of _Phoenix_ in the amount of $ _10,000_ .

5. This contract shall be construed under the laws of the state of _Arizona_ . Time is of the essence.

Signed and sealed on the date first above written.

Joe Delany

Berry Worth

Agreement to Share Litigation Expense

THIS AGREEMENT, entered into this the _____ day of _____ , 199 ___ , by and between:

Name   Address

_____   _____

_____   _____

WHEREAS, the parties are about to commence action against _____ of _____ , city of _____ , state of _____ , and,

WHEREAS, the parties feel it to be in their mutual interest to share expenses in said litigation.

NOW THEREFORE, in consideration of the mutual promises and benefits to be derived by the parties, they do hereby agree to the following:

1. Each of the parties shall pay a pro rata share of all expenses, costs, and charges in connection with the suit according to the proportion of their share in the amount of the judgment recovered by or against them. Until such amount can be determined, all expenses shall be advanced equally.

2. No settlement shall be made that would bind any party without their written consent.

3. Should any party fail to make any payment contemplated by this agreement, the remaining parties may proceed under the cause of action without the withdrawing party's participation.

4. The parties have agreed to open a mutual litigation account with _____ of _____ in the amount of $ _____ .

5. This contract shall be construed under the laws of the state of _____ . Time is of the essence.

Signed and sealed on the date first above written.

_____

_____

_____

Signatures

Consent to Use Name/Likeness

FOR VALUABLE CONSIDERATION, the undersigned consents to the use of my name and/or likeness by _Creative Marketing, Inc._ for _an advertisement promoting the company's service_ .

Check one: ☒ Without limitation as to frequency or duration.

☐ With the following limitations: _____

_____

I represent that I am of legal age and I have every right to contract in my own name.

Heather Jones
Print Name

Heather Jones
Signature
4230 Southland Ave.
Address
Phoenix, AZ 85037
City, State, Zip

Consent to Use Name/Likeness

FOR VALUABLE CONSIDERATION, the undersigned consents to the use of my name and/or likeness by _____ _____ .

Check one: ☐ Without limitation as to frequency or duration.

☐ With the following limitations: _____

_____

I represent that I am of legal age and I have every right to contract in my own name.

_____

Print Name

_____

Signature

_____

Address

_____

City, State, Zip

Permission to Use Quote or Personal Statement

BE IT KNOWN, for good consideration, the undersigned irrevocably and unconditionally authorizes _Creative Marketing, Inc._ and its successors and assigns the worldwide rights to use, publish, print, or reprint in whole or in part the following statement, picture, endorsement, quotation, or other material attached or described as:

"This is the world's best pie."

This authorization and rights hereto __X__ are _____ are not exclusive.

The undersigned acknowledges that the permission granted herein is irrevocable, and that no further payment or consideration is due herein.

This agreement shall be binding upon and inure to the benefit of the parties, their successors, assigns, and personal representatives.

Signed under seal this _8th_ day of _June_ , 199 _6_ .

In the presence of:

Greg Taylor
Witness

Jack Martel

Permission to Use Quote or Personal Statement

BE IT KNOWN, for good consideration, the undersigned irrevocably and unconditionally authorizes _____

_____

and its successors and assigns the worldwide rights to use, publish, print, or reprint in whole or in part the following statement, picture, endorsement, quotation, or other material attached or described as:

_____

_____

_____

This authorization and rights hereto _____ are _____ are not exclusive.

The undersigned acknowledges that the permission granted herein is irrevocable, and that no further payment or consideration is due herein.

This agreement shall be binding upon and inure to the benefit of the parties, their successors, assigns, and personal representatives.

Signed under seal this _____ day of _____ , 199 ___ .

In the presence of :

_____   _____

Witness

License Agreement

THIS AGREEMENT, entered into this _18th_ day of _March_ , 199 _6_ , by and between _Fred Steel_ (Licensor) of _75 West 3rd Street_ , city of _Birmingham_ , state of _Alabama_ , and _Alabama Sign Co._ (Licensee) of _1475 Old Dominion Hwy._ , city of _Birmingham_ , state of _Alabama_ .

FOR AND IN CONSIDERATION of the mutual promises and benefits to be derived by the parties, they do hereby agree to the following:

1. Licensor hereby grants to Licensee the license to _use the roof of his property located at 75 West 3rd Street for the construction and maintenance of advertising signs_ .

2. This agreement shall begin _April 1_ , 199 _6_ , and shall end _March 31_ , 199 _9_ .

3. Payment for the license shall be: _$1,000 per month cash_ .

4. Licensee shall _keep the roof in good repair at all times during this agreement_ .

5. Licensee agrees to secure all proper permits and pay all fees associated with _having the signs_ .

6. Licensee agrees to indemnify and hold harmless the Licensor against all claims for damage to property or injury to persons resulting or arising from _the use of this license granted_ .

7. Licensee agrees to secure and maintain liability and property insurance of no less than $ _250,000_ and to provide licensor with a copy of a paid policy.

8. Upon termination of this agreement, Licensee shall _remove all signs and displays from the roof and restore the roof to a condition no less than when the license began_ .

9. This agreement may not be assigned without the written consent of Licensor.

10. Licensee acknowledges that he enters upon the operation of this license with full knowledge of the danger of the property and that he assumes sole and entire responsibility for any loss of life or injuries that may be sustained.

11. This agreement shall be construed under the laws of the state of _Alabama_ . In any action arising out of the agreement, the prevailing party shall be entitled to reasonable attorneys' fees and costs.

Signed and sealed this the _18th_ day of _March_ , 199 _6_ .

Fred Steel
Licensor

Alabama Sign Co.
Licensee

License Agreement

THIS AGREEMENT, entered into this _____ day of _____ ,
199 ___ , by and between _____ (Licensor) of _____ ,
city of _____ , state of _____ , and _____
(Licensee) of _____ , city of _____ , state of
_____ .

FOR AND IN CONSIDERATION of the mutual promises and benefits
to be derived by the parties, they do hereby agree to the
following:

1. Licensor hereby grants to Licensee the license to _____
   _____
   _____ .

2. This agreement shall begin _____ , 199 ___ , and
   shall end _____ , 199 ___ .

3. Payment for the license shall be: _____
   _____
   _____ .

4. Licensee shall _____
   _____
   _____ .

5. Licensee agrees to secure all proper permits and pay all
   fees associated with _____
   _____
   _____ .

6. Licensee agrees to indemnify and hold harmless the
   Licensor against all claims for damage to property or
   injury to persons resulting or arising from _____
   _____
   _____ .

7. Licensee agrees to secure and maintain liability and
   property insurance of no less than $ _____ and to
   provide licensor with a copy of a paid policy.

8. Upon termination of this agreement, Licensee shall _____
   _____
   _____ .

9. This agreement may not be assigned without the written
   consent of Licensor.

10. Licensee acknowledges that he enters upon the operation of
    this license with full knowledge of the danger of the
    property and that he assumes sole and entire
    responsibility for any loss of life or injuries that may
    be sustained.

11. This agreement shall be construed under the laws of the state of _____ . In any action arising out of the agreement, the prevailing party shall be entitled to reasonable attorneys' fees and costs.

Signed and sealed this the _____ day of _____ , 199 ___ .

_____
Licensor

_____
Licensee

Permission to Use Copyrighted Material

    BE IT KNOWN, for good consideration, the undersigned, as copyright holder, hereby grants _____ exclusive __X__ nonexclusive permission to _Creative Marketing, Inc._ to reprint, publish, and use on its own account for world distribution the following described material: _the first chapter in Letters Across America_ .

    This copyrighted material shall be used only in the following manner: _As a chapter in Letters Across America_ .

    A credit line to acknowledge permitted use of the material __X__ is _____ is not (check one) required. If required, the credit line shall read as follows: _Letters Across America_ .

    This agreement shall be binding upon and inure to the benefit of the parties, their successors, assigns, and personal representatives.

    Signed under seal this _12th_ day of _May_ , 199 _6_ .

In the presence of:

Debi Cade
Witness

Maggie St. Dare
Name
14 Rouge Place
Address
Washington, DC 20016
City, State, Zip

Permission to Use Copyrighted Material

BE IT KNOWN, for good consideration, the undersigned, as copyright holder, hereby grants _____ exclusive _____ nonexclusive permission to _____ to reprint, publish, and use on its own account for world distribution the following described material: _____

_____

_____

This copyrighted material shall be used only in the following manner: _____

_____

_____

A credit line to acknowledge permitted use of the material _____ is _____ is not (check one) required. If required, the credit line shall read as follows: _____

_____

_____

This agreement shall be binding upon and inure to the benefit of the parties, their successors, assigns, and personal representatives.

Signed under seal this _____ day of _____ , 199 ___ .

In the presence of:

_____

Name

_____

Address

_____

City, State, Zip

General Assignment

BE IT KNOWN, for value received, the undersigned hereby unconditionally and irrevocably assigns and transfers unto _Baynes Supplies, Inc._ of _425 Pine Street_ , city of _Boston_ , state of _Massachusetts_ , all right, title, and interest in and to the following: _A contract dated June 14, 1995 between the U.S. Government and Stowe Manufacturing, Inc. to supply specific aircraft parts. A copy of the contract is attached and incorporated herein_ .

The undersigned fully warrants that it has full rights and authority to enter into this assignment and transfer and that the rights and benefits assigned hereunder are free and clear of any lien, encumbrance, adverse claim, or interest.

This assignment shall be binding upon and inure to the benefit of the parties, their successors, assigns, and personal representatives.

Signed under seal this _19th_ day of _September_ , 199 _5_ .

Greg Taylor
Witness

Stowe Manufacturing, Inc.
Assignor

By _Eldgin Stowe, President_

Kathleen Shuman
Witness

Baynes Supply, Inc.
Assignee

By _Frank Baynes, President_

General Assignment

BE IT KNOWN, for value received, the undersigned hereby unconditionally and irrevocably assigns and transfers unto _____ of _____ , city of _____ , state of _____ , all right, title, and interest in and to the following: _____

_____

_____

The undersigned fully warrants that it has full rights and authority to enter into this assignment and transfer and that the rights and benefits assigned hereunder are free and clear of any lien, encumbrance, adverse claim, or interest.

This assignment shall be binding upon and inure to the benefit of the parties, their successors, assigns, and personal representatives.

Signed under seal this _____ day of _____ , 199 ___ .

_____   _____
Witness   Assignor

                               By _____

_____   _____
Witness   Assignee

                               By _____

Assignment of Accounts Receivable

BE IT KNOWN, for value received, the undersigned hereby unconditionally and irrevocably sells, transfers, and conveys all right, title, and interest in and to the account(s) receivable specifically listed on the attachment, to _The Receivable Corporation_ (Assignee) and its successors and assigns.

The undersigned warrants that the said account(s) are just and due in the amounts stated and that the undersigned has not received payment for same or any part thereof and has no knowledge of any dispute or defense thereon, provided, however, that said account(s) are sold without guaranty or warranty of collection and without recourse to the undersigned in the event of nonpayment. Assignee may prosecute collection of any receivable in its own name.

The undersigned further warrants that it has full title to said receivables and full authority to sell and transfer same, and that said receivables are sold free and clear of all liens, encumbrances, or adverse claims.

This agreement shall be binding upon and inure to the benefit of the parties, their successors, assigns, and personal representatives.

Signed under seal the _8th_ day of _May_ , 199 _6_ .

Sarah Barrett   _Baynes Supply, Inc._
Witness   Assignor

                                   By _Frank Baynes, President_

Assignment of Accounts Receivable

BE IT KNOWN, for value received, the undersigned hereby unconditionally and irrevocably sells, transfers, and conveys all right, title, and interest in and to the account(s) receivable specifically listed on the attachment, to _____ (Assignee) and its successors and assigns.

The undersigned warrants that the said account(s) are just and due in the amounts stated and that the undersigned has not received payment for same or any part thereof and has no knowledge of any dispute or defense thereon, provided, however, that said account(s) are sold without guaranty or warranty of collection and without recourse to the undersigned in the event of nonpayment. Assignee may prosecute collection of any receivable in its own name.

The undersigned further warrants that it has full title to said receivables and full authority to sell and transfer same, and that said receivables are sold free and clear of all liens, encumbrances, or adverse claims.

This agreement shall be binding upon and inure to the benefit of the parties, their successors, assigns, and personal representatives.

Signed under seal the _____ day of _____ , 199 ___ .

_____   _____
Witness   Assignor

                                     By _____

Assignment of Copyright or Trademark

BE IT KNOWN, the undersigned, _Barbara Stevens_ of _83 Meadow Lane_ , city of _Dover_ , state of _Vermont_ , being the lawful Owner of a certain copyright or trademark registered in the United States Patent Office under registration number _42132_ , dated _February 12_ , 19 _95_ , for good consideration does hereby sell, transfer, assign, and convey all right, title, and interest in said Copyright or Trademark and all rights and goodwill attaching thereto unto _Stevens Family Partnership_ (Buyer). A facsimile of said Copyright or Trademark is annexed.

The Owner warrants that said Copyright or Trademark is in full force and good standing and there is no other assignment of rights or licenses granted under said Copyright or Trademark or known infringements by or against said Copyright or Trademark.

Owner further warrants that he is the lawful Owner of said Copyright or Trademark, that he has full right and authority to transfer said Copyright or Trademark, and that said Copyright or Trademark is transferred free and clear of all liens, encumbrances, and adverse claims thereto, and that the owner shall sign such other documents as are required to transfer same.

This agreement shall be binding upon and inure to the benefit of the parties, their successors, assigns, and personal representatives.

Signed under seal this _1st_ day of _March_ , 199 _5_ .

Barbara Stevens
Owner

State of _Vermont_
County of _Hills_

Sworn to and subscribed before me by _Barbara Stevens_ , who is personally known to me or who produced _Vermont Driver's License_ as identification.

Debi Cade
Notary Public, state of _Vermont_

My Commission Expires: _August 1, 1997_

Assignment of Copyright or Trademark

BE IT KNOWN, the undersigned, _____ of _____ , city of _____ , state of _____ , being the lawful Owner of a certain copyright or trademark registered in the United States Patent Office under registration number _____ , dated _____ , 19 ___ , for good consideration does hereby sell, transfer, assign, and convey all right, title, and interest in said Copyright or Trademark and all rights and goodwill attaching thereto unto _____ (Buyer). A facsimile of said Copyright or Trademark is annexed.

The Owner warrants that said Copyright or Trademark is in full force and good standing and there is no other assignment of rights or licenses granted under said Copyright or Trademark or known infringements by or against said Copyright or Trademark.

Owner further warrants that he is the lawful Owner of said Copyright or Trademark, that he has full right and authority to transfer said Copyright or Trademark, and that said Copyright or Trademark is transferred free and clear of all liens, encumbrances, and adverse claims thereto, and that the owner shall sign such other documents as are required to transfer same.

This agreement shall be binding upon and inure to the benefit of the parties, their successors, assigns, and personal representatives.

Signed under seal this _____ day of _____ , 199 ___ .

_____   _____
                                   Owner

State of _____
County of _____

Sworn to and subscribed before me by _____ , who is personally known to me or who produced _____ as identification.

                                   _____
                                   Notary Public, state of _____

My Commission Expires: _____

Assignment of Damage Claim

BE IT KNOWN, for value received, the undersigned hereby unconditionally and irrevocably assigns and transfers unto _Recover Corporation_ (Assignee) and its successors, assigns, and personal representatives, any and all claims, demands, and cause or causes of action of any kind whatsoever which the undersigned has or may have against _First Corporation_ arising from the following: _An accident involving Assignor at the offices of First Corp on May 28, 1996_ .

The Assignee may in its own name at its own expense and for its own benefit prosecute said claim and collect, settle, compromise, and grant releases on said claim as it in its sole discretion deems advisable, provided that the undersigned shall reasonably assist and cooperate in the prosecution of said claim to the extent required or requested. Assignee shall be entitled to all judgments, awards, and payments thereon.

The undersigned warrants that it has full right and authority to assign this claim and that said claim is free and clear of any lien, encumbrance, or other adverse interest. Assignor disclaims any representation as to the merits or collectability of such claim.

This assignment shall be binding upon and inure to the benefit of the parties, their successors, assigns, and personal representatives.

Signed under seal this _1st_ day of _June_ , 199 _6_ .

Chris Johnson
Witness

Sue Dentin
Assignor

Assignment of Damage Claim

BE IT KNOWN, for value received, the undersigned hereby unconditionally and irrevocably assigns and transfers unto _____ (Assignee) and its successors, assigns, and personal representatives, any and all claims, demands, and cause or causes of action of any kind whatsoever which the undersigned has or may have against _____ arising from the following: ____

_____

_____

_____

_____

_____

_____ .

The Assignee may in its own name at its own expense and for its own benefit prosecute said claim and collect, settle, compromise, and grant releases on said claim as it in its sole discretion deems advisable, provided that the undersigned shall reasonably assist and cooperate in the prosecution of said claim to the extent required or requested. Assignee shall be entitled to all judgments, awards, and payments thereon.

The undersigned warrants that it has full right and authority to assign this claim and that said claim is free and clear of any lien, encumbrance, or other adverse interest. Assignor disclaims any representation as to the merits or collectability of such claim.

This assignment shall be binding upon and inure to the benefit of the parties, their successors, assigns, and personal representatives.

Signed under seal this _____ day of _____ , 199 ___ .

_____   _____
Witness   Assignor

Assignment of Income

BE IT KNOWN, for value received, the undersigned hereby irrevocably and unconditionally assigns and transfers to _Ed Harrison_ (Assignee) all rights to income, rental fees, profits, dividends, or monies that are now or shall hereinafter be due the undersigned from _Pete Stevens_ arising from the following obligation: _Promissory note dated April 4, 1996 in the principal amount of $5,000_ .

The undersigned warrants that there are no known setoffs or defenses to the payments due. The undersigned further warrants that said obligation to pay is absolute and without modification. The undersigned further warrants that it has full authority to enter into this agreement and that the rights to income assigned hereunder are free and clear of liens, encumbrances, and adverse claims. The undersigned does not, however, guarantee or warranty the collectability of any monies due. This assignment shall be limited to $ _5,000.00_ and no greater amount.

This assignment shall be binding upon and inure to the benefit of the parties, their successors, assigns, and personal representatives.

Signed under seal this _1st_ day of _May_ , 199 _9_ .

Chris Johnson
Witness

Denny Harrison
Assignor

Assignment of Income

BE IT KNOWN, for value received, the undersigned hereby irrevocably and unconditionally assigns and transfers to _____ (Assignee) all rights to income, rental fees, profits, dividends, or monies that are now or shall hereinafter be due the undersigned from _____ arising from the following obligation: _____

_____

_____

_____

_____

_____ .

The undersigned warrants that there are no known setoffs or defenses to the payments due. The undersigned further warrants that said obligation to pay is absolute and without modification. The undersigned further warrants that it has full authority to enter into this agreement and that the rights to income assigned hereunder are free and clear of liens, encumbrances, and adverse claims. The undersigned does not, however, guarantee or warranty the collectability of any monies due. This assignment shall be limited to $ _____ and no greater amount.

This assignment shall be binding upon and inure to the benefit of the parties, their successors, assigns, and personal representatives.

Signed under seal this _____ day of _____ , 199 ___ .

_____   _____
Witness   Assignor

Assignment of Insurance Policy

BE IT KNOWN, for value received, the undersigned hereby irrevocably transfers and assigns to _Ed Harrison_ of _78 Turnview Circle_ , city of _Burlington_ , state of _Vermont_ , all legal and beneficial right, title, and interest in and to the within policy of insurance standing in my name known as policy number _42714_ issued by _First Life_ (Insurance Company), together with all cash values, proceeds, and benefits thereto arising, subject to the conditions of said policy and the requirements of the issuing company.

The undersigned warrants that it has full authority to transfer said policy and shall execute all documents as may be required.

This assignment shall be binding upon and inure to the benefit of the parties, their successors, assigns, and personal representatives.

Signed under seal this _12th_ day of _May_ , 199 _6_ .

Greg Taylor	_Denny Harrison_
Witness	Assignor

Assignment of Insurance Policy

BE IT KNOWN, for value received, the undersigned hereby irrevocably transfers and assigns to _____ of _____ , city of _____ , state of _____ , all legal and beneficial right, title, and interest in and to the within policy of insurance standing in my name known as policy number _____ issued by _____ (Insurance Company), together with all cash values, proceeds, and benefits thereto arising, subject to the conditions of said policy and the requirements of the issuing company.

The undersigned warrants that it has full authority to transfer said policy and shall execute all documents as may be required.

This assignment shall be binding upon and inure to the benefit of the parties, their successors, assigns, and personal representatives.

Signed under seal this _____ day of _____ , 199 ___ .

_____   _____
Witness   Assignor

Notice of Assignment

Date: *May 12, 1996*

To: *First Life*
          3233 87th Avenue
          Denver, CO 80213

You are hereby notified that on _May 12_ , 19 _96_ , we have assigned and transferred to _Ed Harrison_ the following existing between us: _A life insurance policy #3721 in the amount of $100,000_ .

Please direct any further correspondence (or payments, if applicable) to him at the following address:

          Ed Harrison
          78 Turnview Circle
          Burlington, Vermont 05402

Please contact us if you have any questions.

                    Denny Harrison
                    1892 Arbor Dr.
                    Burlington, VT 05404

Notice of Assignment

Date: _____

To: _____

_____

Address

_____

City, State, Zip

You are hereby notified that on _____ , 19 ___ , we have assigned and transferred to _____ the following existing between us: _____

_____

_____

_____

_____

_____

_____ .

Please direct any further correspondence (or payments, if applicable) to him at the following address:

_____

_____

_____

Please contact us if you have any questions.

_____

_____

_____

Arbitration Agreement

Agreement by and between _Baynes Supply, Inc._ and _Stowe Manufacturing_ .

Be it acknowledged, that we the undersigned, as our interests exist in and to a certain contract, dispute, controversy, action, or claim described as: _A certain contract between the U.S. Government and Stowe Manufacturing, Inc., subsequently assigned to Baynes Supply, Inc._

do hereby agree to resolve any dispute or controversy we now have or may ever have in connection with or arising from said claim by binding Arbitration.

Said Arbitration shall be in accordance with the rules and procedures of the American Arbitration Association for the city of _Boston_ , which rules and procedures for arbitration are incorporated herein by reference, and the decision or award by the Arbitrators shall be final, conclusive, and binding upon each of us and enforceable in a court of law of proper jurisdiction.

Signed this _10th_ day of _December_ , 199 _6_ .

In the presence of:

Greg Taylor
Witness

Sarah Barrett
Witness

Baynes Supply, Inc.

By _Frank Baynes, President_

Stowe Manufacturing, Inc.

By _Eldgin Stowe, President_

Arbitration Agreement

Agreement by and between _____ and _____ .

Be it acknowledged, that we the undersigned, as our interests exist in and to a certain contract, dispute, controversy, action, or claim described as: _____

_____

_____

_____

_____

_____

do hereby agree to resolve any dispute or controversy we now have or may ever have in connection with or arising from said claim by binding Arbitration.

Said Arbitration shall be in accordance with the rules and procedures of the American Arbitration Association for the city of _____ , which rules and procedures for arbitration are incorporated herein by reference, and the decision or award by the Arbitrators shall be final, conclusive, and binding upon each of us and enforceable in a court of law of proper jurisdiction.

Signed this _____ day of _____ , 199 ___ .

In the presence of:

_____   _____

Witness

                                 By _____

_____   _____

Witness

                                 By _____

Request under Freedom of Information Act

Date: _August 1, 1996_

To: _Federal Trade Commission_
Federal Agency
25 E. 14th Street
Address
Washington, DC 20024
City, State, Zip

Pursuant to the Federal Freedom of Information Act, I request disclosure of _companies granted trade rights under Treaty 24_ as may be maintained in your files, to the extent said disclosure is required by law.
Please forward said information to the address below.
I appreciate your cooperation.

In the presence of: Very truly,

Sarah Barrett   _Stowe Manufacturing, Inc._

By _Elgin Stowe, President_

7712 41st Street
Address
Boston, MA 02110
City, State, Zip
_812-34-7121_
Social Security No.

Request under Freedom of Information Act

Date: _____

To: _____

      Federal Agency

      _____

      Address

      _____

      City, State, Zip

    Pursuant to the Federal Freedom of Information Act, I request disclosure of _____

_____

_____

_____

as may be maintained in your files, to the extent said disclosure is required by law.

    Please forward said information to the address below.

    I appreciate your cooperation.

In the presence of: Very truly,

_____

                    _____

                    Signature

                    _____

                    Name

                    _____

                    Other Known Names

                    _____

                    Address

                    _____

                    City, State, Zip

                    _____

                    Social Security No.

Notice of Product Defect Claim

Date: _October 5, 1996_

To: _Top Shelf Copiers, Inc._
Manufacturer, Supplier, or Seller
1414 W. 23rd Avenue
Address
New York, NY 10002
City, State, Zip

Notice is hereby provided that we have purchased a product manufactured, distributed, or sold by you and described as: _Super Copier model # 81257_

You are advised of a product or warranty claim in the following particulars:

Date of Purchase: _September 1, 1996_
Nature of Reported Defect: _Doesn't make clear copies as promised_
Reported Injuries or Damage: _None_
Purchased From: _Top Shelf Copiers_

This letter is provided to give you earliest possible notice of said claim, and we request that you or your representative contact us as soon as possible.

We shall advise you upon receipt of any further information on this claim.

Very truly,

Brad Adams

SENT CERTIFIED MAIL, RETURN RECEIPT REQUESTED.

Notice of Product Defect Claim

Date: _____

To: _____

        Manufacturer, Supplier, or Seller

        _____

        Address

        _____

        City, State, Zip

Notice is hereby provided that we have purchased a product manufactured, distributed, or sold by you and described as: _____
_____
_____
_____
_____

You are advised of a product or warranty claim in the following particulars:

Date of Purchase: _____
Nature of Reported Defect: _____
_____
_____

Reported Injuries or Damage: _____
_____

Purchased From: _____

This letter is provided to give you earliest possible notice of said claim, and we request that you or your representative contact us as soon as possible.

We shall advise you upon receipt of any further information on this claim.

                        Very truly,

                        _____

SENT CERTIFIED MAIL, RETURN RECEIPT REQUESTED.

Notice of Product Warranty Claim

Date: _October 5, 1996_

To: _Top Shelf Copiers, Inc._
        1414 W. 23rd Ave.
        Address
        New York, NY 10002
        City, State, Zip

Gentlemen:

Please be advised that we purchased the following product: _Super Copier model #81257_ from _Top Shelf Copier_ on _September 5_ , 199 _5_ .

This product is defective and in need of repair in the following particulars:

Prints streaks in all copies

We understand that this product is under warranty, and we therefore request repair of the product under warranty.

   __X__ Product enclosed
   _____ Please call (_____) _____ for service appointment.

Very truly,

Brad Adams
205 Oakcrest Dr.
Address
Longwood, FL 32750
City, State, Zip

Notice of Product Warranty Claim

Date: _____

To: _____

_____

Address

_____

City, State, Zip

Gentlemen:

Please be advised that we purchased the following product: _____
_____ from
_____ on _____ , 199 ___ .
   This product is defective and in need of repair in the
following particulars: _____
_____
_____
_____
_____
_____

   We understand that this product is under warranty, and we
therefore request repair of the product under warranty.
_____ Product enclosed
_____ Please call (_____) _____ for service appointment.

Very truly,

_____

_____

Address

_____

City, State, Zip

Submission of Unsolicited Ideas

Date: _January 19, 1997_

To: _Jan Adams_
        _1871 1st St. N._
        Address
        Tampa, FL 33619
        City, State, Zip

Thank you for your interest in submitting for our consideration an idea or proposal described as: _A marketing system for widgets_

As you can understand, our company receives many commercial ideas, suggestions, and proposals, and also has many of its own projects under development. Therefore, the idea or proposal you plan to submit to us may have been considered and/or may already be in the planning stages.

Accordingly, we would be pleased to accept your idea or proposal for review, on condition that you acknowledge: (1) Samples or other submissions will be returned only if return postage or freight is prepaid; (2) the company accepts no responsibility for casualty or loss to samples or other submitted material in our possession; (3) the company accepts no responsibility for holding any submitted information in confidence; (4) the company shall pay compensation only in the event it (a) accepts the submitted idea, (b) has received the idea exclusively from you, and (c) reaches agreement with you as to terms and conditions for development of the product or exploitation of the idea.

If these terms are acceptable to you, please sign where indicated below and submit with your idea or proposal. We shall thereafter advise you of our interest.

Sincerely,

Frank Foster, President
American Marketing, Inc.

Acknowledged:
I accept the terms and conditions as stated above.

Jan Adams

Submission of Unsolicited Ideas

Date: _____

To: _____
    _____
    Address
    _____
    City, State, Zip

Thank you for your interest in submitting for our consideration an idea or proposal described as: _____

_____
_____
_____
_____
_____
_____

As you can understand, our company receives many commercial ideas, suggestions, and proposals, and also has many of its own projects under development. Therefore, the idea or proposal you plan to submit to us may have been considered and/or may already be in the planning stages.

Accordingly, we would be pleased to accept your idea or proposal for review, on condition that you acknowledge: (1) Samples or other submissions will be returned only if return postage or freight is prepaid; (2) the company accepts no responsibility for casualty or loss to samples or other submitted material in our possession; (3) the company accepts no responsibility for holding any submitted information in confidence; (4) the company shall pay compensation only in the event it (a) accepts the submitted idea, (b) has received the idea exclusively from you, and (c) reaches agreement with you as to terms and conditions for development of the product or exploitation of the idea.

If these terms are acceptable to you, please sign where indicated below and submit with your idea or proposal. We shall thereafter advise you of our interest.

Sincerely,

_____
_____

Acknowledged:
I accept the terms and conditions as stated above.

_____

About the Author

J. W. Dicks is an attorney by profession and an entrepreneur by choice. In addition to his law practice, Pino & Dicks, he owns numerous corporations and advises small business owners in all aspects of developing their companies, from strategic planning to public offerings.

As a leading seminar instructor on financial topics, J. W. Dicks has traveled the country, speaking to over 150,000 people on small business, stocks, mutual funds, law, and real estate. In addition to his lectures, he has written numerous articles, manuals, and newsletters on the same topics.

Mr. Dicks has authored several business and legal books, including *The American Dream, Financial C.P.R., The Florida Investor, The Small Business Legal Kit, The 100 Best Investments for Your Retirement, Mutual Fund Investing Strategies,* and *How to Incorporate and Start a Business.*

For information about Dicks's availability for speaking engagements, legal business consulting services, or for a complimentary copy of his newsletter, *Small Business Advisor,* phone 1-800-593-4257.